solo

**VENTURING ALONE
IN THE NORTHERN WILDS**

solo

VENTURING ALONE
IN THE NORTHERN WILDS

Dick Anderson

atmosphere press

Published by Atmosphere Press

Cover design by Nick Courtright
Cover photo "Wood Tikchik After the Storm" by Dick Anderson

atmospherepress.com

To Janet, who was with me every step of the way.

Table of Contents

Foreword

In 1998, at age 57, when many begin thinking about sliding placidly toward retirement, Dick Anderson decided instead it was time to go adventuring—and as far from his snug, urbanized cocoon as possible. "I've got to go to the wilderness. Alone," he boldly declared—and did he ever! Wanting to recapture a lost sense of youthful personal freedom, renewal, and connection to nature, he made annual solo trips to Canada and Alaska (and one to the Okefenokee Swamp in Georgia), over the next decade, canoeing and camping in some of the most remote, sparsely populated, and surpassingly gorgeous territory on earth.

This enthralling book encompasses a journal of those singular expeditions—replete with vivid passages describing the spectacular landscape, as well as the abundant energy, skill, and nerve required to explore it, and the dramatic and capricious weather patterns—the latter often determining whether he would spend the day canoeing in the great outdoors or huddled in his tent for days while the elements wreaked noisy havoc just outside.

He also shares with us his up close and personal encounters with the original "natives" of these places—the animals, birds and fish, including moose and grizzlies (who mostly seem more curious about him than threatening). On one occasion, he makes an acquaintance of sorts with a large, complacent northern pike, which puts him off fishing forever—it would be like hooking a good friend!

Finally, we meet a surprising number of welcoming and generous north-woods *human* folk, who pop up serendipitously when he needs them: bush pilots who fly him to his remote destinations and (figuratively) take him under their wings; a forest angel-woman living alone in a rough little cabin, who gives him a seemingly magic potion that saves him from being entirely devoured by mosquitoes; and Inupiat families spending the season in their fishing camps along one of his water routes, welcoming him into their midst and sending word of his arrival onto the next camp downriver.

Solo is finally a contemplation of Anderson's own deepening relationship with nature, of coming to terms with a primordial environment, where *he* is the outsider, dependent upon his own frail resources, his substantial outdoor gear, and the occasional kindness of strangers. Indeed, the passages about the physical details of keeping alive and relatively comfortable are, in their way, as engrossing as the descriptions of flora and fauna. We learn about how to spec out a good campsite and then how to react when a grizzly lets you know your tent is on *his* territory (move your tent!). We learn what compact, lightweight foods to bring that will be decently nourishing if not high-end gourmet (freeze-dried grub, oatmeal, rice cakes with peanut butter, and power bars feature prominently). We are right there as Anderson tries to keep a canoe afloat and himself inside when rough water and high winds have other ideas (barely avoiding catastrophe on one occasion).

And finally, Anderson explores the paradox of learning to relax, to slow down, to just *be* in this harsh and demanding "primeval sanctuary," this often-unforgiving Eden. It is practicing this ultimate extended exercise in mindfulness that allows him in the end to feel genuinely ready to go back home, having fulfilled the old yearning to find his place in the natural world. More than this, he has taken the wilderness inside himself—it is part of him, and he will never again be entirely separated from it.

Mary Sykes Wylie, PhD, now retired and living in Maine, is a former Senior Editor of the National Magazine Award-winning Psychotherapy Networker.

Preface

Far and away
lost in yesterday,
wanderin' down by the brook,
my spirit jumps in
with a crazy grin.
Lord, I just
can't bear to look.

From "Ghosts,"
Music and Lyrics by Dick Anderson

Far and away, lost in yesterday.

As I contemplate sharing my wilderness ventures—my present self paging through my past self—it is hard to discern what is then and what is now, what is real and what is interpretation, my older me translating my younger me.

Did I *actually* do that?

Did I actually do *that*?

Did *I* actually do that?

Which *I* are we talking about? The I then, or the I now? The eye then, or the eye now?

Are there ghosts in this machine?

Fortunately, in this journey through memory, I find the accuracy of my recollections greatly aided by the photographs I took during that time. My original motivation to retreat to the wilderness was to seek a prolonged period of solitude in which I could reconnect with nature and with the essential me—stripped of my workaday responsibilities and concerns. Almost as an afterthought, I took along a point-and-shoot camera, thinking I might want to share where I had traveled and what I had seen.

Over the years, my expeditions took me to ever more exceptional and remote locations. Much as I enjoyed my little point-and-shoot, I decided that only a more sophisticated camera would do justice to the unique and awe-inspiring beauty that confronted me. I chose a digital SLR (Single Lens Reflex) for ease of use and versatility of purpose. Employing this camera for landscape, close-up, and wildlife photography began to work a subtle transformation in my own behavior. As if with new eyes, I became increasingly aware of the intricacies of the late evening sky, the athletic grace of a swan as it dashes across the water to become airborne, the rustic beauty of a dying blossom, or the brooding possibilities of a gathering thunderstorm. Photography became my journal, the camera my pen—instruments for expressing my inner journey.

Little did I know when those photos were taken that I would someday be sharing the story of my wilderness expeditions in book form. But over the years, my friends continue to ask, "How does it feel? What is it like?"

How does it feel to be in a canoe, alone, attuned to the rhythms of the water, the vicissitudes of weather, the mystery of the wild country, and the ghosts that ride along? How does it feel when an eagle escorts you downriver? When a wolf pauses to take your measure? When the caribou approach to see if you are one of the stragglers that can't keep up with the migration? When a couple of grizzlies decide to watch over your campsite? What new wisdom do these experiences have to offer?

Hopefully, this volume will provide more than a glimpse of how it feels to venture alone into the wild.

As I write these words, the world is still engulfed in a pandemic. My hope is that this recounting will offer readers an occasion to explore their own inner resources, and that soon all of us will be able to do this in the wider world once again with an even greater appreciation of the need to care for ourselves and our environment.

In the process of writing down these recollections, I've come to realize that in these journeys I was not the sole wanderer that I had so long considered myself to be. Rather, I was part of a rich inheritance—one in a timeless progression of soul wanderers who have striven to make their way through this expanse of space and time.

Prologue

Routine, in the press of my workaday world, is generally a genial companion. However, at times routine assumes the role of taskmaster, as I doggedly try to keep on schedule and accomplish my agenda. True, I may pause several times a day to breathe and re-center, but eventually my self-imposed hubbub reclaims my life in a cascade of time.

In the wilderness, time stops—or perhaps better said, it slows down, waits for me—becomes my friend, rather than my adversary. The unspoiled quietude invites me to pause, step aside, and listen—listen to the trees, the river, the wildlife, and, most importantly, to myself.

I journey to the wilderness to rediscover my place in the natural world. The city obscures my primordial self. Inventions totally beyond my comprehension shape my everyday life. I flip a light switch to escape the dark. I turn up the thermostat if I am chilly. I open the refrigerator door if I am hungry. If I "click here," I can talk to the entire planet. But none of these conveniences will accompany me to the grave. None can tell me who I am or why I am here.

I need the wilderness to return to my true self: to walk on sand and dirt and rock; to feel the surge of the river; to re-establish my connection with the animals from whom I've become estranged over eons of time; and to stand in the middle of unimpeded horizons that invite the entire universe back into my experience. I need to see that universe with my ancestors' eyes—to cast away the modern myth of invincibility and return to the naked innocence of awe.

I need the wilderness and I need aloneness. I need to be thrown back on my own resources. Not for a day, or a weekend, but for an extended period of time where I can discard the claims of the city and stake my own claim in this special reserve of the self. I need to appreciate once again the beautiful and the terrible that are encompassed in this vast landscape. I need to face the truth of my mortality, and to embrace it.

And finally, I need to return to the comforts of home—to the arms of family and friends and colleagues—and to resume my routine of everyday life.

However, after about a year of this routine, I begin to hear the wild country whispering in my ear once again.

I need the wilderness.

Chapter 1

1997 – THE DECISION

The silence is shattered as the engine roars awake, propeller champing as the pontoons slowly inscribe a perfect arc in the water back to where I stand on the shore. Now, racing over the waves, the small but powerful plane finally escapes the grasp of the lake and lifts gracefully into the afternoon sky. Transfixed, I watch as what once was my chariot becomes smaller and smaller, until it is no more than a speck on the horizon. As far as I can see, there is nothing but water scalloped by the surrounding mountains under a cloudless canopy.

Once again, the great quiet engulfs me.

I am utterly alone.

I shudder.

"Who would want to do this?" I ask myself—the same question I have asked year after year when left behind to fend for myself in the wilderness.

As if mimicking the path of the now-departed aircraft, my mind arcs back more than six decades.

*   *   *

It's 1946.

I'm five years old and squirming uncomfortably on a hard pew in my dad's church in Cedar Rapids, Iowa. Mom shushes me. Dad is up there in the pulpit reading a passage from the Bible. The congregation is listening intently. I'm trying my best to stay quiet, but it's hard. More than once, Mom has taken me out of church before because I got too noisy, so I'm trying to keep extra still. But it's really difficult. I'm getting hotter and hotter in this itchy wool suit as the service drones on and on. Somehow, Dad's voice breaks through my fidgeting, as he intones, "I will lift up mine eyes unto the hills, from whence cometh my help."

Suddenly I can see those hills, and then bigger hills, with snow-clad peaks, and forests and rivers. Then I'm climbing those same mountains. Canoeing the rivers. Roaring through rapids. "Wouldn't that be great?" I think.

"How can a mountain help you?" I whisper to Mom. But Mom has that scolding look on her face as she leans over, holds her finger to her lips, and shushes me again. I try to be quiet.

But I still wonder.

*   *   *

As a grownup, I've set out to answer my childhood question, exploring the mountains and forests and rivers of the remotest areas of North America. My conveyance of choice in this exploration is, unsurprisingly, the canoe. Though I grew up in Iowa, I had one foot planted firmly in northern Minnesota, where, on visits to my Grandpa Ira, I sat rapt as he spun fireside stories of the native Chippewa and the vast wilderness they traveled along the path of the paddle.

In one of these stories, Grandpa described an intriguing lake-saturated hinterland we now call the Boundary Waters. An enormous wild expanse on the Canadian border, it was said you could canoe for days without seeing a single soul. But you had to be careful. One could easily get lost there, or unexpectedly run into a bear, or a moose, or a storm. Naturally, these cautions made me want to go there all the more. But dad and grandpa always said it was too far, and canoeing the Boundary Waters was eventually consigned to the attic of my desires.

Nonetheless, my fascination with adventuring shadowed me. As a kid I had to be satisfied with hopping on my bike and racing through the streets of Cedar Rapids, exploring the adjacent neighborhoods and back alleys, careening along the paths of Beaver Park Zoo, and weaving through downtown traffic and over the Cedar River Bridge—stopping to watch the fishermen who lined the shore in hopes of hauling in a lunker catfish.

When I was old enough to drive, I traded my bike for my dad's car, which allowed me to expand my range. Every evening when I could manage to borrow it, I would take off for the warren of back roads surrounding Des Moines—dad's new pastorate—exploring the myriad farms, fields and woodlands that surrounded Iowa's capital city. Dad and mom would have shuddered to hear about some of my explorations—like the winter night when, misjudging the black ice, my car did a three-sixty and then slid inexorably down the steep asphalt road—sideways!

Often, after one of those late-night excursions, I'd tiptoe back into a sleeping house to do my homework for the following day. As my brother had done, I wanted to go to college, partly because college was yet another opportunity to get away, to be on my own, and to start my own life. When that day finally arrived and I headed off for Grinnell College, it wasn't long before I began to spend my weekends hitchhiking my way around the Midwest, anxious to wander among the skyscrapers of Omaha and Chicago. Eventually my thumb took me as far as New York City.

During my sophomore year at Grinnell, I borrowed my mom's Ford Falcon over the Christmas break and—armed only with the phrase "¿Donde esta un hotel bueno y barato?" ("Where is a good, cheap hotel?")—drove from Des Moines to Acapulco, Mexico. Seeking to immerse myself in the wonders of an unknown landscape and culture, it was on that journey that I finally saw my first towering mountains—edging the far horizon as I drove the desert flatlands south from Nuevo Laredo to Mexico City. After traveling for several hours, those mountains appeared only somewhat nearer. At long last, I was driving through the Sierra Madre—one of several ranges that form the backbone of South and North America.

After I returned to Grinnell, I settled into a life not unlike many of my Midwestern classmates of that time—completing my education, finding a job, getting married, moving to the East Coast, and raising a family. Of course, no life is that simple, particularly if lived in the backdrop of the late sixties and early seventies. Vietnam, racial injustice, feminism, political turmoil, assassination, and social upheaval formed the milieu of my twenties and thirties. Each of these themes reverberated strongly in my personal life as a political activist, and in my professional pursuits as a researcher for the U.S. Senate Foreign Relations Committee, and subsequently as a teacher of Urban Studies in an inner-city high school in Washington, D.C.

By the time I was in my forties I had divorced—though I remained ever after a close friend of my former wife Anne, mother of our three children. After our divorce, Anne and I had shared child-rearing responsibilities equally. Each of us was self-employed, creating the opportunity to spend time with our children on a flexible schedule. Having at last discovered a way to pursue my ideals, I was the co-founder of a small, inner-city graphics design business dedicated to serving not-for-profit clients—happily engaged in a creative, productive and immensely busy life.

My three children—Laurie, Geoff and Kelley—and I had always enjoyed the outdoors, camping in many of the country's national parks, and sharing a particularly memorable canoe adventure in Canada's Algonquin Provincial Park. Camping was one of our favorite activities because it was a flexible and affordable way to pursue our love of nature.

It was Geoff who reawakened for me a way of life I had not tasted since I myself was a young man. Upon his graduation from Connecticut College and before entering grad school at Duke, Geoff took off on his own for a couple of weeks hiking through Canyonlands National Park. He followed this with another trek exploring the mountains and coastline of Oregon. Soon after, he invited Laurie and me to backpack Yosemite National Park. When Laurie returned from Yosemite to her doctoral studies in Boulder, Colorado, Geoff and I extended our expedition to include the Grand Canyon.

That Yosemite/Grand Canyon month began to reawaken a part of me that had lain dormant for some thirty years. I began to consider whether perhaps I could take some time to reprise my youthful solo experiences, to test myself against the elements and to spend some time completely alone. It sounded fun. It sounded inspirational. It also sounded scary—especially for an out-of-shape old guy like me. But mostly it sounded impractical. It simply wasn't feasible.

But the idea kept hanging around.

More years elapsed and I eventually managed to consign these thoughts to the back seat once again. Those few vacancies in my life that still existed were soon filled with new possibilities. I met Janet. We fell in love. We married. Life was busy. And meaningful. And full.

And I continued to grow older.

As fifty became fifty-five, and then more, I began to realize that not only nature, but also life, abhors a vacuum. At this rate, if I didn't soon create time for myself in my overflowing schedule, outside events would be only too happy to divert my attention.

The clock was ticking.

Finally, I sat myself down for a one-on-one. "Just what do you want to do?" I asked myself, "Recreate your youth?" No. I knew that was silly—and not even attractive. I liked who I was now. It was more about not wanting to lose an essential part of me, no matter what my age. I felt that my busy East Coast life had nearly swallowed this transplanted Iowa boy whole.

Whatever happened to that solitary six-year-old who would hop on his bike for hours to explore every backstreet that Cedar Rapids had to offer? The teenager who borrowed his dad's '56 Pontiac and followed the most remote gravel roads just to see where they went? The college student who drove by himself from Iowa to Acapulco and back? The young man who hitched for hundreds of miles just to discover what was over the next hill?

It was as if now, paraphrasing the words of the old Tennessee Ernie Ford ballad, "I owed my soul to the company store"—and I *owned* the company store! I seemed to have slipped into some sort of Faustian bargain in which I had allowed the seductions and satisfactions of modern life to leave me bereft of any connection to the natural order of things. True, my life was full, but maybe *too* full—like a warehouse continually being restocked until it was bursting at the seams.

Whatever the impetus, my decision—to acknowledge this insistent yearning to explore the wilderness on my own not as a dream, but as an imperative that I must bring to fruition before I was no longer able to do so—constituted a turning point. Prior to that late-life decision, I'm not sure I had ever truly understood as a mature adult the need to reclaim a personal space in my life—to commit to make room for my own fulfillment just as I had made commitments to family, friends, work and community.

Of course, this was not an easy decision. I was assailed by questions and doubts. Was I merely being selfish, going off on my own and leaving my responsibilities behind? What if something happened at home while I was away? What if something happened to me? Was I putting my family and myself at unnecessary risk? Was I simply acting out childish fantasies?

I finally concluded that these questions only led to more procrastination. The only sure way to find the answers was to head for the wilds and see what transpired.

What, I wondered, will Janet think of all this?

* * *

"I've *got* to go to the wilderness. Alone. It's something I've been harboring in the back of my mind all my life. It's 1998 and I'm already fifty-seven. If I don't do it now—while I'm still able—I'll never do it."

At last, I think, I've said it out loud. My hunched shoulders relax, relieved to finally articulate what has been nagging me for years. I'm standing in our bedroom trying to explain this need—this necessity—to Janet. She quietly listens while I pour out my urgency.

Since we met in 1991 and married three years ago, Janet and I have shared a love of travel. We've already logged many miles together. On our first trip we held hands as we drove all the way to her hometown of Pensacola, Florida and back— blasting out Glen Frey's "True Love" while singing at the top of our lungs. That adventure was followed by an excursion to Grand Manan—a little-known gem of an island in the Bay of Fundy—where we hunkered down in a tiny cabin, occasionally venturing out to enjoy the island tradition of afternoon tea or to explore the rocky, wind-blown coastline. Presently, we are formulating plans for visiting friends in Denmark and eventually taking a long-delayed "honeymoon" in Italy.

Now, as we stand in our bedroom, Janet looks pensive. "Why alone?" she asks. "You're sure you aren't just feeling a need to get away from us?"

"It's nothing like that," I reply. "I've been feeling this urge to spend time alone in the wilderness long before there was an 'us.' One reason I can even consider going off by myself is because I've got 'us' to come back to."

"Going alone," I continue, thinking out loud, "would give me a chance to find out how I react when I'm forced to rely entirely on my own resources."

"You mean like testing your manhood?" says Janet, only half teasing.

"Well I guess that's part of it," I shrug, a bit embarrassed. "But only a part," trying not to sound too defensive. "It's more like there's some primordial self that I've lost track of. I want to leave behind my civilized self and get back to 'me'—whatever that means."

I can feel myself searching for the words. "I need to put aside my never-ending schedule and just stop. And look. And listen. And prioritize. I want to truly distance myself from work, from the city, and from all the distractions and conveniences of my life."

Finally all the feelings that I've never quite been able to articulate come pouring out. "I want to rediscover my place in the universe—find out just who I am when I strip away everything else. I want to experience what happens when I go to an isolated, wild place without any expectations. And not just for a weekend, or even a few days. If I'm going to do this thing, I want to give it the time it deserves—maybe like a couple of weeks."

Janet sums it up quite simply: "Sounds like you've really got to do this."

"Yeah. I guess it does." I nod, grateful for her understanding. "It feels really important!"

We step toward each other and enjoy a warm embrace.

Sitting down on the bed, we begin to talk about where, when, and how.

Chapter 2

1998 – MAIDEN VOYAGE – BOUNDARY WATERS

This is embarrassing.

The breeze is gusty, but not too bad. A sunny, cloudless sky looks down on the pristine expanse of Moose Lake, surrounded by balsam, pine, birch and spruce. Aside from the wind, the lake is actually pretty calm. In fact, this could be where they shot all those beer commercials I remember as a kid. The jingle plays anew in my mind as if fifty years were nothing: "From the Land of Sky-Blue Waters."

Nonetheless, the bow of my canoe swings uncontrollably back and forth, side to side, no matter how I try to compensate. I suspect that all those guys sitting back there in their rockers on the front porch of the lodge are getting a real kick out of this as they look out over the water—watching this grizzled old man desperately paddle, first on one side, then the other, in the stern of his sleek yellow Kevlar, as the wind whiplashes his bow first leeward and then windward. In a final humiliation, I am spun in precisely the opposite direction from that I wish to go.

"Must be his first time in a canoe," I can imagine one of them saying, his eyebrows raised derisively.

"Sure looks that way," his companions are probably chuckling, and leaning forward for a better look. "Betcha he don't last a day out there."

About an hour ago, when my outfitter had walked me down to the dock to select a canoe, he said proudly, "We've got some really nice Kevlar options. They're light and super tough." Pointing to one in particular, he continued, "This here fourteen-footer weighs only fifty pounds. Perfect for solo."

"I'm going to be out there for ten days," I remind him. "I've got quite a bit of gear. I think I might need something larger."

"Then how 'bout this seventeen-footer over here?"

We walk over to take a look.

"Seems perfect," I say, appraising its sleek lines. "Should be plenty. How much does it weigh?"

"'Bout sixty pounds, as I recall," he replies. "Go ahead and try 'er out."

And so, after quickly throwing on a life vest, I step down from the dock and into the canoe, feeling it rock skittishly under my six-foot-two, hundred-ninety-pound frame. Lowering myself down carefully onto the stern seat, I can tell right away that it is different from any canoe I'd been in before—like a high-strung thoroughbred compared to my old nag back home—an aluminum Grumman.

Getting a feel for this new beauty, I proceed out a hundred yards or so into the calm waters while my outfitter saunters back to tend the lodge store. I am pleased with how responsive it is, and I begin to practice various new solo canoeing strokes I have studied.

"I can't believe it!" I exclaim to myself, excited as a kid. "I'm finally doing it!"

"After all these months of planning I'm really here—on Moose Lake, in a new Kevlar! In a couple of hours I'll be on my way. Solo! Alone! All by myself! In the wilderness! Incredible!"

As if in response, the wind kicks up.

I now realize my first mistake was to sit in the stern of an empty canoe, with no gear to act as ballast. At least in the bow, the canoe's center of gravity wouldn't be so extreme. Better yet, I should have just knelt in the middle, but my fifty-seven-year-old knees do not like kneeling. So here I sit, at the whim of the wind, my bantamweight canoe swinging around the fulcrum of my heavyweight body, like water circling a drain.

Cautiously, hunching down and grabbing the gunwales, I inch towards the center of the precarious craft, keeping my body low, lest my first attempt at canoeing the Boundary Waters ends up with me in the drink. As I move forward, two things happen: I feel my first glimmer of success as the canoe stabilizes; and, the wind, mercifully, dies down to a gentle breeze. Like a kid learning to ride a bike, I test my balance, gingerly shifting my weight from side to side, gauging the response of my craft.

"It isn't as if I'm a novice canoeist," I chastise myself. But, I quickly discover I am a novice soloist, and when Kevlar is added to the mix, I've got a lot to learn—and quickly! Also, I have to admit, I'm not a young father anymore, and my confidence, like my body, is a bit shaky. Nonetheless, I'm determined to forge ahead.

Finally, with a bit more practice, I'm able to paddle a relatively straight course. With renewed conviction, I practice my J-strokes, draws, prys and sweeps, gaining assurance as the canoe responds. Finally, much more comfortable, I turn towards shore.

"How'd it go?" asks my outfitter as I step through the screeching screen door of the camp store.

"Fine," I lie, as the rickety door slams shut behind me. "A little tricky at first, but I think I've got the hang of it."

"So I noticed," he replies, covering his mouth to hide a spreading grin. "I'm sure when you load up your gear it'll help stabilize it."

"That's what I was thinking," I say, relieved he is being so circumspect.

Living the Dream

My initial experiment with going off by myself—all expectations checked at the door—is this canoe trip to Minnesota's Boundary Waters, a wilderness area so named because it sits on the boundary between north-eastern Minnesota and Canada. It's understandable that I would choose this destination, given the fact that I have spent many cherished childhood days in the company of my northern Minnesota relatives, trolling through the pine-scented air of Blackduck Lake with my dad and his dad, fishing for walleyes and northerns.

With great anticipation, I begin elaborate preparations for my maiden solo. Though I am a reasonably experienced occasional paddler, I know going alone will be a different challenge. I intently scrutinize legendary Canadian canoeist Bill Mason's instructional video on solo canoeing, *Path of the Paddle*—playing it over and over, until I have internalized a host of maneuvers. I research outfitters until I find an experienced Boundary Waters outdoorsman with a sympathetic ear who agrees to help me plan the best route for this first solo venture.

Once I finalize my route—I carefully mark it in yellow on my pristine, newly purchased US Geological Survey topological maps (maps that will be dog-eared, battered, and damp by the end of my journey). Each night, I spread out the topos on my side of the bed—Janet sometimes glancing over quizzically from her reading. I pore over each twist and turn of the water-surrounded terrain—envisioning my journey over and over—estimating the time it will take to paddle the lakes and portage my gear overland on the trails between lakes.

As zero hour nears, I spread my camping gear throughout our basement (in what will prove to be an annual ritual) in order to inspect every article and pass judgment as to whether it is essential for my journey. I shop for food, balancing issues of weight, nutrition, and necessity—envisioning myself hunkered over a cozy fire or huddled in my poncho in a pouring rain (later, I will learn to imagine days of blustery wind and even occasional flurries of snow).

As part of my preparation, which consists mostly of riding my bike on the country roads surrounding Poolesville, Maryland, for about fifty miles each week, I struggle into my backpack—fully loaded with fifty pounds of gear—and climb Virginia's Old Rag Mountain, preparing my lungs, my legs and my psyche for the long portage trails ahead by scrambling up its formidable boulder fields. I berate myself for not doing more, but the demands of my graphics design business do not abate, and I have to steal whatever time I can to whip my body into some sort of shape.

In the years to come, late summer will increasingly become a focus of my year. After returning from my trips, I settle back into the routines of fall and winter like a hibernating bear, hunkering down during the increasingly shorter days approaching the winter solstice. Hunched over my computer, I am constantly busy with the demands of my clients.

However, come spring, my body and spirit inevitably begin to reawaken and I somehow create the time to prepare for the journey I know is to come. Emerging from the cave of winter, I hop back on my bike at dawn and begin to train for the inevitable demands of my upcoming odyssey. A familiar sense of anticipation returns, and I begin my research: making plans, contacting outfitters, and envisioning new possibilities.

But this is my first journey, and finally, prepared or not, my late August departure day arrives and Janet drives me to the airport. We agree that I'll call from my outfitters just as soon as I return. I board a Northwest Airlines flight bound for St. Paul/Minneapolis, the first leg in a personal journey that will transport me to a broader, yet simpler, experience of myself in the world.

Once I arrive at my outfitter, on the shores of Moose Lake, just outside Ely, Minnesota, I haul my two fifty-pound packs into the bunkhouse for one last overnight inspection. Early the next morning, filled with a home-cooked Northwoods breakfast of ham, eggs, pancakes, sausage and coffee, my outfitter and I head for the lake to select a canoe.

Not So Great Expectations

My initial solo practice in a Kevlar now thankfully behind me, my outfitter loads me and my canoe into his high-speed motorboat for a dashing ride across Moose Lake to the point where I will be dropped off to continue the journey on my own. As we bounce over the waves, I ruminate on my decision to explore this unknown wilderness.

What will happen? How will I react? What lessons will I learn? Will I embrace each moment? Or will I become fearful—and shrink back into myself and the comforts of daily life? Just what is to be learned from being alone? Will I be tentative? Scared? Bored? Will I unearth things about myself that I would rather not know?

Before long we reach my point of departure. This morning's lesson in the real-world practicalities of solo navigation fresh in my mind, my wilderness adventure officially begins. I remind myself not to entertain any expectations for what lies ahead. I've placed myself in this unknown wilderness to see what presents itself—not to create, but to witness.

The first thing I witness is a host of other adventurers and not a little noise. Far from being a sanctuary of untrammeled isolation and quiet, I'm surrounded by other nature enthusiasts. In fact, an entire Boy Scout troop raucously races their canoes, excitedly calling back and forth to each other across the water. "Oh, no!" I despair. "I've come all this way to the Boundary Waters only to find a traffic jam!" In fairness, there are only three or four canoes in the vicinity, but it feels like a multitude.

Clearly, I realize, I expected immediate solitude to be the hallmark of my Boundary Waters experience. Hungry for escape from the noise of the city—I'm more than ready to experience a world where silence reigns. Over the course of my urban life, I have sought places of respite, and in this instance I had hoped to create an instant, private communion with nature, free from distraction. Obviously, I need to learn patience. "No expectations!" I remind myself and turn my attention inward, away from the others around me.

From this point forward, this initial day of solo canoeing becomes a process of discovery. Tentative at first, I begin to identify my paddling cadence, experimenting with my ability to control the canoe with the slightest movement of the paddle or shift of my body weight. I can feel the current beneath my feet, along with the insistence of the wind, and I learn how best to adjust my labors to their rhythms. Stroke by stroke, as my paddling becomes more graceful, I feel increasingly at home in my surroundings.

Looking around, the beauty of the surrounding pines, spruce and birch is undeniable. Nonetheless, it is hard to let go of my disappointment in not being completely alone. However, one by one, the others drop away, claiming one or another of the enticingly located campsites. I try to stifle my resentment at finding so much competition for these sites—many already filled with earlier arrivals—and I soldier on.

I decide to practice my compass skills and award myself hearty congratulations when—with no little sense of relief—I manage to locate my first overland portage. On my topo maps, the starting points of the portages are clearly marked, but I soon learn the difference between maps and the shifting environs of these northlands. Islands that appear on the topo are now covered with water. Shorelines have shifted. And portage points—so easily identifiable on the maps—are frequently overgrown with reeds and brush, concealing their rough-hewn paths from even the most practiced eye. I quickly learn to use the map as a general guide, but rely on my compass readings to pinpoint my location.

My deep-seated desire for isolation is, as yet, unfulfilled. However, I am relieved to discover that when I deviate from the main canoe route, I soon have little company. A couple of strenuous, lengthy portages leave me, suddenly, completely on my own, and I will not see another soul for a number of days. And no wonder! I'm soon to discover that each portage is a daunting challenge—especially since I'm the only Sherpa.

After spotting my first portage sign—a slash on a tree—I hop out and pull the canoe up on the bank. Now let's see. I've got two fifty-pound packs, a sixty-pound canoe—plus incidentals such as paddles, camera bag, tackle box and fishing poles. Off-loading the canoe, I lean down and heft one of the packs on my back, staggering from side to side until I get it centered, struggling to adjust the shoulder straps.

Then I lean over and try to pick up the other pack. But two packs are too heavy. I can't take them both. Same for the canoe. No way I can lift it overhead and portage it with this pack on my back. I'm beginning to feel my age. I'm going to have to grab the paddles, portage this first pack, and come back for the rest.

Off I go. Ducking under low-hanging tree branches and occasionally stumbling on roots, I head down the trail. A couple of times, I have to stop—head hanging down with hands on knees—and catch my breath. Finally, I see the next lake through the trees. My heart lifts. Once I get there I sling off my burden and flop down, panting. Only two more trips to go: one for the other pack and the tackle box, and one for the canoe and camera bag.

I think, "What did I get myself into?"

"You made this bed, now lie in it!" I reply, beginning a conversation with myself that will last the duration of the trip.

However, after resting a while, I'm soon recovered and off

I go to retrieve the next load.

Back and forth, stubbornly counting off each of the five laps. On the last trip, my legs are rubbery and burning as, balancing my canoe overhead like an oversized hat, I duck-walk under a low-hanging branch. I careen and lurch, until— at long last—I've completed my first solo portage.

Gasping for breath, I gingerly lower the canoe onto the ground and flop down against a tree. I haven't worked this hard since the summers I spent as a college youth, employed as a Gandy dancer for the Chicago, Burlington and Quincy Railroad, digging out ties and wielding a spike maul. I vividly remember how that job instilled in me a dogged determination for accomplishing difficult tasks. Now, some forty years later—though physically and emotionally spent—I feel that self-same pride of accomplishment that I'd nearly buried in my past. I close my eyes and thank my seventeen-year-old self for teaching me perseverance.

Dance of the Hours

By my fourth day out, I'm completely alone, gliding lazily through the sun-spackled and becalmed late afternoon. And how is it to finally be truly alone in the wilds? In a word, exquisite! The vast silence fills my senses—a silence no urban dweller can truly know or perhaps even imagine. A silence made for being alone with your thoughts—or perhaps, even better, for no thinking. At times, paddling feels like a continual meditation, the unconscious rhythm of each stroke bearing silent witness to the manifestations of nature.

I try to make as little noise as possible, not wanting to disrupt the stillness. Drifting into the emptiness of time and space, the constant editorial chatter of my mind quiets until it is nearly struck dumb. Later there will be time for missing my wife, for wondering how things are going back at the office, for wanting to share this experience with my friends. But for now, I surrender to the seductive elegance of my surroundings, through which I glide like the hawks riding the thermals far above me.

Finally, the dimming light and pangs of hunger impel me to look for a place to camp. Far down the windward side of the lake, a majestic boulder rises up—likely a gift from the ice age—offering an imposing pinnacle on which to pitch my tent and survey my surroundings. It's quite a slog hauling my camping gear to the top, but eventually I manage it—thanking myself for scrambling up the boulder fields of Old Rag Mountain that previous summer.

Once arrived, I discover a clearing at the far end with a fire pit, which has obviously hosted other campers before me who were undaunted enough to make this climb. I build a fire and devour a hastily cooked evening meal of freeze-dried chicken and noodles. After hanging my food stash from a high branch to discourage the bears, I lay back to count the emerging stars, grabbing a nearby rock for a pillow.

After an hour or so—the pine-filtered wind having swept all thoughts from my mind—my bones begin to succumb to the chill of evening. I manage to rouse myself, douse the dying embers of my fire, and crawl into my tent—having now fully cast aside my late-night city routine and capitulated to the daylight/darkness rhythms of the wilderness.

I brought a headlamp and a book to read, but such activity has no appeal this night, feeling like a distraction to my empty mind. A nearly full moon floods my tent with a soft glow. Across the expanse of night, the owls commence their questioning calls. The wind rustles the birches and small critters scurry here and there in the undergrowth, their tiny footfalls magnified by the brittle fallen leaves carpeting the forest floor.

The night sounds are a comfort. Rather than wary, I feel at home in this great, solitary expanse. Not sure how I would react to being alone for such an extended period, I am happy to find myself so at ease as I settle deeper into the cocoon of my sleeping bag.

Since my thirties I have learned to live with the chronic pain of peripheral neuropathy, a condition no less present because I am in the wilds. But the exertions of the day and the stillness of the evening are soothing antidotes, and eventually—despite the insistent burning and prickly feeling of the neuropathy assaulting my feet—I drift into sleep.

Early the following morning, the pre-dawn forest begins to awake. Pinks and oranges and yellows elbow their way through the blue-black horizon. Jays, warblers, chickadees and waxwings (nature's most insistent alarm clocks) sing a discordant cacophony, and woodpeckers add an oddly syncopated accompaniment. I crawl out of my tent to join the emerging day.

After groggily rummaging through my backpack and locating my water filter, I climb down from my boulder perch to the lakeshore, find a handy rock to sit on, and absentmindedly begin my routine of filtering water for the day. Apparently satisfied that the day has officially begun, the birds are now hushed, and—aside from the occasional call of a loon echoing across the lake—all is once again quiet. Mist-laden shafts of sunlight pierce the surrounding spruce, balsam and birch, casting lengthy shadows and chasing the chill from the air—promising a brilliant day to come.

Suddenly this tranquility is jolted by a clumsy stomping of hooves not fifty feet away—across a little cove directly opposite from where I hunker on the shore. There, cavorting in a circular dance like thousand-pound nymphs from *A Midsummer Night's Dream*, are a bull moose and the cow he is obviously attempting to impress.

I stop my labors, afraid that my presence might be discovered, and watch this unexpected *pas de deux* in awe as these two giants engage in their morning frolic, dipping their ponderous heads at each other while kicking up their hooves. In this pre-iPhone era, I am blissfully ignorant of treating this event as a photo op. I simply sit quiet as a stone and treasure this early morning ballet. Eventually, the frolickers retire to the forest and, rejuvenated, I return to my task.

I scramble back up the rock face and prepare a breakfast of wild blueberry pancakes. In the morning stillness, concentrating on the task at hand, my focus is interrupted.

Snap!

A twig? The hairs on the back of my neck stand in primitive alert. I have an eerie feeling of being watched. Turning slowly, carefully, I peer into the shadowed forest surrounding my campsite.

Nothing.

I listen, straining to hear the slightest sound. Again, nothing. Unconvinced that I am alone, I rise furtively and edge over to inspect the woods in the direction from which I think the sound came.

Suddenly, from the corner of my eye, I glimpse a startled toss of antlers and hear the frantic galumphing of hooves as the bull moose I had earlier witnessed in his mating ritual scrambles back down the rise from my campsite. A little shaken, but mostly relieved, I stand thoughtfully, trying to make sense of this experience. How long he has been watching me? Obviously he had climbed the steep rise to my elevated site and stood noiselessly, until I finally noticed that slight snapping of a twig. I shake my head, amazed. Amazed about how quietly this giant creature had approached. Amazed that a moose could even climb such an incline.

And finally, amazed at what had brought him here. I did not sense menace (belying the warnings I had received about the dangers of encountering a moose). Rather, this behavior feels more like curiosity—as if he is investigating my presence. As if his instincts are to ascertain who I am and what dangers I might present.

Although this is my first encounter with a wild animal that appears to exhibit such curiosity, in later journeys—to locales where animals had little, if any, interaction with humans—I will witness this apparent curiosity again and again—with caribou, wolves, and grizzlies, as well as with other moose. Given descriptions I have since heard regarding similar encounters, it occurs to me that perhaps I am only beginning to comprehend the instincts, intelligence, and behavior of our four-footed cousins.

Rules of the Wild

Of course, not every day in the wilderness presents a dancing moose experience. This lesson hits home just a couple of days later when I arrive at a stream that joins two lakes. Along the course of this stream, the water cascades in serpentine fashion through a field of small boulders. Rather than try to canoe through this obstacle course, I decide it's best to make a short portage around it. I nudge my canoe into a niche between several large rocks and prepare to disembark. Standing up carefully, I grab a backpack that I have stowed behind me and sling it over onto the boulder on which I am stepping.

Mistake!

Mid-step, my lunging motion pushes the canoe sideways, and now I'm straddled between canoe and boulder. The canoe rocks precariously, causing my foot to skid off the slippery boulder. As my leg plunges downward, I scrape my shin on the rough stone and splash heavily and unceremoniously into the water.

Sitting in the shallow water, drenched and wounded, I howl in pain and curse my stupidity at the top of my lungs. Fortunately, nobody is around to hear my raging. I am discovering that the freedom to shout, howl, bellow, rail, fulminate and inveigh, as well as sing, laugh, hoot, and yodel is one of the therapeutic aspects of journeying solo in the wild. With nobody present to offer comment or criticism, I can talk to myself with gusto, and even hold lively debates!

Feeling some relief after thus exorcising my feelings, I carefully stand up from my watery seat. With more than a little trepidation, I bend over my leg to inspect the damage. The bad news is that I have sustained a long, deep, ugly gash of some six inches on my right shinbone. It is bleeding profusely. The good news is that I cannot see any exposed bone. I inspect the gash closely and I see no observable break. Testing my weight, I don't feel the pain of a fracture. All in all, I feel fortunate to have suffered no worse.

Only after completing this self-inspection do I notice that all this time I've been standing in a small cascade of water rushing by the boulder I had attempted to step onto. As I stand here, the water surges over my legs, cleansing the wound. The flowing cold water seems to staunch the bleeding and alleviate the pain. Rather than rush for my first aid kit, I sit on a nearby rock and watch appreciatively while nature nurses the gash in my leg.

After about fifteen minutes the bleeding has ceased and my leg actually feels pretty good, even though the injury looks bright red and ugly. I step out of my watery cascade and, wedging the canoe snugger to the shore, grab my first aid kit and, wincing before I even touch the wound with a swab, force myself to liberally apply the stinging antiseptic to the laceration.

My first thought is to bind the wound, but since it is a scrape and not a cut that separates the skin, I decide to leave it exposed to the open air. Gradually, over the next few days, the red slash looks less and less angry.

As it turns out, over the years my leg will display a slash of dark discoloration, similar to the slashes on trees that mark trails. It serves as a constant reminder that traveling solo in the deep wilderness comes with a constant responsibility to be self-aware. Even in my simplest movements, the rules of the wild must be obeyed.

On this trip, only one other minor mishap comes to mind.

The very eve of my last night in the Boundary Waters, I am paddling slowly through some reeds into shore, looking for a clearing to set up my final campsite. It looks as if beyond these reeds hides the perfect spot, but I can't quite see over the vegetation. So, I carefully stand up in my Kevlar and—finicky as it is to the slightest shift in weight—the canoe rocks sideways and I fall headlong into the drink.

Fortunately I'm near the shore. Soaked to the bone, I stand up and discover the water is only about four feet deep. True, no one is around, but still I feel more than a bit sheepish. Gathering what dignity remains, I inspect the damage. Fortunately—aside from my soaked gear—I seem to be the only casualty, until I notice that the contents of my opened tackle box have spilled out of the canoe and drifted to the bottom of the lake. A bit too far to reach, I have no choice but to dive continually to gather up the spillage, piece by piece. Luckily, the water is clear, and I seem to have retrieved everything. From this point forward to midway in my very last expedition, I manage to stay inside my canoe.

By the way, the campsite is indeed quite nice.

My Fish Story

The final morning of my Boundary Waters expedition, I wake up early—about 4:30 AM. The birds are just beginning to discover the dawn, and I decide I might as well get up and try fishing for my breakfast. Shaking the stupor of sleep from my brain, I stumble out of my tent, grab my pole, and launch my canoe—venturing only fifty yards or so from shore.

The lake is silent, dozing in the morning mist, and—obeying the sanctity of this quiet—I dip my canoe paddle noiselessly. Even the sometimes-raucous loon is circling silently on the lake's surface some twenty yards off my bow. As I repeatedly cast my line, the loon repeatedly dives from the surface. Clearly, both of us are looking for our morning meal.

Loons fascinate me—not solely because of their unique

vocalizations. Sometimes you'll see a vigilant mother gliding watchfully through the water, her chicks huddled safely on her back, hitching a ride. Loons can plunge to depths of two hundred feet, stay underwater for up to five minutes, and then emerge some fifty yards or more down lake. I am getting an up-close and personal demonstration of this—and more. Just as I am anticipating where he will next surface, the loon breaks the water with what appears to be a two-pound walleye in his beak.

He sits there, displaying the fish as if to say, "Is this what you're looking for?" At that same instant, I hear the distant but telltale whistle of a bald eagle. Scanning the lake, I spot the great bird swooping in rapidly from the east—clearly taking aim at the loon and its catch. Talons down, the eagle swoops in and makes a swiping pass at the loon, who, just in the nick of time, dives—fish still in mouth—as the eagle grabs nothing but water, kicking up a mighty spray.

The loon surfaces and the hunt is on again, the eagle banking sharply and making two more fruitless passes while the loon repeatedly dives to protect himself and his catch. Finally, the mighty bird gives up and flies off, his once ominous presence diminishing to a flapping speck on the distant horizon. Seeing this, the loon wastes no time and deftly tosses the pike into the air, catches its vertical fall in his mouth—and swallows it whole, the fish bulging in his gullet.

I return to my campsite to prepare oatmeal, my morning fishing expedition no match for the success of the loon. But far more meaningful than catching any fish, I feel privileged at what I have witnessed. Bringing myself to this remote place, I have been part of a scene that is—in spite of my many years of camping and trekking with family and friends—an entirely new experience on my own. Somehow, this raw tableau awakens in me a renewed respect for the everyday struggles that comprise survival in the wild—and I am grateful to be alive.

And I myself have been a participant in this scene. In my somewhat meager endeavors over the past ten days, I've sought to find my place in this world far beyond the city: to reemploy my own senses and rediscover my relationship with a simpler, sometimes harsh—and always challenging—environment. Each moment has been a learning experience, discovering my rhythm not only in the cadence of my canoeing, but also in my daily routine. I have learned that I can survive on my own and be comfortable with my own company. Never boring, some incidents have in fact proved foolhardy and scary. But I managed to summon resilience and calm in the aftermath.

And I have found that though I am nearing my seventh decade, I am not too old to experience awe. With this first solo journey to the Boundary Waters, I have embarked on a new expedition of the spirit, and it feels like I have much to learn.

It is as if this odyssey has opened a passage to a more expansive way of being—a sort of meditation—a taking in with my eyes that has created new space in my heart. I have challenged a body that has grown city soft, and frequently despaired in the process. But, in the end, I have discovered a welcome calm and peacefulness in the midst of this wild life of give and take.

If anything, I am discovering that I crave this seclusion more than ever. Remembering the beginning of this Boundary Waters expedition—was it only ten days ago?—I recall that it took me a couple of precious days to find myself truly alone. I've been told that Quetico, the Canadian side of these waters is even more isolated.

"After this initial voyage," I tell myself, "I might just be ready to raise the stakes."

With that in mind, I begin to envision my next journey—to the backcountry of Quetico.

Chapter 3
1999 – ROUGH WATER – QUETICO

The wind is relentless. Trees bow low under its insistent force. Whitecaps roll, lashing the shore with unbroken rhythm. What's it been now—three days? If I wait any longer I'm going to miss my pick-up. But how am I supposed to take my canoe out in this water? I'll capsize before I get ten feet offshore. My stomach is knotted. Can't seem to stop shivering. I try bouncing up and down on my toes to release the tension and get warm. This must be what a horse feels like at the starting gate. As far as I can see, the lake roils. Two miles of cascading whitecaps. I'm imprisoned by a boundless barrier. The funny thing is, as I look up, the day is beautiful—sparkling under an azure autumn sky. And the sea is beckoning.

* * *

A year has passed since my first solo canoe expedition to the Boundary Waters. I'm here at Quetico—the Canadian side of those same waters—to once again abandon the cacophony of the city, to test my mettle in an even more remote location, and to open myself even wider to the wisdom of the wild country.

On my maiden voyage to the Boundary Waters, it had

taken two precious days to remove myself from the company of other outdoor lovers—families, scouts and groups of friends whose excited chatter and whoops echoed over the lakes as they settled in for a night around the campfire. So, this year I arrange to have a motor launch haul me, my gear and my canoe to Prairie Portage—Canada's point of entry into Quetico. My research indicates that this location should put civilization at an acceptable distance and deliver immediate isolation.

We have traveled nearly an hour, and the monotone drone of the seventy-five-horse Evinrude vibrating the boat over the rolling waves rocks me into a sleepy trance. Finally, the motor slows to a throaty growl and then a raspy purr. Scanning the shoreline as my guide throttles down the engine, I shout from my perch in the bow of the launch, "Where's my lake?" All I can see is an endless line of trees. "Just beyond those evergreens," is his laconic reply. "You'll have to portage a ways. This is as close as I can get you."

I can't say this is welcome news. I had imagined that I would simply be plopped down on my own private lakeshore, hop into my trusty Kevlar—now my go-to canoe whenever I can rent one—and immediately start paddling. Instead, I will have to begin my adventure by hauling the canoe and my gear over rough terrain—the least fun and the most physically challenging part of any solo canoe trip. Suddenly, I feel a year older!

I disembark the launch and, wading through the water, schlep my gear and canoe ashore. With a farewell nod, the captain restarts the hulking outboard, backs off the shallows, swings the launch around, revs up to full power, and leaves me in his wake. I stand stock-still, listening to the receding sound of the engine as it fades into the horizon until the launch becomes a speck. And then—nothing. Silence. Alone. A familiar and not unwelcome stillness. But nonetheless, being left alone on a distant lakeshore does feel a bit final. No cell phone. No radio. No contact. Just me.

Suddenly, I'm more aware than ever of my vulnerability. There's no changing my mind. No turning back. I'm on my own again—and that's that. I shake my whole body, trying to rid it of this sense of trepidation. I breathe deeply of the crisp, invigorating air, seeking renewed strength, energy and resolve from each inhalation.

The good news is that this portage proves far shorter than I feared—only seventy-five yards or so to where I can put into the lake. The bad news is the swarming mosquitoes. The really bad news is that, after frantically rifling through my gear—twice—it's clear that I've forgotten to pack bug repellant (perhaps the number one necessity on any outdoor person's checklist)! So my second solo canoe venture begins with me fighting off the swarms—swatting and flailing in a manner that only seems to invigorate their attacks.

Swearing a blue streak (both at the mosquitoes and at my stupidity), I feel a profound sense of discouragement, fearing my entire trip will collapse into an unending war with these marauders. But at this very moment of despair—out here in the middle of nowhere—I hear what could only be described as the voice of an angel calling out, "Hey! You! Git yerself on over here and come on inside!" I look up, and there, not fifty yards away, stands a sturdy young woman on the porch of a small, rough-cut shack tucked back in the trees. And yes, she's beckoning to me.

I am about to meet someone who, unlike me, had elected to forsake the city permanently and take up residence in this incredibly remote bush country. She laughs sympathetically as I bolt through her front door to escape the swarm chasing after me. I glance around at this sudden but welcome haven of civility. The inside of her cabin is as spare as the outside—a few shelves stocked with basic camping supplies surrounding a modest living quarters consisting of a couple of chairs, a woodstove, table, and loft. But it's pleasant—I guess you'd call it cozy—and it's mosquito-free! Without bothering to introduce herself, she goes straight to the problem.

"This here's the best thing in the world for skeeters," she announces, reaching for a small bottle on the shelf. "It ain't even skeeter repellent, but it works better'n anything I ever found."

"Fact is," she says, handing it over for me to inspect, "it's shampoo. But it ain't just any shampoo. It's got some sort'a ingredient that for whatever reason all kindsa insects don't like."

She doesn't know why it works and I don't care—as long as it works.

"Jist go on down and jump in the lake an' wash your hair and your body an'—you know—everything. It won't keep 'em away, but they won't land on you neither. Here."

Skeptical, I take the proffered bottle, searching for where I had secured my money. "Keep it," she says, waving my money away. And at that moment, it feels like the most generous gift one human being could give to another. She wishes me a good journey, and, almost bowing with thanks, I back toward the door, and say my goodbyes.

I grab my gear quick as I can—swatting vainly at the insect hoard every step of the way—and precede helter-skelter back to the lake. There I strip off my clothes, leap into the water, and scrub myself from head to toe with the shampoo. My skepticism turns quickly to surprise. It actually works!

The mosquitoes still swarm, but they don't alight and they don't bite. (No, I can't tell you the name of the shampoo—on my return home I misplaced the bottle and have been kicking myself ever since!) I can't believe my good fortune. It's as if my whole trip has been rescued. Dressing hastily, I load my gear into the canoe and begin my two-week journey into the unknown.

During these first few Quetico days, necessity teaches me what most outdoor veterans already know: when the mosquitoes are swarming, if possible, camp on a barren, windswept peninsula. Wind is perhaps your best friend in keeping the critters away. Fortunately, the weather grows windier and chillier, and before long I bid goodbye to the insects for the remainder of my trip. The chill is bracing, especially cooling as I spend most of my day paddling—exercising muscles that have lain dormant through the preceding year.

I further conclude that one of the best ways to avoid mosquitoes is to embark on these trips in the chillier days of early September rather than those of late August. In future years, this becomes my *modus operandi.*

Of course, nature's gifts are often double-edged. The wind is my friend when at my back, but a stiff challenge when I face into it. Some days it blows so strong that I find myself paddling with every ounce of my strength—kneeling into its force and digging my paddle deep with broad strokes, all the while railing against the elements, woefully noting that despite my Herculean efforts the shoreline has barely receded.

But there are also days of quiet calm—lilting days under a sun that streams pathways through the mackerel sky and dances on the undulating water. On such days there is a meditative quality to paddling—the rhythm of my thoughts attuned to the arc of each stroke—reinforcing a canopy of quiet that is interrupted only by the occasional fluttering of a bird or fish. On these days, hours pass unnoticed, until finally necessity reasserts its demands and I scan the shore in search of a protected space to cook and camp for the upcoming night.

On such peaceful evenings, I sometimes feel inspired to set pen to paper. But when the light fades, I fade as well—succumbing to my sleeping bag just after sundown and rising with the dawn. Nature is once again dictating my daily routine.

Mornings I crawl out of my two-person tent (one side for me and the other side for my gear) and wander down to the lakeshore to take in the sights and sounds. Often, a gentle breeze sighs its way through the red and white pines of Quetico's boreal forest. A red squirrel might scold me from an overhead branch, lest I get too close to his winter stash. As often as not a loon will come silently floating by, ignoring my presence and occasionally dipping her black and white head in the water. Now and then she dives, as if to test out her morning muscles—just as I am doing.

Three such loons swim by one particular morning, calling with their ocarina voices. It's difficult to tell if the distant identical "o-o-o-o-ah-ah-ah-ah-o-o-o" response originates from another loon the next lake over, or is an echo rebounding back across the mirrored water. Whatever the case, the three do, after a time, succeed in attracting a fourth loon, who swoops down, splashes a noisy landing, and instinctively falls into formation.

Stillness returns, and I reluctantly take leave of the lakeside to cook breakfast and prepare to break camp once again.

Not all mornings are so pristine. One day I arise somewhat later than usual and crawl sleepily from my tent. Suddenly, it dawns on me that it is too quiet—no birds rawking, no loons calling, no chipmunks scurrying, no squirrels scolding—only a windless calm. Immediately I scan the skies.

Looming in the south I see a daytime darkness the likes of which I had seen only in my childhood visits to Blackduck Lake. It appears as if a newly formed dark purple mountain ridge has suddenly erupted on the northern horizon. As I stand transfixed, the ridge swells ominously, slowly advancing in my direction. Clearly, I'm in for a storm. A chill runs over my body, and I feel both awestruck and vulnerable—naked against these elemental forces.

As I watch the darkened massif inexorably advancing, the trees begin to announce its approach with a moaning that eventually swells to a low roar. I duck back into my tent to fetch my camera, determined to record this show of nature.

But almost immediately the pines are bending under the coming blast and, realizing this is no time for a photo op, I scurry back out to secure my meager belongings.

Fortified with stories of canoes being tossed like toothpicks in a super storm last year, I make sure my canoe is pulled up far enough on shore. To doubly ensure my only transportation isn't smashed into the trees, I tie the straps of my backpack to the canoe struts and anchor the bow rope to a stump. For good measure, I pile heavy stones on top. Finally, I gather some dry wood I had previously collected and stash it in the tent.

Satisfied with my hurried preparations, I stand by the lake (just as I used to stand at the edge of Blackduck Lake with my father while my mother begged us to come inside the safety of the cabin) to admire the approaching fury. Soon, a cold, pounding rain drives me back into my tent, which I have battened down in a young grove of protective pines. I lie there in the mid-morning darkness, listening to the wind tear at the trees, the rain pounding on my tent fly, which flutters as if it will tear to shreds. Thunder caroms across the lakes, echoing across the heavens like a disgruntled freight train.

Curiously, I soon drop into a peaceful sleep.

As it turns out, this is only the first of three days of challenging weather. No canoeing now—just hunkering down and waiting it out. Later that first day, the skies again swell with darkening clouds. Between squalls, I erect a tarp-covered cooking shelter that hopefully will protect from the rain, though I realize a heavy wind could easily rip it from its moorings. Nonetheless, it offers the possibility of a hot meal, in place of the power bars and peanut butter.

Once again the late afternoon and early evening bring a calm, while yet another storm gathers on the horizon. Taking advantage of this lull, I cook a hot meal of freeze-dried teriyaki chicken and coffee, resecure the campsite, and again seek the shelter of my tent to await the coming onslaught. Exhausted,

I nod off.

The first inkling of a new assault comes as I awaken in inky darkness to feel an insistent breeze stiffening the walls of my tent as the whispers in the pines became a higher-pitched whistle. As the gusts kick up in the surrounding blackness, I have visions of the "hundred-year" storm that had left whole forests blown down like matchsticks—thousands of giant spruce and pine stripped of their needles and laying side by side for miles on end.

I had witnessed this blast zone two months after the event on my inaugural trip to the Boundary Waters. Apocryphal stories grew out of that storm—one being that of a hunter who had taken refuge beneath a protected embankment on the shoreline. When the gale had finally blown itself out, the hunter arose, as did a moose, which had—unbeknownst to his startled companion—shared the same foxhole.

All this swirls through my mind as I lie here. The wind begins to howl. Then the rains come. Sheets of it. The pines groan under their burden. I try not to imagine one of these towering but shallow-rooted behemoths that surround my campsite—a campsite selected for the very protection they seem to offer—crashing down and smushing my tent. Who would ever know? When would they find me—flat as a pancake?

Most of my times in the wilderness, I have successfully disciplined myself to avoid such obsessing. But occasionally— as now—I am not immune to such unwelcome but recalcitrant musings. Even so, as the storm and the wind picks up, my exhaustion overcomes my worry, and once again I fall asleep.

But not for long.

The storm proves to be a fierce one. For hours the deafening thunder echoes across the night sky, accompanied by merciless lightening, and a constant, unforgiving downpour. I spend much of the night checking for leaks and laying plastic protection on the tent floor—just in case the outside rain fly and tarp don't hold. Fortunately, they do fine. I awake glad I had the foresight to pitch the tent in a protected, well-draining area. Lesson from Algonquin learned! There, years ago, on the final night of an outdoor adventure I had shared with my three children in a remote area of this Canadian Provincial Park, I had carelessly selected a depression in which to erect our tent.

Later that night—during a similar thunderstorm—I woke to discover that, strangely, the ground beneath us felt as soft as a pillow. Turning on the flashlight to check for leaks, I found a rapidly expanding puddle forming on the tent floor. There was no denying it—our tent was flooding. In my stupor, I stumbled outside to see what could be done to staunch the flow. As I did so, Geoff and Laurie groggily came awake.

"What's happening?" they called to me.

"Get me some towels," I called back in my refusal to accept the reality of what was a soaking downpour. "I'm going to stuff them under the tent to soak up the puddle," I explained— not realizing just how ridiculous this solution must have sounded.

They dutifully handed me all the towels they could locate as I frantically stuffed them under the tent. Looking around in the dark with my flashlight, it was only then that I realized I had erected the tent in a swale—a fine location as long as the weather stayed dry. Now it was the site of quickly enlarging pond.

Finally, I came to my senses and crawled back into the tent. "We've got to go now," I announced. "No use waiting 'til morning. We're just going to get drenched"—as if we weren't already soaked. The three of us looked at Kelley, who continued to snooze peacefully, her sleeping bag now having become a floating island in the tent.

"Let's not wake her 'til we have to," we agreed. Gathering all our now waterlogged gear as quickly as we could, we heaved it into the trunk of the car. Fortunately, our canoes were already loaded on the roof rack, since we had planned to leave in the morning.

Finally, we woke Kelley. "What's happening?" Kelley yawned as we hustled her through the downpour and into the car.

"It's raining," I replied in perhaps the understatement of the trip. "We're going to drive to the nearest town and get dried out."

"Where's that?" Kelley wanted to know.

"About a hundred miles," I replied.

"What time is it?" she asked.

"A little after three at night," I said.

"Oh," she said, and then nodded off to sleep in the back seat of the car.

Soon we started our middle-of-the-night drive—all of us soaked to the bone. Geoff was soon asleep, and Laurie, typically, sat up front chatting with me as we followed our headlights through the dark. "Maybe we'll see a moose," said Laurie excitedly, ignoring the downpour.

Early that next morning, about 7:00 AM, we reached a town. Spotting a laundromat, everybody woke up and helped haul our soaked clothes and gear inside. I removed my hiking boots so I could dry my wet socks, and the kids pitched in with washing and drying our clothes and wiping down our gear with paper towels supplied by the laundromat. Bedraggled as we were, we must have looked especially pathetic to the townspeople who began to filter into the establishment, laden with their laundry baskets.

A gentle-looking woman tentatively approached me. "Would you like to have these boots I found?" she offered sweetly, noticing my stocking feet.

"That's very kind of you," I responded, not bothering to tell her that they were the boots that I had removed just a half-hour previously.

After that, I always made sure I erected my tent on high

ground.

Meanwhile, here in Quetico, after a fitful—but less disastrous—night, I rouse myself and peek out on a rain-spattered, overcast, grey day. I walk down to the shoreline, and notice that last night's wind did indeed shred my cooking shelter. Gazing along the waterline, I am amazed to observe that the lake has risen at least one full inch.

While the brunt of the storm has passed, there is still an unrelenting wind kicking up impressive white caps, roiling the lake. Watching these four-foot swells crash onto the beach, I realize that for a third day in a row, there will be no canoeing. In planning my trip, I had left room in the schedule for a couple of "down" days, which should, I had hoped, allow plenty of wiggle room to meet my launch at the pre-arranged hour on my pick-up day.

A couple of down days? Ok. But three days? Not so good! At this point, my rendezvous is in serious jeopardy. And who knows how much longer this blow will persist? All I can do is hope tomorrow will allow me to resume my journey. I resolve not to worry about events over which I have little control. Returning to my campsite, I batten down the hatches once again, crawl into my tent, and spend the day reading, writing, and snoozing—occasionally leaving the shelter to wander my peninsula and photograph the flora. This activity provides a welcome respite. As evening darkens, I return to my shelter to spend yet another night.

Stormbound

So here I stand, anchored to the shore as I have been for each of the past three mornings—gauging the wind and eyeing the whitecaps—torn between playing it safe and trying my luck despite this weather. The rain has finally ceased and the sun is shining like the first day of the rest of my life. But the wind still howls.

Alone in the wilderness, I understand there is no margin

for error. Capriciousness will not be kindly rewarded, but neither will diffidence. Replaying Bill Mason's *Path of the Paddle* video in my mind's eye, I can see Bill propelling his canoe into fearsome rapids—negotiating the waters as smoothly and efficiently as if he'd stepped out for a stroll in the park. Giving myself a pep talk, I think, "It *can* be done! I've seen it." And the fact that it *can* be done is, for me, the key that unlocks my indecision—the critical understanding that moves me to action.

Resolving to resume my journey, I break camp and load my gear, lashing it extra-tight into the canoe. I walk back to check my campsite and bid farewell to the sheltering woods that, throughout the storms, has given me safe haven. Turning, I head back down to the wave-lashed shore.

My first few attempts to launch my canoe are exasperating, infuriating, and (in hindsight) laughable. How to hold the canoe steady into the breakers, leap in, and paddle all in one motion? The answer? Try again. And again. The first time, my canoe is slapped sideways into me with incredible force, knocking me off my feet and nearly under the water—requiring me to exert every muscle to scramble back to my feet, thoroughly soaked, and keep the canoe upright.

Second try—same result. There's an old Midwest expression, "Mad as a wet hen." Now I understand the reference.

On the third try I manage to stay on my feet, but my canoe is thrown askew and nearly swamped. Now I am furious. Iowa-stubborn—red-faced and railing at the wind, the waves, and the gods in general—I try once again.

This time, much to my surprise, I manage to hop into the canoe and—flailing furiously with my paddle—gain a slight forward momentum into the foaming whitecaps which break mercilessly over the bow of my slight craft, drenching my face with a cold spray.

Clearly, there's no going back now. I paddle with all my

strength, alternating urgent, bold strokes first on one side of the canoe, then on the other, trying to maintain the bow straight into the wind. If the wind turns me, I will surely swamp. I manage to proceed ten yards—then twenty—off the shore where I have spent the last three days. I'm encouraged with my paltry progress, but exhausted! The discouraging truth, I realize, is that I cannot possibly keep up this frantic paddling.

Suddenly, in my mind's eye, I once again see Bill Mason calmly paddling through the whitewater. Counterintuitive as it seems, I slow my pace to match his. I replace my flailing with measured, steady, almost meditative strokes. As I do so, my mind calms with a new awareness. I am in a cocoon of silence and my spirit warms as I experience a quiet, yet exuberant, elation.

The canoe glides forward almost effortlessly through the churn. It's as if my internal calm has arrested the external turmoil. Suddenly, I realize that the two miles of lake that stretches before me is not a barrier, but a beckoning pathway. Rather than my nemesis, this lake is my companion and guide. It's the road on which I will continue my journey, leading the way home.

Despite the clamor of the wind and the breaking whitecaps, I'm paddling in smooth water.

Labor Day

"I miss Janet."

This is what I set to paper that Labor Day—a holiday where I find myself alone and still far from my journey's end. I am ready to be reunited with my life companion. Tired and weary, but immensely satisfied with my second wilderness solo trip, I've confronted the challenges I had hoped for—both physical and mental—and come through it all with a greater confidence in my ability to appreciate and inhabit the wild country. But enough! Now I just want to go home. However, there's still one final challenging day to negotiate.

Now, tomorrow has arrived and Quetico's waters prove to be no less formidable than in previous days. Once again, I waken to grey, threatening skies and a menacing wind. At least, I tell (delude?) myself, the lake isn't capping quite as much as yesterday.

When I emerge from my tent, I discover a squirrel has gnawed into my food pack. It hadn't occurred to me that the pack might be vulnerable to a night of sharp, persistent teeth, but clearly it was. I should have remembered the time Geoff and I lost most of our food to chipmunks in the depths of the Grand Canyon, forcing us to ration the final pack of ramen and one last scoop of peanut butter as we climbed up to the North Rim over the next couple of days. Fortunately, today's loss amounts to only a handful of trail mix, so I count myself lucky and repair the pack with everyone's favorite fix-anything solution—duct tape.

Next, I set about filtering drinking water and sit down to prepare breakfast. As luck would have it, in one last gesture of farewell, the mosquitoes return *en masse* and, flailing them away, I am forced to retreat to the tent. There I cobble a breakfast consisting of a power bar, a portion of unexpectedly delicious dried fruit, a piece of raspberry jerky, and remnants of the trail mix that the squirrel has left for me.

After emerging from my breakfast tent, it's clear that the wind is picking up and the skies are again threatening rain. I'd better pack up while I still have a chance to stow a dry tent before taking my leave. This next lake is the final obstacle to reaching my rendezvous. My heart sinks a bit as I realize the wind has swung around and is now blowing from the southwest, promising an arduous journey to my pick-up location. I'm weary and my hopes for a sunny, breeze-aided day are proving to be wishful thinking. However, by this point in my journey, I have learned to forgive my desires and play nature's capricious cards as best I can.

By the time I dismantle my campsite and load my canoe, the waves are capping, threatening—much as they had the other day—to beat back my launching. This time, improving on my previous experience, my second try proves to be the charm. After much wrestling to set the canoe's bow directly into the pounding surf, I manage to scramble in and get underway—all this time trying to quell my resentment that this last day will clearly require another supreme effort.

Once under way, I attempt to apply the lessons I learned just days ago—breathing deeply, calming my mind, and slowing my paddling to conserve my strength. Once again, I experience a satisfying sense of accomplishment as I manage to hold the canoe on course—not allowing the wind to turn me.

Ah hubris!

Having thus managed to reprise that success for a couple of hundred yards, a steady blast of wind suddenly catches the bow and begins to sweep it sideways. Impatient and frustrated, I am suddenly my old self, screaming and cursing as I attempt to correct my course, straining every muscle of my arms and back. I am losing the battle and once again find myself unwilling to give nature her due without a fight.

But willpower is not the solution, and as the wind turns my canoe a full one hundred eighty degrees, it threatens to undo all of the progress I have made. Unable to accept this fate, I back-paddle furiously, first on one side and then the other, swinging the canoe from ninety degrees back around to one-eighty, hoping in vain for the wind to abate for just one moment and allow me to propel the bow back into its face.

For a good five minutes I labor thusly, spending my last resource of energy, only to find myself no further along than when the wind first turned me. Finally, resentful but spent, I bow to nature's caprice and my limitations. Slumping forward and laying my paddle across the gunnels, I give up and ride the waves as they push me shoreward. In one final act of stubbornness, I try to set a course across the waves and I manage to gain some forward progress—perhaps, in the final result, recapturing some twenty yards.

But eventually I am thrown back to shore, dangerously slapping against the rocks. Disembarking, I wade through the foaming breakers, hauling my canoe behind me. Once on dry land, I flop down on the pebbly shore, gasping—my heart pounding like the surf. After resting a few minutes, I screw up my determination to have another go at it. Once again I point my craft into the whitecaps, wedging my body against the canoe to hold it steady. Swinging my leg like a high jumper, I climb in, and forge stubbornly back into the fray.

This time, I feel cautiously optimistic after about a hundred and fifty yards of forward progress, until the wind once again slaps my bow and my optimism sideways. Once again, I curse my fate, screaming into a wind that could care less. I flail for some time—spending my reserves of energy in the process—and finally give in. While drifting sideways towards the shore, seeing the absurdity of my efforts, I begin to rethink my strategy.

Clearly, there is little point in exhausting myself further. Instead of trying to head on a straight course through the open sea with its cross-currents and changeable winds, I will have to cut across the waves as best I can, hug the ragged shoreline of the inlets and bays surrounding the open water, and—perhaps most importantly—adjust my "poor me" attitude and be mentally prepared to be blown aground and restart as necessary. True, following the shoreline will increase the distance I have to travel about threefold, but the only other alternative is to wait for the winds to calm, which almost surely will make me late for my scheduled pick-up—prompting a search for my whereabouts.

This strategy works even better than I had hoped. I am blown aground into a bed of reeds only once, and when I finally gain the far side of a bay, the shoreline there is somewhat more protected from the wind by a bordering stand of pines. When a stalwart bald eagle abandons its perch atop one especially tall spruce and sweeps across the sky above me, I choose to view this as a good omen. It is not lost on me that this raptor is the national symbol of the country towards which I am fitfully navigating.

However, behind this inspiring sight is a build-up of ominous purple clouds, promising more wind, perhaps heavy rains, and—most intimidating—lightning. I keep close to shore, taking heart that at least I have yet to hear any thunder, which invariably announces electrical activity. No sooner have I processed these thoughts than a clap of thunder tolls overhead and heavy sprinkles splotch the water.

Needing no further warning, I paddle hurriedly through a patch of willows to the shore, beaching my canoe. Eyes on the heavens, I hurriedly untether my hiking boots and backpack—items which can ill stand a soaking—from the forward canoe thwart and throw them on the shore. I quickly recover the tent tarpaulin from the backpack, throw it over my belongings and myself, and—thus huddled in my makeshift shelter—prepare for the onslaught.

It never comes! After a few heavy sprinkles the storm moves north and west. Relieved, I repack my canoe, buoyed with a sense of cautious hopefulness, and resume my journey. My spirits are further lifted when a pair of bald eagles now tilt high overhead and my erstwhile companion on this entire journey, the stalwart loon, escorts me ten yards off my leeward bow.

But the elements do not abide omens. As I steer my canoe around the next point of land, the wind—perhaps trying to see if I am napping—threatens to blow me back across the bay I have just traversed. This time, paddling steadily in long sweeps, I hold my course.

Finally, peering through my binoculars, I can barely make out, about a mile distant, the small sign that marks my destination—Prairie Portage. I am now more confident that I will make my rendezvous on time, but I am not sure at what expenditure of effort. I still have a lot of open water to cross, and following the shoreline any longer will mean a detour of many miles and hours. But will the elements now be kinder?

Nature is quick to provide her answer. The wind abates somewhat, but it is still playing crosscurrents with the waves. (It has always seemed peculiar to me that waves can come directly at you while the wind gusts from skewed angles—but this is not an uncommon phenomenon.) Thus, while the waves are now calmer, the wind occasionally bursts across my bow and threatens to turn me—first one way, then the other. I paddle vigorously from one side to counter this action, switching the next instant to paddle just as vigorously from the opposing side. Occasionally, fear of being blown all the way back across the bay threatens to intrude on my work—but I thrust these thoughts aside.

Finally, when I am only a couple of hundred yards from my destination, I can see the piece of land marking the far shore where my guide deposited me nearly two weeks ago. Suddenly, I am aware of how ravenous I am. Since I am this close to the finish, it might be a good time to stop and eat. Remembering the armada of mosquitoes that had greeted me when last at Prairie Portage, I beach my canoe on a small, wind-swept peninsula to assemble a lunch.

Eating the last of my cheese rice cakes topped with peanut butter and jelly (which I heartily recommend—it has been a staple during my thirteen days) and munching on my ever-present supply of ginger snaps, I gaze across the expanse of lake at my journey's end with mixed feelings. The sun is finally breaking through and the seas are calming. I am ahead of my pickup time by a couple of hours.

Then a gust of wind reminds me of why I had not waited for a calmer departure. Even though my destination is in sight, I should not dally. Satiated, I rise from the rock that has served as my picnic table and climb back into my canoe, fortified for the last stretch of paddling, amazed by how my body responds to just a bit of nourishment. In a couple of hours I will meet the young man who had left me at this same location nearly two weeks ago.

The final crossing is relatively uneventful, with one exception: As I approach the Prairie Portage shoreline, two men have just launched their canoe and are starting their own adventure into the Quetico outback. During this entire trip I've had no contact with the outside world and have marked the passage of days crudely on a piece of paper. Suddenly, I experience a pang of doubt. What if I have miscalculated, and I am actually here on the wrong day? As our canoes approach each other, I shout, "Is this Tuesday?"

They laugh good-naturedly and call back, "Yep." Then I overhear the bow man say to his partner in the stern, "That's what I want to be able to ask when we get back," delighted with the idea of losing track of time. We salute each other and continue on our respective journeys.

A few minutes later, I am pulling my canoe onto the last Canadian soil I will touch, I presume, for some time. Upon my arrival, I feel emotionally and physically spent, my mind and my body ready for respite. Summoning a last reservoir of determination, I unload my gear onto the beach, and prepare to portage my belongings to the American side of the Boundary Waters.

Only now do I realize I have no hiking boots for the portage. The boots are in the grass where I left them when sheltering from the storm under the tarp. Should I go back for them and risk missing my connection? No way! I sadly bid the trusty boots farewell and prepare to portage in my Tevas.

The three round-trips it takes to haul my gear and my canoe consume the next hour. Foot-weary, I finally plop down against a log and await my launch. Soon enough, I hear the moan of the Evinrude across the water and catch sight of a dark speck growing on the horizon. It's a welcome, reassuring site, and I greet my young pilot with hugs and slaps on the back.

I climb into the launch. Unpracticed in the art of conversation after all this time and bone-tired, I can only slump on my seat and smile dumbly. Soon after taking off, the rhythm of the waves and the droning of the motor rock me to sleep.

Chapter 4
2000 – WHAT CAN GO WRONG? – WABAKIMI

Nothing really prepares you for this moment. The train recedes. You stand in the morning chill. The clacking sound of the wheels fades and the train grows more and more distant. As it gets smaller, you feel smaller. Both you and the train seem to be shrinking, while the trees and the sky and the vast expanse seem to grow larger and larger. And the distance between you and anyone else becomes greater and greater.

Once again, here I stand, ready to experience the sun, moon, earth and stars in a manner not permitted to the city dweller—seeking a silence interrupted only by the occasional call of the loon, howl of a wolf, or splash of a pike as it leaps from the lake in its unceasing search for food.

This is my third solo canoe venture to the wilds—each time seeking a remove one step further from civilization. My mantra, repeated to rangers and outfitters alike, has become, "Will I be truly alone in the weeks I am gone?" If the answer is, "Yes," my only further concern is, "How do I get there?" and "How do I get back?" Thus it is that I have come to the Wabakimi area of Canada's Ontario Province, some three hundred miles north of the Minnesota border.

The answer to my "How do I get there?" was, "By train!"

"Really?" I say. "Take a train to a wilderness lake?"

Following these instructions, I find myself early one September morning in the year 2000 loading my gear and my canoe into a boxcar of the Canadian National Railway's northern route from Armstrong Station to Savant Lake. I share a passenger car with a handful of other sleepy-eyed riders; most of whom I presume to be members of the Ojibwa Nation, through whose lands we are traveling. Slowly, as the train serpentines through the surrounding forest and lakes, each of us will debark until, at last, it's time to drop my gear and me at my appointed lake.

It has been drizzling rain off and on throughout the ride. As I stand watching the train recede into the pines, a momentary respite of early morning sun breaks through. But soon the rays yield to the overcast, and it begins to sprinkle once again. The cold drops on my face break my trance. I bend down and sling one pack over my shoulder and, staggering sideways a bit under the weight, hike to the lake—about a hundred yards from where the train has deposited me, my canoe, and my gear.

Dumping the pack heavily on the lakeshore, I trudge back for my second pack, and repeat the trek back to the lake. Finally, I go back one last time to retrieve the canoe. Unable to secure a Kevlar for this trip, my outfitter has provided me with a durable, but heavier, three-ply polyester seventeen-footer.

Reaching across the thwart, I roll the canoe up onto my thigh and then, with a grunt and a jerk, lift it onto my shoulders. Hitching it into place to get the proper balance, I raise the bow so I can see my way forward. Lumbering back to the lake I turn to take one last look at the tracks that brought me to this remote Ontario country and away from the last vestiges of community life that I will see for the next couple of weeks.

But the moment is brief, for the icy September rain is increasingly insistent and I need to locate my poncho, pack my gear into the canoe and—after securing it under a protective tarp—get underway before I get too chilled. Shivering to thread the last guy rope through the remaining tarp grommet, I push the loaded craft into the shallows of the lake. Once launched, my Maple Leaf baseball cap tilted low under the hood of my poncho to protect my glasses from the slanting rain, I hunker down and begin to paddle, soon falling into the familiar rhythm that had propelled me through the Boundary Waters and Quetico. The lake is long and begins to froth under the wind, reminding me of Quetico's challenges. As if tuning a long-neglected instrument, I adjust my body and mind to the demands of the wild.

Under the Rainbow

A rainbow is forming on the northeast horizon.

Amongst the baggage I have brought for this journey is my brain—a handy, portable device featuring thousands of years of development. During that time, it has undergone many revolutions—agricultural, scientific, industrial, and now digital—to the point where my prefrontal cortex can say to this rainbow, "You are beautiful, but actually you are light refracted on water droplets resulting in a spectrum of color." Dorothy dreamed of going over the rainbow. Now anyone can do it—just hop a jet! At least, that's what the "baggage" part of my brain tells me.

But this is the wilderness, and one of the reasons I come here year after year is to listen to the other part of my brain— the part that is easily five times older than my civil-eyed intellect. It's the part that hunted and gathered long before it settled into villages and cities. The part that formed the DNA that still governs me today—keeping a wary eye out for bears and wolves and storms and wind and rain. That primordial part of me seeks to be under the rainbow, mantled by its protective arc.

The darkening mountain of clouds, which had loomed before me and prompted me to bear down on my paddle to secure the distant shore, has now moved hesitantly to the south, giving way to a more hopeful sky. As the rainbow appears, my entire nervous system seems to recline, and I have to resist feeling giddy with hope. It's easy to understand how my ancestors might view the rainbow—and the serenity it imparts—as a blessing from the gods.

My mental and physical energy revived, I begin to scan the shores for a possible place to cook a meal and bed down for the night. It has been a long day of paddling in the rain and I'm ready to reward myself with sustenance and rest. And so, I decide to make camp among the sheltering spruce and pines along the shoreline over which the rainbow seems to hover. After pitching my tent, gathering what dry wood I can rescue from beneath layers of pine needles, and cooking a modest meal of freeze-dried chicken and noodles, the late afternoon sunshine warms to an almost balmy fifty degrees.

I shed all my clothes and spread my wet gear along the rocky beach. Naked and alone, I lie spread-eagled on the shore, soaking up the warmth, surrounded by the stillness. As my breathing quiets, I allow myself to drift into a well-deserved nap. Eventually, an evening breeze goosebumps my skin, and, reluctantly, I pull on my clothes and return to the fire pit, adding a log or two for the evening. The sky now populated by stars, I gaze at the emerging Milky Way—like my ancestors likely did—and, satisfied that all is well, crawl into my waiting tent.

Once settled in my enclosure, I put on my headlamp and pore over my topo maps, planning the next day's adventure. But soon I put tomorrow's plans aside and lie here contemplating the gifts of this day. Thinking about the rainbow, I recall the wonder and delight I felt as a child on Grandpa Miller's Iowa farm some fifty years before. A late August thunderstorm had interrupted the wheat threshing— an annual event wherein extended family and neighbors would work together to harvest the crop. It was my job to carry the water bucket and offer a dipper to the sweat-soaked men working the combines. When the storm had passed, steam rose from the fields. Expectantly, I scanned the skies and, sure enough, there was a rainbow spanning across the heavens. I was filled with awe and joy—just as I had been today.

Years later, I was to pen a song about those days—a song I eventually played for Grandpa Miller:

> *I was wonderin' just where*
> *all the rainbows begin,*
> *and where the sun sets again,*
> *after being where he's been.*
> *Where the moon and the stars*
> *plan the night we'll be seein'*
> *while they're waiting for daytime to end.*

> *From "Waiting for Daytime To End,"*
> *Music and Lyrics by Dick Anderson*

The arc of the rainbow seems to have traced the arc of my life.

My eyes grow heavy-lidded and I switch off my headlamp, wriggle down into my sleeping bag, and listen to the night. Occasionally a fish will leap hungrily out on the lake, or an owl will announce its presence. One final time, the owl hoots. Other than that, it is quiet. And quieter.

And sleep.

Lost?

In the wilderness, nothing focuses the mind like the threat of being lost. Allowing yourself even the suspicion that you might have made the wrong turn, or misread your compass, or mistaken a landmark, feels like marching inexorably to a self-inflicted doom. Somewhat akin to Kübler-Ross's five stages of grief, one fights against the certainty of the notion.

At this particular moment, only my second day in Ontario's Wabakimi wilds, I have just moved beyond denial to anger, and am approaching bargaining. The problem is that my compass readings are at odds with my topographical map. Theoretically, all is well. Supposedly, I am headed in the right direction, but it seems like I should have long ago received confirmation of that fact by the appearance of a slash on a tree marking the beginning of the portage trail to the next lake.

So far—no such slash.

Earlier this day I made what now appears to have been a turning-point decision. I had come to a junction where a river-like tributary wandered away from the lake I had been paddling. My topo did not acknowledge the existence of this juncture, let alone any such tributary branching away from the lake. However, my compass reading indicated that if I did not follow this non-existent waterway as it meandered to the east/northeast, I would not achieve my destination. Finally, siding with Korzybski's dictum, "the map is not the territory," I chose to believe the compass reading.

Instead of continuing on the lake, I veered off and headed up the tributary. Happily, the aid of a swift current made my paddling much easier. Less happily, it also cemented my choice of this route—promising increasing difficulty if I should try to retrace my journey back to my decision point.

Thus, as the minutes now stretch into hours, I feel I've reached a point of no return—the idea of backtracking is more and more inconceivable. I am committed. I take some comfort in the fact that after two years of solo expeditions, I am slowly becoming a savvy paddler. The fact that I had remembered to check my angle of declination before starting this journey reinforces my decision to trust my compass over my map. Nonetheless, I will feel much better only if and when I catch sight of the slash marking my next portage.

And the further I paddle, the less confident I grow.

Depression, Kübler-Ross's next stage, while understandable, is simply not acceptable. It will only contribute to a stage that Ross may have skipped—panic! What if I've somehow made the wrong choice? If I have wandered off course, is there an alternate way forward? True, it's still hours before nightfall, but I've already been traveling far longer than I expected—and at this rate, I will have to make camp and refigure my options.

As these thoughts assail me, I realize that what is most important at this moment is not to let my apprehensions become obsessions that can cloud my judgment. And so, taking a deep breath, I continue—one stroke of the paddle at a time—allowing the hypnotic rhythm to calm my body and quiet my mind.

After thus proceeding for another half hour or thereabouts—rocking forward and back again with each stroke, allowing my body to follow the pendulum of my paddle—my patience is finally rewarded with a tenuous clue from the shore ahead. There, on the trunk of one of the taller pines that fronts the forest, is a faint grey slash—weatherbeaten over the years to near invisibility—but unmistakably man-made and marking the beginning of my next portage. I let out a jubilant "whoop" of relief, celebrating my decision to stay the course my compass has dictated.

As it turns out, I will have no grand adventure to relate about being lost in the vast expanse of the great Canadian Shield. However, I've discovered something of much greater value. This near-miss experience will serve as a touchstone for my future wilderness travels. I have no desire or need to repeat the dread that I have experienced over the course of this day.

In subsequent journeys, I will double-check all preparations—including my assumptions. But most importantly, I know that certain circumstances defy preparation—instead requiring on-the-spot observation and real-time decisions. It is important to remember that relaxing best resolves such moments—slowing my breathing to the cadence of my paddling and allowing my mind to discover a course of action.

Never—then or now—will I confuse myself with those TV adventurers who are dropped into the middle of nowhere with only a fig leaf and a fig, somehow surviving desert storms or arctic blizzards. However, as a city denizen approaching my sixtieth year, I am beginning to experience a resurrection of a self that has been lost in urban routine. I respect the instinctual alerts that challenge my self-assurance. At the same time, I am learning that adapting my body to the rhythms of my surroundings predictably results in a calm, reasoned approach that will rescue me in what otherwise might be times of great peril.

Fishing Without the Pole

Getting lost is, of course, only one of the hazards of solo wilderness travel. Losing things along the way is another. Having learned this the hard way, I try to be very conscious of my gear, checking campsites thoroughly before leaving them. Not only do I want to "leave no trace," but I do not wish to be surprised later in my journey by the absence of some key piece of equipment. Every item I bring on these trips is there for a reason, and usually will be sorely missed if misplaced. Nonetheless, try as I may, almost every trip features some item either left at home or lost along the way.

This morning—fresh from feeling elated about keeping my bearings yesterday and locating the slashed tree that marked my next portage—I reward myself with a hearty breakfast of wild picked blueberries, hot chocolate and fresh eggs that I had cracked into a plastic bottle for the journey. I break camp, checking my site thoroughly, and prepare to portage my gear to the next lake. As usual, the portage requires three trips to slog two fifty-pound packs, my canoe, and assorted fishing gear and tackle. I figure I can attach my fishing pole to one of the packs, thus leaving my hands free to carry my tackle box and a dry bag.

Off I go, trudging over an overgrown, rock-strewn path that looks as if it hasn't been traveled in years. Frequently, I have to climb over deadfalls, clear away bramble, duck walk under overhanging branches, and scramble over boulders deposited during the last ice age. After nearly a mile, I spot a patch of blue water through the curtain of pines. A familiar relief radiates through my entire body as I stop to admire this first glimpse of my destination. The crazy suspicion that I am on the wrong path flees before a wash of assurance. No matter how many portages I make, that first sight of my objective is always a comfort—like meeting an old friend.

Once I attain the lake, I back up against a sturdy spruce, carefully sit down, and wriggle out of my burden. I find this dismount much easier on my back than trying to remove the heavy pack (which by now has worn a groove in my shoulders) by awkwardly slinging it sideways to the ground. Stupefied after this mile-long trek, I sit for a while gazing out at the lake, unconsciously registering the route across these waters that I will travel from this point—the pattern of the waves, the velocity of the wind, and the gathering clouds overhead. Rousing myself before I get too comfortable, I hobble to my feet using the spruce as my crutch to stand up, and then as a wall to lean against—stretching my legs like a runner preparing for a marathon. Thus limbered, I start back to retrieve my second pack.

Repeating the portaging, resting and stretching routine, I eventually return from my third circuit bearing my canoe overhead. I carefully roll it off my shoulders and into the shallow waters of the lake. Once more exhausted, I flop down by my familiar spruce and take a nap. The entire portage—about a mile in length—has taken most of the morning, and I sleep for a good half hour.

However, my dreams are interrupted by a loud splash near the shore, and I awake to see a northern pike leaping for its lunch. Speaking of lunch, by now I am quite hungry and decide this will be my chance for some fresh fish. I had tied my fishing pole to my backpack and go to grab it.

No pole!

No pole?

Perhaps I tied it on the other pack? I look. No pole. Feeling more than a bit disoriented, I examine each pack again, but looking again doesn't make the pole appear.

Clearly, it has torn loose somewhere along the portage trail. Disheartened, I run back along the trail to look, carefully checking the sides of the path. No pole. Back and forth I wander, in a stupor of disbelief, sure that the pole must be somewhere along the trail. No pole. Finally, worried about wasting too much of my day and growing very hungry, I return to my gear. What a shame. My favorite pole! And now I really have a hankering for fresh-caught fish.

Suddenly it dawns—do I really need a pole? Did people always fish with a pole? Of course not. I can't expect myself to wade into the water and catch a fish with my hands, but I do still have my tackle box. It contains all I really need: a reel, fishing line, leaders, weights and lures. Soon enough, I fashion a casting line, and, twirling it over my head like a lasso, heave it out where my pike had leaped.

I jig the lure and reel in the line. No luck. I try again. And again. Maybe this is silly. But much to my surprise, after my fourth try, my line unexpectedly speeds out of my reel and dives into the water. I jerk back on the line and set the hook. A good-sized northern suddenly breaks the water, twisting and turning in the noonday sun. I'm as excited as a twelve-year-old on his first fishing trip. Casting the reel aside (which really doesn't have much leverage without the rod), I pull the fish hand-over-hand to the shore.

Who knew? I've just caught my dinner with no pole!

The excitement over, I clean my catch, dig a fire pit, wrap the pike in foil, and cook it over a makeshift grill of wet sticks, eventually allowing it to fall into its own coals. It's a feast for a king—or at least for a tired outdoorsman, armed with yet another lesson in adaptation.

Mindful Traveling

When traveling solo, I've discovered the hard way that while paying attention need not be an obsession, I do need to cultivate it as a habit. Thus, I've developed a routine of double-checking my campsite or portage site before I leave it, of marking my entry point into a lake or river, of noticing the contours of the surrounding territory as I travel through it, of scanning ahead, or even of analyzing my next footfall.

Many of these lessons in mindful traveling come home to roost during this Wabakimi pilgrimage. A few days after losing my fishing pole, I experience a much more potentially disastrous event. While paddling peacefully, enjoying a warm sunny day after a previous afternoon filled with thunderstorms, I hear a faint sound of cascading water in the distance. Peering ahead, I see nothing unusual, but I notice that the current is picking up speed. Soon, a definite roar announces an impending waterfall. Wasting no time after feeling my tiny craft increasingly caught in the sweep of the current, I quickly paddle for shore. None too soon, for by the time I achieve take-out, the roaring waterfall, about a thirty-foot drop, is swiftly drawing the river into its vortex.

I scout for a portage around the falls and determine that my best route follows along the river for the next hundred yards or so. At that point, I will have to detour well away to find a suitable route to the lower level beyond the cascade where the river resumes its natural flow. I follow my usual procedure of first portaging my two backpacks. I proceed with particular caution because the spray from the water has slickened the rocks along the shore, creating an ever-present danger of slipping. After some exploring, I am able to find a route that will allow me to scramble from boulder to boulder down some thirty feet to the lower level and leave my gear in a protected area, downriver from the churning rapids at the base of the falls.

Making one final climb back up to retrieve my canoe, I hoist it onto my shoulders for the final portage. Proceeding with great caution along the slippery rock shield that comprises the shoreline, my canoe is buffeted by a swirling wind generated by the cascading water. Nonetheless, I maintain a sure footing. Suddenly, a gust of wind catches my canoe like a sail and tilts me toward the river. As if in slow motion, still holding the canoe firmly on my shoulders, I topple sideways. What is most curious about this moment is that I begin laughing hysterically, as if I were watching a cartoon of myself being blown over like a stick figure. When I land in rocky shallows of the river shore, I lay there, still in a walking orientation, with the canoe on my shoulders as if it were a large hat. I continue to laugh uproariously.

Somehow, both the canoe and I survive the tumble without incident—perhaps because I am so remarkably relaxed during the fall, laughing throughout the incident at how silly this scene would appear to an outside observer. It was as if I was both participant in and witness to this spectacle. Whatever the explanation, I scramble to my feet, re-shoulder the canoe, and march off again—happy to have suffered no further consequence. However, it is one more experience that I will catalogue in my mind for future reference. In this case, I had focused on my footing, not appreciating how my canoe might act like a parasail catching the gusting wind.

Fortunately, all these incidents—the brush with losing my way, the lost fishing pole, and my fall with the canoe—will serve as lessons in being mindful. However, I haven't fully learned my lesson, because a few days later, I nearly contribute my favorite chamois cloth to the woods of the Wabakimi. Upon discovering that it was missing, I confess that

I canoe back nearly a half-mile to retrieve it. This behavior might be considered a bit more than eccentric; however, chamois are invaluable on expeditions—to keep one's hands clean, wipe down a wet tarp or tent, sop up the ever-present water underfoot in a canoe, and for untold other mundane uses.

Additionally, I must confess that when one is off by oneself for a considerable length of time, there is a tendency to anthropomorphize even the most insignificant of objects. I apologize profusely to my abandoned chamois, which had accompanied me on so many previous trips, and promise to look after it more carefully in the future. For justification of this peculiar behavior, I can only refer you to *Cast Away*, and Tom Hanks's rather endearing relationship with his soccer ball, Wilson.

Reconnecting

These last few days—filled with gusty winds, rough water and long portages—have tested me to the point of exhaustion. So much so that I must stop a day or two and rest. Last night I stumbled through the routine of setting up camp, fixing dinner and falling into my tent. This morning I've slept late— a distinct break in my outdoors habit of rising at dawn. The temperature has fallen and I'm in no mood to leave the comfort of my down bag.

Reluctantly jump-starting myself into gear, I layer up and step outside to pick a few of the ubiquitous blueberries that surround my camp and proceed to mix them into flapjacks. As I gulp down this normally tasty meal, I stare absently at the now quiescent lake. A slight breeze sends shivers over its surface. I still feel tired and grungy.

"A dip in the lake'll wake you up," I tell myself. But the thought causes me to shiver, as if reflecting the ripples on the lake. I glance overhead. The sun is losing its battle with the clouds and the chilly breeze kicks up, rattling the poplars.

When I've felt this sluggish in the past, my solution has been to strip everything off and just leap into the water, allowing the bracing cold to bring me alive. But today I'm out of sorts.

"Come on, Dick. It'll be good for you," I chide myself.

Slowly, reluctantly—chastened by my own words—I peel down, layer-by-layer, absently placing my clothes in a neatly arranged pile near the lakeshore. Hugging myself, my hunched body is aswarm with goose bumps.

"Why am I doing this?" I grouse.

Hobbling carefully over the sticks and pebbles that populate the shore—my plantar fasciitis complaining with each step—I arrive at the lake's edge and hesitantly stick one foot into the water, followed by the other. The icy water takes my breath away. Shivering almost uncontrollably, I splash water over my face and body. Finally, with sudden resolve, I fling myself into the frigid lake. Gasping after I surface, I take a deep breath and dive back below the surface, entering the strange water-world of muffled sound and liquid light. This time I emerge whooping with delight as adrenalin shoots through my system, seemingly kick-starting every cell of my being.

Plunging back down, I swim back and forth with strong, powerful strokes until exhaustion and the freezing water forces me back to shore. Once out, I hunt for my chamois to towel off, but then think better of it. Instead I stand, arms and legs spread, allowing the breeze itself to dry me. Rejuvenated, strangely calm and peaceful, I feel at one with all that surrounds me. As if to join in the feeling, the sun finally breaks through.

There is a large rocky ledge behind me. I lie back on it, spread-eagled, eyes slit, and bask in the mid-morning warmth of the now-bright sun. The temp is still no more than the mid-'40s, but I'm no longer chilled. As I rest there, I breathe deeply, inhaling the crisp smells of autumn, the early falling leaves beginning to carpet the adjacent forest floor. Soon I'm in that twilight realm of near-sleep—aware of my surroundings, but on the edge of dreams.

Ten minutes later (an hour later—who knows?), I open my eyes, stand up and stretch. I try a few yoga poses to loosen up, and as I do, an involuntary release of tears begins to flow—a sort of spontaneous letting go. I realize what a trial this old body's been through in the past few days, as if preparing for this moment.

Reconnected with my old friends—the sun, the trees, the wind, and the water—I remind myself, "This is why I keep coming back, year after year: this solitude, this peace, this conversation."

Finally, the breeze picks up again and my teeth begin to chatter. I step into my clothes, layer by layer, and prepare for the rest of the day.

The Plane

Days later, the morning dawns bright and blue. No rain. About as perfect as one could ask.

As the sun pours through my tent flap, I breathe a sigh of relief. It could have turned cloudy, or rainy, or windy. But fortunately it's sunny and calm—one of those sparkling September mornings that implies all is well with this beautiful world. My good fortune with the weather means that rather than have to wait around for a day—or two, or three—this is the day I will head home. And am I ever ready! Incredible as these last two weeks have been, I've had enough. Enough paddling. Enough portaging. Enough slogging my gear, and setting up camp, and building fires, and breaking camp, and loading the canoe, and—enough!

So if my compass calculations are correct (and I've double and triple-checked them), I'm only an hour or two away from where I will meet my bush plane—and the plane shouldn't arrive for another couple of hours after I get there. That leaves plenty of time to cook a leisurely breakfast, clean up, paddle to my pick-up lake, and wait for my ride.

"Don't be too blasé," I tell myself. "This is no time to miscalculate!" I've never done this before—rendezvous with a plane in the middle of nowhere, some two weeks after having a brief down-and-dirty discussion with my pilot about when and where we would meet. I rerun that conversation in my mind.

"I should be there around midday, but you might want to get there a couple hours before."

"What if the lake's white capping?"

"Shouldn't be. That lake's pretty well protected by the pines. If it's too choppy, I'll waggle my wings and we'll try again later in the afternoon."

"What if it's *still* capping?"

"Then we try again the next day. Don't worry. The weather's got to be pretty rough before we call it off. We'll keep trying."

"I'll paddle out into the lake so you can see me."

"Yeah. Just don't get in the middle. I need plenty of space to land. Don't worry. I'll see you. Not too many white canoes where you're goin'."

So here I am. As usual, I don't carry a watch with me, but by the sun it must be around ten—well before noon, at least. The lake quietly ripples. Not a cloud in the sky. I scooch down so I'm lying in the bottom of the canoe, using my gear for a backrest. I pull out my map and triple-check where I am. No particular features on this lake—nothing to distinguish it from other lakes. Surrounded by pines and spruce, there are a few rock shelves, but nothing to set it apart. But compass-wise, it's right where it should be.

I rummage through my camp pack and get out a book. Pulling my cap visor down, I begin to read and relax in the warming sun—my canoe rocking oh so gently. The sky, the woods, and the water are completely silent. Dozing and waking, I let the peace of the wilderness wash over me—hug me, cradle me, and cleanse my brain of a thousand unnecessary thoughts.

Finally, some hours later, I hear the telltale buzz of a small plane beyond the horizon. Slowly, slowly, the sound grows in intensity and eventually rouses me to sit up and scan the skies. Finally, a spec appears, growing larger and larger until I can make out the wings and tail.

It circles my lake, scouting for the perfect landing spot as I wave a greeting, realizing this is the first contact with another human that I've had in a couple of weeks. Suddenly, the motor grows more insistent and the plane banks sharply, throttles down, and glides into a perfectly executed landing, the pontoons throwing up twin plumes of spray in their wake. The nose rocks forward and the pilot brings the craft back around while I paddle out to meet it. Cutting the engine, the pilot swings open the cockpit door and steps out onto one of the pontoons. Squatting down while holding onto a wing strut, he grabs the bow rope that I throw in his direction and eases my canoe parallel with the float.

I scramble out of my canoe onto the pontoon with a tinge of nostalgia—as if I were abandoning an old friend. After a quick handshake—each of us grinning our relief to see the other—my new friend invites me to climb into the plane and hands up my gear. While I stow the equipment in its new home, he secures my canoe to the struts and pontoon, then climbs aboard for the journey back.

Once we don our headgear, he revs the engine for takeoff. Suddenly the tiny plane rears back and becomes a roaring beast. Circling the lake to the far side, we rumble down our watery runway and the surface begins to race beneath us faster and faster. We are aimed directly for the jack pines encircling the lake, as if playing a game of "chicken" and one of us had better move! At the last possible moment, with a burst of air beneath us, the plane lifts out of the water and sweeps so near the tips of the pines that they seem to shudder in our wake.

Now aloft, we circle the lake one final time and from this new perspective I appreciate the vastness of the wilderness that has encompassed me for the past two weeks. I seem to see the reflection of my ghost paddling over the sparkling water and trudging through the dense forests. I am tired and ready to return to hearth and home. But I know that soon again, I will be seeking out this wandering spirit that I am leaving behind.

Chapter 5
2001 – LESSON LEARNED – MURTLE LAKE

Seeking the Mountains

I choose Wells Gray Provincial Park in British Columbia for my 2001 wilderness sojourn to surround myself with the peaks of the Cariboo Mountains, west of the Canadian Rockies. A beautiful, meandering, five-hour drive from the Vancouver airport, the park's Murtle Lake offers isolation, grandeur, and a unique canoeing experience.

This being a Provincial Park, I leave my name at a rough-hewn registration station located at the head of the first portage trail. The park provides a rather unusual amenity at the beginning of the trail—a two-wheeled portage cart, which sort of reminds me of an old oxcart with bicycle wheels. Wrestling my canoe onto one such cart, I load it with my gear, then precariously steer it down the steep incline of the trail until I reach the lake.

The obvious advantage of the cart is to make it possible to portage the canoe and gear in a single trip. The difficulty is wheeling my canoe, loaded with about one hundred fifty pounds of equipment, without it running off down the hill with me chasing behind. As I struggle to keep that from occurring, I wonder just how burdensome the return trip up the hill will prove to be. Eventually, I reach the lakeside and off-load the gear onto a small floating dock. I carefully lower the canoe into the lake, lash it to the mooring cleats, climb into the boat, and—careful to keep my balance in the rocking craft—load my gear into the canoe, and prepare to shove off.

The cart-aided portage and the dock from which to load and launch the canoe seem like a luxury compared to my previous experience of trudging back and forth over overgrown portage trails, strewn with rocks, roots and deadfall, followed by wading into icy, wind-blown waters when shoving off from my launching point. However, I soon discover that these amenities have been provided to accommodate a steady stream of adventurers from around the world who come here to enjoy this pristine lake and its surrounding trails and streams. Thus, I realize I will have to paddle some distance before finding the isolation that I seek on these trips. For now, I appear to be the only person around as I paddle away from the receding dock looking for a designated campsite (actual camping areas being another feature that I had not experienced since the Boundary Waters).

Tired from a day's travel that began early this morning in Washington, D.C., I pull into the first such area I come across and rekindle the routine of setting up camp and shaking off my citified habits. A sign reminding me to beware of the bears (both black and grizzly)—like a dash of cold water in the face—helps complete the transition from my suburban existence of the past year to the wilds of Wells Gray.

After pitching my tent, I begin searching for a high branch from which I can hang my food well out of reach of hungry bears. This is my first venture into known grizzly country, and I must admit that I am feeling a bit wary and more than a little vulnerable. However, I decide that worrying about bears will not keep them away, and finally locate a suitably high branch.

I attach a hefty carabineer to the end of my climbing rope. That accomplished, I wind up like a baseball pitcher and attempt to throw the weighted rope some fifteen feet up and over the branch. Twice my efforts fall short, but the third time I manage to heave the rope over the limb and feed it back down to where I can grab it. Rigging my food sack to the carabineer, I haul it into the air, watch it sway pendulum-like over my head, and tie the trailing rope as high as I can reach around the trunk of an adjacent pine tree (knowing full well that bears are notorious for figuring all this out, untying the rope, and feasting on your vittles). As my food bag rocks back and forth below the branch, I nonetheless feel a rather embarrassing sense of accomplishment.

I stroll back to the lakeshore and sit on a convenient log to watch the sun lowering on the southwest horizon. My mind drifts lazily, still adjusting to the fact that early this morning I was in my own bed thousands of miles distant. For someone as old as myself who grew up before the era of jet airplanes, this business of traveling great distances so quickly will always seem amazing, if not surreal. Regardless, here I am, back with the silence, breathing in the fresh fragrance of the pines, unencumbered by time and necessity. I sit absently, gradually letting my memories drift away, and think of nothing at all.

Finally rousing myself, I amble over to my tent and search my supply dry bag for my WhisperLite and my fuel bottle. But wait, the fuel bottle feels awfully light. I shake it. Empty! I shake it again, as if shaking it will change the fact that I had clearly forgotten to fill it once I landed in Vancouver. Taking filled fuel bottles aboard commercial aircraft is forbidden and carries substantial fines, thus necessitating filling such bottles with fuel on arrival. I had failed to do so, and now I realize that I will spend my next couple of weeks building wood fires. Fortunately, there is plenty of relatively dry wood under the pine needles even though it had rained earlier today. Forgetting my fuel is no immediate problem.

However, as a precaution, I fill a spare dry bag with kindling, just in case the rains return. "Is there anything else I have forgotten?" I wonder. I spend the next hour anxiously sorting through my gear, making sure that nothing else is missing (remembering how I had failed to bring mosquito repellant on my Quetico trip). Fortunately, all seems to be in order, and I set about gathering additional wood for my evening meal. Long past midnight, I creep into my tent, zip the flap, and yield to the night.

Murtle Lake

It takes two hours of steady paddling to attain the north end of Murtle Lake, but it's worth it. This distant venue, some eighteen miles removed from other campers clustered in the west arm, proves to be a welcome respite for the next week or so. As it turns out, I won't meet another soul during my entire stay on the north arm.

This trip is unique from my previous wilderness expeditions. I had been attracted to this particular lake not only because it was set deep in the cradle of the Cariboo Range, but because it was world-famous for being the largest canoe-only lake in North America. Rather than break camp, paddle and portage from lake to lake each day, I can stay put and use my campsite as a base from which to explore my private kingdom.

I soon fall into a routine. Each morning I rise, gather driftwood and kindling for my fire, erect and put in place the ladder supplied by the park service, and climb to the overhead platform that has been constructed for the purpose of storing my pack and food supply away from inquisitive bears. Hauling down my gear, I cook a leisurely breakfast of pancakes, eggs and hot chocolate with marshmallows. After breakfast and cleanup, I replace my food cache on its platform, remove the ladder, and hike each day in a different direction, exploring the surrounding environs.

On one such day I follow a small stream that drains the Murtle River, which arises from a glacier nearly twenty miles distant. I meander upstream for a couple of miles, armed with my camera, binoculars, and a daypack containing snacks. Sloshing through the reeds in my trusty Tevas, the September-cold water numbs my feet, ankles and calves (nothing new, since my feet have long ago gone numb from peripheral neuropathy), while a welcome sun warms and tans the rest of my body. The uneven surface of the streambed makes it slow going, but I'm in no hurry. I'm a kid again, bent on discovery—squatting down to examine even the smallest pebbles, marveling at the smoothness of their multicolored surfaces, ground down and eroded since the last ice age.

Another day I choose to explore in the opposite direction. Lacing up my Gor-Tex-lined hiking boots, I attempt a steep and challenging climb up a boulder-strewn waterfall. Exhausted and daunted by the slippery trek, I cling to outcrops, saplings, small trees, and roots—whatever I can grab to keep from falling back. Finally, I abandon the waterfall and work my way over to the equally sheer slope of the bordering forest. As my climb becomes increasingly sheer, I stop frequently, wheezing and gasping, often hugging a tree for support while trying to find purchase for my feet.

Taking a breather, I sit with my legs encircling the base of a small pine to prevent me from sliding back down the mountain. Shedding my daypack, I use it as a pillow to lie back against and, thus perched, enjoy an afternoon siesta.

Eventually, I cautiously struggle to regain my feet—grabbing the pine to pull myself up—and press on, one step at a time, into the late afternoon, all the time wondering if a grizzly is foraging this precipitous slope. As the shadows lengthen, I calculate that I'd better start back for camp if I want to arrive before night falls. Long ago I learned that no solo hike is worth risking the onset of darkness.

"What a different mindset I have when traveling alone," I think, recalling when Geoff and I hiked through the sequoia cathedrals of Yosemite, the ghostly cliffs of the Grand Canyon and the laurel-lined trails of the Great Smokies. In each of those instances, we enjoyed a full moon and each other's reassuring companionship. But here on the steep trail by myself, especially given the promise of a moonless night, I am not in the least tempted to linger.

The following day I decide to rest my aching body and stay in camp. Occasionally, I write in my journal—lounging onshore in the September sun—lulled by the rhythm of the waves lazily lapping the rocky shore. Binoculars by my side, I let nature come to me. It's a day to remind that doing nothing often brings rewards equal to the most industrious activity.

Scanning with my binoculars, I see a darkening sky on the distant horizon and wonder about the possibility of rain. I am reminded of the storms I have faced on past trips, from the times when I was a kid on Blackduck Lake to my more recent experiences in Quetico.

Suddenly, I'm smiling to myself as I recall an occasion where equally dark clouds gathered in the distance on a large reservoir in Tennessee—part of the massive TVA project initiated by Franklin Roosevelt in the 1940s. My young children and I had ventured far out on the lake in a motorboat I had rented. Kelley was just a toddler. Spotting the ominous clouds on the horizon, Laurie and Geoff asked, "Should we turn around and go back to shore?"

"I think we've got plenty of time," I replied.

"I think we should go back," said Laurie.

"So do I," chimed in Geoff.

"We're fine," I tried to reassure them.

Soon the wind whipped up and the clouds approached rapidly. Laurie and Geoff looked at me with questioning eyes.

"Ok," I admitted. "We'd better hightail it," as I revved the motor and we swung around in the direction of shore.

As we raced along, the rains came. First the sprinkles. Then a steady patter. And finally it let loose. We spotted a nearby island, beached the boat and, with Kelley huddled under my poncho, ran for the shelter of some nearby trees to wait out the storm. Some twenty minutes later, the sky cleared once again and we headed for home.

All the way, Laurie and Geoff repeated gleefully, "We were right and you were wrong! Right? We were right and you were wrong!"

"Right," I answered each time, properly sorry for the drenching. "You were right and I was wrong."

To this day, whenever I get too sure of my judgment, they remind me, "We were right and you were wrong!"

Tonight, here at Murtle Lake, the rains never come.

Anderson Lake

After some days using this location on the north arm as a base camp for exploring, I begin to feel the tickle of my old restless need to move on. I gather my gear, load the canoe, and decide to meander my way toward the west arm of Murtle. After being camp-bound for so many days, it's good to reacquaint myself with the mesmerizing rhythms of the water. My canoe gently glides through the slap, slap of the waves against the bow.

About mid-afternoon, I round the bend into the west arm of the lake, and eventually beach my craft at a trailhead on the far end of the west arm. Bending my back to the task of pulling a fully loaded canoe well up onto shore, I turn around to discover a trail marker announcing that Anderson Lake is two and a half miles distant. Ready to stretch my legs after many hours in the canoe, and curious about a lake that bears my name, I secure my gear, shoulder my daypack, and strike off down the path.

Eventually, I notice patches of blue water through the dense growth of spruce and pine and once again feel the familiar anticipation of reaching my goal. Anderson Lake does not disappoint. By now, tired from the exertions of a long day, I sit down on an inviting deadfall to a belated lunch, munching absently and gazing at the mirror-calm lake reflecting the surrounding mountains. It isn't long before, heavy-lidded, I sink lower and lower until, cradling my head on the fallen log, I doze off in the late afternoon breeze.

As I awake, the declining sun casts long shadows. I struggle painfully to my feet and stretch out the kinks. It's time to get back to my canoe and look for a campsite on the west arm. This proves to be no mean feat.

I had enjoyed a week of solitude while camped at the far end of the north arm of Lake Murtle. No such fate awaits on the west arm. As late afternoon gives way to evening, campfires dot the shoreline, as well as the islands that seem to float eerily in the darkness. There is no room in the inn. I circumnavigate the west arm two and three times to no avail, finally beaching my craft on one of the islands and cautiously hailing two campers who are huddled around their fire.

Stepping into the circle of their firelight, I explain my plight: "Hi, fellas. I'm sorry to intrude, but I'm getting kind of desperate. Could I possibly pitch my tent at the far perimeter of your island? I realize there's no designated campsite there and I promise to stay well out of your way. It's hard to believe, but every possible campsite is taken. I'm about done in and I need to stop for the night."

At first they appear a bit apprehensive. Then, they must figure I look legit and stand up to shake hands. "No problem. There's a spot over there that you can use" gesturing to a clearing about twenty yards distant. "You're welcome to join us for coffee."

"Thanks. I really appreciate your generosity," I reply, knowing what lengths I generally go to in order to be off by myself.

And so, for the next hour or two, three men huddle in the firelight, sharing coffee and swapping stories on this eleventh day of September.

Here, in the pristine wilderness, all is quiet. Even the wolves are silent.

The following morning, after bidding my newfound friends adieu, I spend my final two days exploring Murtle Lake and slowly making my way back to my launch point.

My World Turns Upside Down

"Are you Dick Anderson?"

This greeting by one of Canada's Northwest Mounties is an unexpected jolt. It's September 14, 2001. I have just emerged from my Murtle Lake sojourn and am unloading my gear for the last steep, uphill portage to where I had parked my truck some ten days before. The fact that this policewoman knows my name is not surprising, since all wilderness travelers are required to register with the park service, but it is troubling nevertheless. Had something happened to my family during my extended absence? Suddenly, I can feel my heart racing.

"I have some bad news. You might want to sit down," she advises with little fanfare. Then she continues. "Your country is at war, but we want you to know that Canada stands beside you!"

I am utterly stunned. At war? But I've been gone for barely two weeks! She then proceeds to tell me that the Twin Towers in New York City, from whose rooftop I had recently observed all the spectacular landmarks of Manhattan below, have been destroyed in a terrorist attack three days ago, while I had been obliviously sipping coffee around a campfire.

Fortunately, she carries a satellite phone, which she kindly offers so I can call Janet, who—I later discover—had watched billows of smoke rising over the Pentagon from her downtown Washington, D.C. office window. Unable to reach her, I call a mutual friend, who agrees to locate Janet and pass along a message that I will call again as soon as possible.

Of course, 9/11 proves to be a watershed event for the entire world, and its impact on my trips to the wild is immediate. While I was making my first foray into grizzly country, Janet was part of a mass exodus of downtown Washington, D.C., trying to sort out rumor from fact about the harrowing attacks in New York, Pennsylvania and Washington. Eventually, my friend and his wife located her and invited her over, knowing this was no time to be alone.

Clearly, I realize, my arrangement with Janet about being incommunicado on my expeditions will be a thing of the past. My being unavailable at a time of such great uncertainty and distress cannot bear repeating. My needs to be present as a husband trump any fantasy I might still entertain of being a solitary adventurer. On all future trips, we agree that I will carry a satellite phone and we will formulate a plan for regular contact.

Going Home

Having finally reached Janet, I begin to make preparations to journey back to Washington, DC.

First comes an agonizing night in a motel halfway back to Vancouver—a night where I fight off busy signals for some five hours while trying to make telephone arrangements for a flight from an airport that is closed for the next week (Vancouver International) to an airport that would be shut down for the next month (Washington National)—all the while watching the television replay repeated images of planes flying into the towers, of panic in the streets, and of the towers crumbling in massive plumes of dust and debris.

I feel heartbroken for my country and utterly ineffective.

Finally, I am astonished at three in the morning when an airline agent actually answers my repeated calls and I am able to make arrangements to fly one week hence first to Houston, then on to Dulles International.

Then comes a week of hanging around one of the world's truly beautiful cities, wanting only to get back to my wife and family and somehow try to atone for my absence during these traumatic times. Without much enthusiasm, I decide to spend my waiting days scouting Vancouver—walking its waterfront (one of the few cities in the world where you might find a coyote doing the same), visiting its art gallery and Museum of Anthropology, and exploring the nearby mountains.

At long last, after nearly a week, it is time to go to the airport and board my plane—just another in a series of surreal events. Approaching the airport, I am astonished to see hundreds of planes still parked on the tarmac—many of them international jumbo jets, awaiting permission to fly—while thousands of bedraggled would-be passengers wait with their luggage in a line stretching outside the terminal building for a half-mile or so.

Even more unreal is the fact that, because I had, unknowingly, secured a reservation on one of the first flights out of the country, I am allowed to bypass all this. Remarkably, I walk through a nearly deserted terminal and board a half-full flight. I now realize how my perseverance had paid off that long night on the phone after I had emerged from Murtle Lake. I feel lucky to be headed homeward, even if I do have to detour through Houston, Texas. I am finally on my way home to join in the national nightmare and, hopefully, the national healing.

Chapter 6
2002 – HUNKERING DOWN – SASKATCHEWAN

Dawn breaks. Still rubbing the sleep from my eyes, I reluctantly abandon the comfort of my bed and step outside into the frigid October morning. Shivering, I mumble "mornin'" in response to my host's too-cheery greeting. Grunting, we hoist my canoe and gear into his battered pickup, clouds of condensation escaping with each exhalation we breathe. We climb into the cab, and drive north in sleep-dumb silence for an hour or so to a remote landscape of water, rock, conifer and birch—the landscape of Saskatchewan's pre-Cambrian Shield.

No sooner have I been dropped off at my launch point, watching still bleary-eyed as my outfitter's taillights fade into the steel-colored distance, than the first snowflakes begin to appear, accompanied by a stiff breeze. Determined not to be daunted by this worsening weather, I hurriedly load my gear into my canoe, flapping my arms back and forth against my body to ward off the cold. Quickly, I push off from shore, hopping into my conveyance in the same motion.

Less than a hundred yards offshore, I slow my paddling to a stop. I am freezing. My fingers and toes are already numb, starting to ache. My face feels raw. It's as if all motion has slowed to a halt in this frozen tableau.

"What am I doing here in October in the outback of Saskatchewan?" I ask myself. Truth be told—as usual—I'm here living out a fantasy. For most of my young life, the name "Saskatchewan" fascinated me. In my imagination it suggested a wild country, far away and mysterious. And with a name like "Saskatoon" as the city where I will begin this journey, who could resist? The fact that these names found their origin in the Cree language only added to the mystique.

Additionally, aside from exotic names, my research into challenging solo canoe circuits had drawn me to this Canadian prairie province. I had thought to come here the previous year, but decided instead to experience the beauty of Murtle Lake and the Cariboo Mountains of British Columbia. Now, armed with a satellite phone after being incommunicado during the traumatic events of September 2001, I am once again ready to take on the challenges of portaging lake to lake in a wilderness that is far removed from other adventurers.

And why October? Because, given 9/11, I did not wish to spend any part of September away from Janet and home. The early part of the month marked the first anniversary of that tragic event, and the latter features a happier celebration—our wedding anniversary. Rather than go north in August with its crowds of mosquitoes and outdoors enthusiasts, I chose October, when the colder, harsher conditions would drive reasonable folks to their firesides. And so, having found the perfect outfitter for my needs, I set off for the Saskatchewan bush.

Now, here I sit, freezing in the snow and biting wind, reaping the benefits of my decision. "How can I go on in this bitter cold?" I despair. "You don't have to," I answer myself reassuringly. "You can simply turn around right now, head for a warm cabin and nestle in for a couple of weeks. It's okay with me. You don't have anything to prove."

"However," I add, my inner voice now resolute, "if you do decide to go on, get used to this! It's going to be this way for the next two weeks!" (Such dialogues are a constant, and often helpful, feature of my wilderness solitude.) "We're doing it," I decide then and there. "No further discussion!"

My mind made up, I unexpectedly experience the wet and cold in an entirely new way. The snow and wind continues unabated. I am just as cold as before my decision. But all this I pay little mind. Somehow, my brain and body have flipped a switch and these conditions become my new normal. For the next two weeks, the snow is frequent and the sun only occasional. My trip becomes a lesson in adaptation. Fire building is a frequently honed practice.

Until that snowy October morning, I hadn't truly appreciated how much attitude facilitates accomplishment. This realization becomes a touchstone for a mindset I learn to employ when confronting future obstacles: Lamenting doesn't help; better to accept, adjust and carry on.

Thus begins my first day. As the snow perseveres, rather than eat my lunch on the water (I often will munch M&Ms and trail mix while paddling), I soon stop and build my first fire of the day, making hot broth while warming my hands and feet. Mid-day fires become my routine for the duration of the trip. Later this afternoon, succumbing to the cold, I stop early, immediately build a fire, and—somewhat warmer (at least in spirit)—set up my campsite. I spend the first hours of this shivering night huddled by a blazing fire, watching the gently dancing snowflakes descend, shimmering into the glow.

At some point my near trance is disrupted by splashing sounds, and I look up to discover a family of playful otters— curious about my presence—popping their heads above the icy surface of the lake and frolicking some twenty yards offshore. My spirits buoy as I watch them watching me. Thus heartened, I crawl into my waiting tent, snuggle deep into my sleeping bag, and bid the world goodnight.

The following mid-day brings a brief but welcome respite from the snow. I come upon a narrows that joins Calder and

Buchanan Lakes, and as I round a ledge of large boulders, I look up to discover it is covered with pictographs, rusted by time but still remarkably preserved. The upper right-hand portion of this message features crossed arrows, as if it might be a compass pointing the way for future paddlers. The lower left portion seems to depict a hunting expedition.

Mouth agape, I shiver, but this time not from the cold. I am both filled with awe and bowed with humility. It's as if I've stumbled upon a sacred space, and I am the recipient of greetings from a long-vanished era. I can easily imagine the relief travelers over the centuries must have felt upon discovering this signpost. I linger for some time in this cocoon of history, staring up at this communication from ancestral times, reluctant to leave.

Finally, I continue on.

Later that afternoon I realize I am approaching a decision point. Before starting this trip, my outfitter speculated that I would not likely run across anybody during my two weeks on the water—unless I wanted to stop in and say hello to Rick and Deb, an adventurous husband and wife team who had constructed a remote "eco-lodge" called "Forest House."

Generally, I plan my routes so that I can enjoy complete solitude, but this couple and their unique project piques my curiosity. Approaching the point at which I will have to detour a few miles to canoe to their outpost (otherwise accessible only by float plane), I decide to drop in on Deb and Rick and see for myself what they have created.

Proceeding, I am at first unsure that I have correctly negotiated the labyrinth of lakes that my outfitter hastily indicated on my topo map. Finally, I spot a canoe landing and a path leading off through a meadow. Sure enough, upon disembarking and following the path, my snow-speckled vision soon reveals a remarkable log lodge in the distance.

I approach, and tentatively rap on the door with a gloved hand, my fingers nearly numb. "Welcome," grins by Rick, who has thrown open the door and beckons me inside, acting as if it is nothing unusual to find a stranger trekking through this wintry scene and knocking on his door so far from any other habitation. Deb joins in, receiving me enthusiastically—as if I were a long-lost friend. Wasting no time, they usher me through their eco-lodge, proudly explaining the composting toilet and solar panels that they have painstakingly installed. Out back there is an extensive vegetable garden and some small, presently unoccupied, cabins for guests.

After this grand tour, we sit by the fireplace in this serene setting, trading stories of our love for the wilderness. As the late afternoon shadows lengthen, it is all I can do to excuse myself from this comfortable setting and return to the raw elements that await me. Laden with as many of Deb's freshly baked chocolate-chip cookies as my pockets will hold, I trudge back through the persistent snow to my canoe, reluctant to leave the warmth of the lodge and its enthusiastic proprietors.

Night Vision

Once in my canoe, I retrace my paddling back to the lake some miles distant where I had diverged from my planned route. By now nightfall is beginning to overtake the landscape. It's high time for me to locate a campsite and build a warming fire. I paddle, searching for a place that will accommodate the modest footprint of my tent. I am well aware that dusk is deepening, but I still see nothing that promises a possible campsite. All around, the boulder-packed shore offers little repose, as the steeply sloped banks plunge into the depths of the surrounding lake.

My search for a location to build a fire and pitch my tent takes me deeper into the evening shadows, until finally daylight gives way to darkness.

Still I search.

Still no campsite.

Hungry, tired and growing numb from the cold, I decide

that a protein bar will have to suffice as my dinner. I am growing increasingly anxious to find a place—any place—to lay my body down and sleep.

Finally, shining a flashlight that trembles in my shivering hand, I find an indentation in the shore sufficient for me to tie up my canoe and unload my tent. Surrounded by boulders, I have little choice but to erect my tent on the rocky crevices, without the benefit of stakes. I crawl in, and spend a miserable night wedged between the boulders at rather impossible angles, catnapping as best I can.

Thankfully, though I sleep little, I am able to huddle in my sleeping bag and stay somewhat warm, the unanchored tent with its precariously askew poles at least protecting me from the wind and snow outside. That next morning I am able to scramble up a rather precipitous slope farther back into the surrounding woods, build a fire, warm myself, and cook some hot food.

The weather is still blustery with intermittent snowfall. Nonetheless, with a good meal under my belt, I feel somewhat restored. I clamber back down the steep slope, load my gear into the canoe and cautiously step aboard, careful not to tip myself into the freezing water. As the day progresses, taking no chances, I begin my search for shelter in the mid-afternoon. I eventually find the perfect clearing to pitch my tent on Hornet Lake. Gathering a supply of relatively dry wood and logs from beneath the snow and groundcover, I build a roaring fire. Enticed by my newfound safety and relative warmth, I stay anchored to this spot for a couple of days, drying my wet clothes and gear and allowing frozen hands and feet to thaw.

Occasionally venturing out on mini excursions for an hour or two, I return to my campfire and hunker down for long periods, adjusting my activity to the allowances of the weather. Occasionally a beaver will swim past towing a willow branch, or a mink will slither along the shore, each keeping a wary eye on my camp as they go about their preparations for the winter months.

Here Comes the Sun!

Most of my Saskatchewan adventure is a lesson in learning and accepting my limitations. Days are filled with snow and daunting winds. More than ever, I am very careful and methodical, lest a mistaken footstep incur a fall or worse. Patience truly becomes a virtue. This means proceeding at whatever pace is within my capabilities, allowing my plans to change as needed. Some days I stop to build a fire and rest two and three times between morning and evening. If I do not travel the distance I had planned, I find it's better to realign my expectations than become a slave to them. After all, am I not out here to give myself over to nature, rather than try to bend conditions to my presuppositions?

Eventually, I learn to appreciate, if not enjoy, the demanding weather. True, sometimes I find myself railing against it. One time while paddling my canoe into a strong headwind, I stand up, leaning into the wind to gain leverage, and arc my blade with sweeping motions deep in the water in an effort to propel myself forward. Glancing up from my efforts, I notice that one particular tree along the shore has remained in place for the past five or ten minutes. All my expended energy has gained me no forward momentum.

Screaming my frustration, I redouble my efforts. Still the tree remains where it had been. Finally, remembering my Quetico experiences, I slump down to my knees and paddle gently. In truth, neither method produces the desired result. I am no further along. However, as in Quetico, it becomes clear that I am not here to do battle—but rather, to learn to surrender. This is neither the first nor the last time that I will have to relearn the lesson to cooperate with nature and be guided by circumstances—for such cooperation does eventually yield rewards. Finally, the gusting wind subsides sufficiently for me to resume my forward progress. As usual, the long-term solution is patience.

After days of snow and cold, and too many nights of finding only rough boulders on which to pitch my tent, I am finally coming down the homestretch of this journey. I wake up one morning, some two days from my prearranged pick-up time, and notice a small break in the gray clouds on the far horizon. Thinking little of it, I quickly build my fire and eat a breakfast of pancakes and hot chocolate. Later, I load my gear into my canoe and start toward my destination. The wind still blows, but the snow has abated.

Soon a break in the cloudy horizon reveals a patch of blue sky. Suddenly, as if a miracle, the sun breaks through. As its warmth anoints my body and soul, I burst into song: "Here comes the sun! Here comes the sun! It's all right!" Even the Beatles couldn't have sung this anthem with more gusto. I have never been happier to be alive and to experience the blessings of nature. The spirit of this song remains my inspiration during these last days on the water.

Now the sun has gone away, but not the warmth it has brought my soul. I've survived two bitter weeks in the Saskatchewan wilderness. Never am I so happy as when I spot the pick-up truck that approaches in the far distance this final afternoon. I am cold, weatherworn and spent. But somehow I've never felt better.

So what is my plan for next year after spending two weeks in what my son Geoff would later describe as this "freezeateria"? Head north by northwest!

Alaska, here I come!

Chapter 7
2003 – TRUE NORTH – THE KENAI

Anchorage

What's in a name? A whole world if you're a kid growing up in the 1940s in Cedar Rapids, Iowa. Anchorage—the gateway to the far north. The land of icebergs and glaciers, grizzly bears and polar bears, and Sergeant Preston of the Yukon! Actually, Anchorage is nowhere near the Yukon and you have to travel several hundred miles north to see polar bears. However, a nine-year-old boy can be forgiven for conflating these images. And it is true that now and then a grizzly will wander into the edges of town. One fact is indisputably true—the name Anchorage loomed large in my childhood imagination—but was a gazillion miles away.

Now here I am, some fifty years later, a passenger in a silver bird that has brought me to the *real* Anchorage—as I resume my annual September migration northward to find solitude and beauty. Looking down on the sun-dazzled sea, the silver bird prepares to swoop down and land, thus completing the first leg of my journey to the Alaskan wilderness. My plan is to immerse myself in autumn's kaleidoscopic colors in the upcoming weeks, canoeing the remote lakes of the Kenai Peninsula. I press my face against the oval window, and watch as the chilly waters of the Cook Inlet rush upward toward the fuselage—replaced suddenly by a runway. With an abrupt jolt, we touch down at Anchorage International.

"Where's My Sat Phone?"

A couple of Septembers prior—on the 14th of 2001 to be precise—I emerged from the wilds of British Columbia, only to be greeted by a member of the Royal Canadian Mounted Police, who somberly enquired, "Are you Dick Anderson?" I was about to hear about an event the world would come to refer to as "9/11."

From that point on there was no more going into the wilderness incommunicado. Last year I had carried a satellite phone into Saskatchewan. This year I plan to carry one once again. However, not wishing to risk a repeat of last year's snowy, bone-chilling adventure, I have chosen to once again travel in September—leaving late in the month, well after Janet and I have celebrated our anniversary.

As I step into the unfamiliar environs of the Anchorage terminal, I crane my neck to find John Norris. Among the many hats he wears, John is president of SatComAlaska, and he and I have arranged to meet at this spot, where he will hand over one reliable, dependable satellite phone with an extra battery. I look for the next ten minutes. No John. I retrieve my luggage. No John. Impatient, I flip open my cell phone and dial John's number.

John answers, as cheerful as I am apprehensive.

"No problem," he assures me. "I'm running a bit late, but I'll be there in a few."

And, in a few, there's John—striding through the terminal doors, walking directly my way, shaking my hand vigorously with an infectious laugh, and welcoming me to The Last Frontier.

"Can I help with your gear?" John offers as he reaches for one of my backpacks.

"Thanks, but I've got a flight to Kenai in about an hour," I remind him. "If you'll just give me my sat phone, I'll pay you and be on my way."

"Oh, I don't have it here. But don't worry. It'll arrive soon. Meanwhile, why don't I give you a quick tour of Anchorage?!"

"But where *is* the phone?"

"Oh, it's out in the bush."

My concern is written on my face. Here I am, in a distant city, with my connecting flight due to leave soon, about to disappear for two weeks into the remote woods and waters of the Kenai Peninsula, and my phone is "in the bush."

"No worries," John assures me, "I talked to the guys who've got your phone this morning. They were only a couple hundred miles out. They should be in the air right now. I'll show you around town and then we can meet up with them at the airstrip," he says as if he does this every day (turns out, he does). "Besides, if they're late and you miss your flight, I'll take you down to Kenai myself."

"Welcome to Alaska," I thought. "When in Rome." Clearly, things are a bit different here—pretty much go with the flow— and that, I realize, I could learn to like!

We pile all my gear into John's SUV, and off we go to see the *real* Anchorage. We take a quick pass through downtown (which, strangely, reminds me of downtown Cedar Rapids when I was a kid), and then swing by the seaplane-mooring base (which is nothing at all like Cedar Rapids)—where John proudly shows me his four-seater Cessna.

Sweeping his arm to take in the view of hundreds of planes moored around the lagoon, John explains that since there are only a handful of roads linking an area the size of Texas, California and Montana combined, Alaskans depend on air travel far more than those who live in the Lower 48. Alaskans, I would come to understand, took smug satisfaction in differentiating themselves from their fellow Americans to the south.

Stepping off the dock onto the seaplane's starboard

pontoon, I swing up into the passenger seat while John gives me an enthusiastic tour of the instrument panel and explains how the GPS works.

Checking our watches, we pile back into the SUV and head for a dirt and grass landing strip. As we stand there on what seems to be a vacant stubble field, I wonder how we can possibly get back to the airport in time for my connection. Finally, straining my eyes, I make out a beetle-like dot on the far horizon and hear the growl of a small craft.

"That should be them," says John, as the wings and fuselage come into focus.

Sure enough, in just a couple of minutes the plane glides downward and taxies toward us, bumping along the rough landing strip and kicking up dust behind. Once the engines are cut, out jump four camo-clad hunters, the excitement of their wilderness sabbatical still emanating in their hearty greetings and adrenalized chatter. No strangers here—all of us are reflexively bound in unspoken camaraderie. The sat phone is handed over, and with no further ado John and I wave our goodbyes and race for the airport, just in time for me to make my flight to the Kenai.

By the time I buckle my seatbelt and prepare for takeoff, I realize that I have just made a remarkable new friend—one who will, as it turns out, become an important participant in my future Alaskan sojourns. In the years to come, I will meet John's wife and children, stay in their Anchorage home, visit their fly-in cabin, and—thanks to John's generosity—have an opportunity to take aerial photos in some of the most spectacular and remote regions of the state.

Like a Tree

Seen from the air, Alaska's Kenai Peninsula is a carpet of trees, interspersed by lakes and streams. The canopy is so dense that you cannot imagine yourself alone in a canoe—far from the throngs of the salmon-besotted fishermen lining the shores of the Kenai River—winding through this maze of wildness.

But now I *am* in my canoe, the fishermen long behind, and that same community of trees that I marveled at from the air now reveal their individual character—stately Sitka spruce, standing tall and proud, claiming their space, sometimes embracing massive boulders with their roots; sun-spangled aspen, clacking rhythmically in the crisp autumn breeze; and paper birch, peeling and bleached white, casting a battalion of lengthy shadows in the late afternoon sun.

A bald eagle perches high in the tufted apex of a cedar, and as my canoe draws near, it swoops down, as if guiding me forward, alighting on a treetop far down the lake—repeating the process over and over as I approach. Thus, I am escorted on my journey, as if a spirit animal were leading the way. Finally, the magnificent bird soars off, leaving me alone and strangely bereft, as if to remind that companionship is ephemeral, and only I can determine my ultimate destination.

Sometimes the trees are guideposts, an objective to mark my progress. Other times they are a haven of shade for a noonday repast, a cradle for a nap, or a terminus for the day's journey—providing shelter for the night's camp. From my canoe, as the late afternoon shadows lengthen, causing the tree-filtered sun to dance on the water, I search for just the right spot, where the forest encircles protectively, the wind is diminished, and a patch of level ground awaits my tent. Taken together, these sheltering conditions are rare along Kenai shores, and I think back on last year's journey—canoeing through the remote warren of lakes that saturate northern Saskatchewan—when I learned the perils of waiting too late in the day to search for a suitable campsite.

Camping in the Kenai

The lessons of Saskatchewan are fresh in my mind as I scan the shoreline. I have come to appreciate that each wilderness campsite is a personal haven, a respite for body and soul—a place you make your own, if only for the night. This time, my search is quickly rewarded, and I set about the chores of establishing my temporary home. I gather rocks for the fire pit. Next I collect wood—first the twigs for the cooking fire, and then larger pieces for later this evening.

After I am satiated on a meal of country-fried steak and rice, topped off with a Power Bar, I cozily settle by the now roaring fire. I gaze into the leaping and falling flames—an ever-renewing experience that warms the body and hypnotizes the mind.

As the flames slowly become embers, my eyelids grow heavy. Hobbled from a long time sitting, I stand up laboriously, douse the flames, and bid my surroundings goodnight. Only then do I look up and realize that the late evening Alaskan sun is enveloping the horizon, painting the fading Indian-summer sky with a palette of pinks and purples and reds, radiating out from its yellow-white center behind a dappled silhouette of birches.

I crawl into my tent.

Somewhere a jay chirps its evening lullaby, serenading me to sleep.

Morning

Dawn breaks in a frigid chill, and with drowsy reluctance I climb out of my body-warm sleeping bag and race to pull on long johns, socks and boots, and add the layers that I know will later be peeled off as the day progresses—a daily ritual which is the price for communing with nature at this time of year. Emerging from the tent, I am greeted by the sight of my own breath, fogging a world covered with the icy crystals of a first September frost. Caught unprepared, I discover that the firewood I've left unprotected shines with the hoary sheen. I am forced to drop to my hands and knees and rummage beneath the ground cover to locate reasonably dry kindling.

Are snakes keeping warm down here? I don't recall snakes in Alaska. What I do recall is finding myself in a similar posture in a Virginia state forest one foggy, drizzly evening some years before. I had arrived at my campsite after dark and needed to collect dry firewood. Copperheads and rattlers shared those environs, and with nervous caution I warily proceeded to forage for tinder. Fortunately, none of the sticks I gathered began to writhe.

Snapping myself back from this reverie, I shake off the memory. Despite my gloves, my fingers are growing numb, and without further delay, I feel my way beneath the spruce needles that cover this sub-arctic forest floor. Eventually, I assemble a modest collection of dry twigs and muskeg. With hands that now feel like clubs, I try to strike a match.

After two unsuccessful attempts, I produce a tiny flame. Willing myself to be patient, I nurse the fragile flicker— blowing as steadily as my shivering breath will allow—hoping the sparks will catch the neighboring kindling. Finally, my efforts are rewarded and the tiny flickering flame slowly becomes a glowing fire. Soon I will be feasting on coffee and flapjacks. Though it is hardly the dead of winter, I nonetheless can't help but recall Jack London's cautionary tale of a fire not built.

Sipping the last dregs of coffee, I finally rise to survey the environs surrounding my camp. The distant mountains that were purple the previous evening are now white with snow.

Suddenly, the morning quiet is torn by a deafening sound—similar to the report of a rifle—and my body involuntarily tenses in prickly alert. Not thirty feet from shore, a bright silver coho has broken water and leaps high into the air. My heart leaps with it, and as the great fish plunges back into the water, I am suddenly seized by the desire to engage this beauty, which I estimate is easily upwards of twenty pounds. My rational mind knows this is foolishness. The light tackle I've brought with me is no match for this prodigious salmon.

Nonetheless, I grab my pole and feverishly rig the line, selecting my largest orange-spotted Lazy Ike as the lure of choice. I scramble into my canoe and push off for the spot the coho has so recently vacated, his leaping body still etched in my vision. Casting the line, I decide to troll back and forth over the area. Rather than hold the rod with one hand and try to paddle with the other, I lean the tip of the rod on the deck of the stern, thread the handle and reel under my seat and hold it tightly in place between my boots. Even though the likelihood of a strike is negligible, I am ready to grab the pole in an instant.

Well, maybe not an instant. No sooner have I begun paddling than my pole leaps from between my feet—reel protesting noisily as the line shoots out. Before I can even grab for it, my pole rockets over the stern and dives into the water, far from my reach and instantly out of my view. My "engagement" with this adversary is brief and humbling. I have lost my favorite rod and reel, my favorite lure, and more than a bit of my pride. I paddle back to shore, still excited though chagrined, and begin to break camp. Another day in the Kenai has begun.

The Forty-Mile Trek

"With longer portages, extra time and physical effort are required for exploring this system. Generally, these challenges mean fewer people visit here creating better wildlife viewing, excellent rainbow trout fishing, and a more compelling wilderness experience. This route covers 80 miles including 40 lakes and 46 miles of the Swanson River."

—U.S. Fish and Wildlife Service description of the Swanson River Canoe Route

I'm the kind of person that salivates on reading the above description. More challenge? Few people? Just what I'm looking for! I have come to the Kenai precisely to get away from the Alaska of tourists, sport fishermen, and hunters. What I am looking for is solitude—and boy did I get it! I meet precisely one person while canoeing the Swanson system. He is kind enough to take one of the few photos I have of myself during these years of wandering the wilds of the north. He too is traveling solo, and—true to our natures—we exchange brief pleasantries and go our separate ways.

I spend about ten days canoeing the waters of the Kenai, with some forty miles of that trekking the trails between lakes. When the USFW Service promises long portages, they deliver. Many of these portages are a mile or more in length over rugged terrain. As an oldster traveling alone, I can only handle about fifty to sixty pounds while making the trek from one lake to the next. I haven't had to do this much portaging since Quetico. Like then, I shoulder one fifty-pound pack for the first leg of the portage, generally carrying a paddle in each hand, and leaving behind my canoe and other gear.

Upon reaching the launch site at the next lake, I leave the pack and paddles and return to fetch another load—consisting of a second fifty-pound pack, the camera bag, and other gear such as my tackle box and spare fishing pole. I wearily return one final time to heft the canoe onto my shoulders and haul it to where my other equipment is stashed. I have no fear of my gear being commandeered, as there is no one around to do so! My main precaution is to make sure the food packs are safe from bears or other critters. Fortunately, the rather complicated procedure of hanging these packs from the highest available limb is a skill I have mastered in previous journeys.

But What About the Bears?
One can hardly think about Alaska without thinking about

grizzly bears. Stories abound, especially in our media-saturated, voyeuristic environment. Realizing that I am planning a trip into bear country, I spend as much time as I can researching how I might best prepare myself. It is clear to me that the sometimes-romanticized attitude that "bears are our friends" can prove naïve, dangerous, and irresponsible.

However, advice from rangers and other experienced outdoor advocates is sometimes conflicting: Make sure your campsite has a small perimeter, so you are not claiming too much territory; mark your territory just as the animals do and claim a large space; clean your fish at least a hundred yards away from your tent; no, clean your fish and cook your meals near your tent so you're not claiming too much territory; stand tall if you come across a grizzly on the trail; avert your eyes lest the animal think you are challenging it; always carry a firearm; use bear spray; don't use your weapon unless the bear charges; remember, black bears are generally more aggressive than grizzlies; take a bear bell with you and make a lot of noise on the trail; carry all your food in a bear-proof canister; travel in blueberry season when the salmon are running and the bears have plenty to eat.

It will take several journeys and many years for me to come to my own conclusions about how to stay safe and feel at ease in bear country. In preparation for this trip to the Kenai, I visit a sporting goods store to explore the possibility of purchasing a rifle. There I learn about various weapons and ammo I will supposedly find indispensable. "This beauty'll bring down an elephant," I'm advised. I also compare a variety of pepper sprays that I might employ to ward off a charging animal. "This one shoots fifty feet, but this one only has a range of twenty-five. 'Course that presumes the wind is with ya."

For a number of reasons, most of all my lack of experience with firearms coupled with an aversion to inflict harm on an animal in whose territory I am an uninvited guest, I choose to carry bear spray. Thus traipsing the trails of the Kenai, I have a large aerosol can of spray clipped to my belt, always fearful that I may catch the activating lever on a shrub and accidentally envelop myself in a cloud of pepper. Actually, there is little chance of that happening because the activating mechanism is so safeguarded that by the time I manage to unclip the spray, remember how to deploy the activating lever, gauge the wind, aim, and spray, the bear will likely be long gone—or on top of me.

To avoid this possibility, I make noise by singing at the top of my lungs a tune based on a childhood ditty. Thus, "Rain, rain, go away," becomes "bears, bears, go away." Actually, I'm conflicted because, as a photographer, I would love to come across a bear (at a safe remove)—but how is that going to happen when I'm making all this racket? After a few days of feeling rather silly, I lapse into relative silence, deciding that the bears will easily hear me tramping through the undergrowth.

Do I actually run into a bear on this trip? I do hear what I guess to be a quite large animal moving through the brush about fifty yards ahead of me. When I arrive at a small intersection of two animal trails, I come across a freshly steaming pile of bear scat. But that's as close as I come. No bear sightings today.

A Larger Life

Folks like my friend Harry shake their heads and wonder why I put myself through this tortuous and somewhat risky routine year after year. I certainly have as well. I've never come up with a simple answer. All I know is that somehow the rewards far outweigh the difficulties. The aches and pains fade with time, but, for me, the experience of reconnecting with the natural world and the larger universe is essential for feeling whole and complete. Over the course of a year, I inevitably find the routine of work and city life self-focused. No matter how fulfilling the work or stimulating the urban environment, the center of this activity is "me." I schedule my time. I have appointments to keep, tasks to fulfill, self-imposed obligations to meet.

My remove to the wilderness—usually for a couple of weeks—frees me from this encompassing cycle. My pace—reflecting my experience of time—slows, sometimes to a near standstill. Inevitably, when I return to these wilds, I find myself standing in solitude—in a forest, or a glade, or by a river—letting the realization wash over me that I am no longer the center of my universe. Rather, I am simply a denizen, along with the other animals, plants, waters and rocks. The longer I stand in stillness, an atavistic sense of belonging recurs—as if returning to a way of being that I have forgotten. I am a part of a continuum—a flow—small but not insignificant. I am revisiting my ancestral home—a home to all who have come before and all who will come in time.

This annual discovery reinforces my willingness to continue my travels, enriching my life with a renewed awakening — always knowing that encountering the unexpected makes each journey unique — well worth the aches and pains.

And so it is with the Kenai.

Ghosts

After a September night that featured no more than three hours of honest-to-goodness darkness, another dawn breaks in Alaska's Kenai.

A fog is looming over the lagoon—spreading a gauzy blanket that muffles the lapping of the icy water. I stand on a rocky outcrop jutting out from the shoreline, my hands cupped around a steamy mug of coffee. The earth is shuttered, still asleep. On my right, patrolling the edges of the lake, a regiment of tall pines stretches skyward, the pinnacles of these guardians obscured in the ghostly atmosphere. Overhead, escaping the haze, the southwest sky yawns, a blue expanse promising a crystalline, sunny day. Directly eastward, the sun is still fog-bound, a silver disk bathing the rocks and trees in a phantasmal glow of bleached light and ebony shadow.

Free from the cacophony of the city I've left far behind, my mind seizes this opportunity to slow down and meander through time. I recall how last night I was standing here on this identical rock, serenely surveying this same scene, aided by a waxing moon. The contours of the shore were then plainly visible, and now, trying to reconstruct the details of that vista, I find myself suddenly transported, as if my present self were merging with my self of last night. It's a strange, eerie, yet not unfamiliar feeling—not déjà vu, but time collapsed—my past and present selves becoming one.

I close my eyes and purposefully slow my breathing to probe this curiously harmonious connection, and soon am drawn even further back—into a memory of another September evening many decades ago in Virginia, when I had written "Ghosts," a song whose lyrics sought to capture this selfsame sense of time folding back upon itself, past and present overlapping.

> Stars shining bright
> mirror my night
> and view my reflection sublime.
>
> My ghost sits up there
> watching me stare
> down through the spaces of time.

Earlier that long gone autumn day, I had ascended Old Rag—a mountain beloved by outdoors enthusiasts—near the hamlet of Sperryville. At the summit, after scrambling over the last challenging boulder field, I beheld a breathtaking fairyland—ice crystals adorning the entire mountaintop with diamonds. Choosing an inviting boulder, I sat down to luxuriate in my surroundings and take in the valley below. Gazing down, I spotted in the distance the old farmhouse where I was spending the night. Through my binoculars, I was just able to make out the broken down iron-wheeled horse cart reclining forlornly in the front yard.

That evening, after completing my descent, I would be resting on that very horse cart and gazing back up at the summit, where only hours before I'd been marveling at the valley below. It was there, sitting on that dilapidated cart, that I had experienced the same sensation I was now feeling in the Kenai—time and my two selves gently merging, as if I were looking up at a ghost of myself—a ghost who, across the expanse of time, was looking back at me.

Now, these many years later, as I stand here absorbed in this hypnotic Kenai morning, my thoughts return again to last night—a night in which only the occasional shiver of ripples on the lake and the howling of a wolf had interrupted the stillness. I remember how, reluctantly, I had broken the spell and begun the noisy job of setting up camp—erecting a rain tarp, chopping wood, staking the tent, rattling pots and pans, building a fire.

I had eaten supper in silence, transfixed by the blaze, drawn deep into the flames that were morphing red to orange to yellow, shuddering skyward and then falling back into themselves. As I sat thus entranced, time again shifted and I found myself imagining how fires like mine must have comforted those ancestors who crossed Beringia—the Siberia-Alaska land bridge—as they journeyed here from Asia thousands of years ago, seeking food and shelter. Then, as now, fire must have been a shield against the night—a haven for all who shared its warmth and light. I could almost feel their ghosts and wondered if they had dwelt in this very place.

As my campfire slowly embered, satiated and sleepy from my evening repast and the labors of the day, I had stretched out, wriggling my shoulders and butt into Kenai's forest floor until I'd fashioned a comfortable cradle. Grabbing the nearest rock for a pillow, I had scanned the heavens, enveloped by the deepening silence of the night—a silence broken only by the mourning of that distant wolf.

Gazing up from my prone position, searching the heavens for falling stars, my thoughts once again began drifting, this time to the past of fifty years ago, where my seventeen-year-old self, also looking skyward, huddled against the chill and watched these same stars as they flickered over Blackduck Lake in northern Minnesota. That night I had also stretched out, but in the bottom of a rowboat, anticipating my older brother's arrival the next day.

I'd invited Lyle to join me for a week at the lake to share a cabin I had rented with my summer savings, hoping we might reprise for one last time the summers we'd spent together as kids. He would be arriving in the morning, but that night was mine alone to savor. Luxuriating in my solitude, I'd rowed out onto this beloved moonlit cradle of my youth.

I was a pipe smoker back then. (It was my teenaged conception of maturity.) I'd lit my pipe and lain back—a cushion under my head and a blanket thrown over my legs—gently rocking with the waves. My fishing pole dangled over the side of the boat, but I was hoping I would not have to respond to any sudden pull on the line. Half a century later, I still recall the fish had obliged.

After some time—perhaps a minute, perhaps an hour—I'd roused myself from this fifty-year-old memory. The night's fire had turned to ashes. Pulling myself up from my prone position with the aid of a nearby sapling, I had hobbled back over to my Kenai lakeshore, like old men do after sitting too long.

I'd stood by the shore quietly, bidding farewell to the day. Another wolf call sent a thrill down my spine and suddenly I had the irrepressible urge to howl in answer to his plaintive cry. I threw back my head, cupped my hands around my mouth, and, inhaling deeply, howled to the heavens.

"A-r-o-o-o-o-o-o-o-o," I had wailed, over and over. "I'm here too! I exist! I'm part of this!"

The night swallowed my howls, but I had felt content—even a little giddy. Smiling to myself in satisfaction, I returned to douse the campfire, crawled into my tent, and slept 'til just before dawn broke.

Now, as I once again stand here on this misty Alaskan morning, I deeply breathe in the crisp, refreshing air. I no longer need to howl. Howling is for nighttime. Morning invites gentleness to usher in the new day. I bask in the surrounding tranquility, and reverentially tend to my morning duties, as if tiptoeing through a cathedral. I cook my breakfast in silence. I strike my tent in silence. I load my gear in silence.

Wading into the fog-shrouded water, I launch my canoe, and the rhythmic pull of my paddle deepens my morning trance.

Suddenly, an enormous slapping sound crashes through my reverie, followed by a prodigious spray of water. With this fierce warning to steer clear, a beaver has announced his presence on the lake.

I obey, giving him a wide berth. Gliding forward, I welcome another day canoeing the Kenai.

Chapter 8

SPRING, 2005 – STARTING OVER – OKEFENOKEE

Best Laid Plans

My plan was to canoe Alaska's Tetlin National Wildlife Refuge in September of 2004, but cancer argued otherwise. In the spring of 2004 I received the news that, regardless of a low PSA reading and no discernible warning signs, I was in fact in the advanced stages of prostate cancer.

Was I shocked? Absolutely, especially given the fact that I felt fine. In fact, if it hadn't been for an alert doctor (whose specialty was oncology) suspecting my condition after a yearly physical, I'm not sure when I would have discovered the cancer. However, after the initial blow of receiving the news— never being one to dwell on matters over which I had no control—I subsequently began weighing my options. Thus, instead of planning for the wilderness, I spent that spring researching treatments, finally concluding that radical prostatectomy surgery was my best approach.

My surgeon suggested September as a time that would best fit his calendar. I asked, "Could we wait a few weeks so I can go on my annual wilderness expedition?" He just shook his head at my denial. Rolling her eyes, Janet shook her head in agreement with him. So that September I traded the wilderness for a hospital bed. However, determined to make up for this sleight of fate, I decided to return to my outback canoeing just as soon as I healed. I began making plans not to go north, but south, to Georgia's renowned Okefenokee Swamp in May of the following year.

Why the Okefenokee? For one thing, it was too early in the year for reasonably predictable canoeing weather in Alaska. Additionally, I had been to the Okefenokee—a bird-watcher's paradise—years before with my family. It had left an indelible impression. We had camped on the fringes of the swamp and canoed for a day through the edges of this alligator-patrolled region.

Recalling the wild beauty of Okefenokee's marshlands, my research revealed a canoe circuit through the glade that allowed paddlers to spend days in its environs, taking advantage of elevated pole-supported platforms for overnight camping above the reach of the gators and other critters. It seemed like a great change of venue and an exciting opportunity to re-hone my wilderness skills.

And the Okefenokee offered one final advantage: no portaging. Only six months away from my prostate surgery, I was leery of the physical exertion required to schlep my baggage from one destination to the next—especially after my experience in the Kenai, where I had hiked some forty miles. My research showed only one brief portage through the Okefenokee. Otherwise the main challenge would be hauling my gear up the ladders to the various platforms.

Perhaps the fact that most impressed me from my previous visits to the Okefenokee—and the Everglades as well—was the exotic, abundant bird life. During those trips, I had also carried a point-and-shoot camera and, unfortunately, experienced its limitations. It possessed neither the resolution, the shutter speed, nor the telephoto capabilities to capture the splendor of the many varied herons, egrets, storks, cranes, kites, gallinules, spoonbills, and other water birds—let alone the surrounding flora and fauna.

As a sort of congratulatory present for resuming expeditionary life, I decided that now was the time to buy the new camera I had been considering for the last couple of years. I chose a new SLR (Single Lens Reflex) camera, with all the bells and whistles—including a telephoto lens paired with a heavy-duty Manfrotto tripod—and a large, waterproof backpack to protect this precious cargo. I selected a digital Olympus E-300 because it offered the lightest, most affordable, most compact alternative for solo use. However, it added nearly forty pounds to my gear, including the thirteen-pound tripod.

Notwithstanding the added weight, this investment would mark a new dimension in my explorations. Like a person with new glasses, now more than ever I began to pay precise attention to the details of my surroundings, whether they be distant or nearby, grandiose or minuscule. The camera also had the unanticipated benefit of focusing my inner experience, sharpening my appreciation for that which was truly meaningful in my post-prostate existence.

*   *   *

Finally, after purchasing a mosquito-net hat and a snakebite kit, and packing plenty of repellant and sunblock, I wing my way south. Landing in Jacksonville, Florida, I rent a van and head north for the Georgia Parks canoe rental location. Once there, given that I will be traveling alone, I am required to demonstrate my ability to load my rental canoe atop my van by myself in order to assure the Park Service that both I and their canoe will return safely.

Still a bit tender from my surgery, I struggle to roll the heavy canoe onto my thigh, jerk it over my head, balance it on my shoulders while my legs wobble and stagger beneath me, and finally slide it into place on the van's roof rack. The Park Ranger who oversees this test shakes his head doubtfully as I sweat and pant, but, seeing my rather pathetic determination, gives his permission for me to proceed with my journey.

Driving to a remote area of Okefenokee National Park appropriately called Kingfisher Landing, I struggle once again to unload my canoe and portage it to the launching dock. This accomplished, I load my gear, slather myself with repellant, and step into the craft. Once launched, I whoop with joy. It feels like a first step in resuming a normal existence after the drawn-out drama of the cancer.

The Okefenokee is reverberating with life—trumpeting bullfrogs and calling birds overlay the constant screech of insects. This cacophony of natural exuberance is exhilarating, contrasting with the silent canoe as it slices through the coffee-dark water.

Though I don't meet another soul during my paddle through the swamp, I have the feeling of being constantly watched. Not infrequently this is true. Suddenly among the lily pads, alligator eyes will appear just above the waterline only yards in front of my glide path, quietly appraising me as the prow of my craft bears down upon them. Just when it appears that a collision is inevitable, the eyes sink soundlessly beneath the surface, as my canoe seems to skim over the long, plated body. Somewhat disconcerted, I turn and look behind me, but, in every such instance, all trace of the creature has disappeared. This happens so often that soon I grow to anticipate this somewhat unnerving confrontation.

My journey through this verdant outdoor aviary—pulsating with insects, amphibians and birds—stands in marked contrast to the sounds of the Northwoods, whose quiet was only occasionally broken by the high-pitched cry of an osprey, the wind in the pines, or the rhythmic dip of my paddle.

Only once in the Okefenokee do I tread upon dry land—Floyd's Island, where a rustic cabin stands welcoming the weary traveler. Otherwise, the raised camping platforms scattered throughout the swamp offer protection for the night. Each evening I tie up at one of these open-air shelters, schlep my gear up the ladder to the platform surface, and pitch my tent. After a day traversing the swamp, these platforms are a welcome respite, equipped with a sheltering roof, picnic table, an outhouse, and plenty of space for a photographer like me to set up a tripod.

From this vantage point, it's a shutterbug's paradise. Wait long enough, and most of the Okefenokee's wonders will come to you: a sunset, yawning across the horizon; a full moon overhanging the mangroves; a hazy, mist-shrouded sunrise weaving through the swamp; and, of course, all manner of frogs, chameleons, dragonflies, butterflies, and exotic birds—in full voice and proudly displaying their plumage.

At nighttime, a muted but steady cacophony of buzzing insects and foghorn-like croaking bullfrogs settles over the swamp, and soon lulls me to sleep. The spring peepers announce the morning and I arise, cook breakfast and coffee and then sit back for a spell—scanning the morning mist with my binoculars. One particular morning, I spot a group of frolicking sandhill cranes in the distance, wings spread and scarlet-slashed heads bobbing in a courtship display.

About an hour later when the mist has fully lifted, I grab my gear and descend the ladder back to my canoe. After loading all my paraphernalia, I push off noiselessly into the swamp, allowing the canoe to glide silently forward before quietly dipping my paddle into the dark water—unwilling to disturb the peace of this sanctuary. I consider myself lucky that the spring weather is mild (often, it can be oppressively hot) and the mosquitoes are correspondingly few. My netted hat has yet to be employed.

Though rain is an occasional visitor, only once—several days later—do I find myself on the open water with billowing, black storm clouds approaching rapidly. It is mid-day. Realizing I am far from the nearest platform or any other kind of refuge, I quickly locate my tarp and throw it over both my gear and myself. The temperature drops rather dramatically. Soon the wind is rocking my small craft and rattling my tarpaulin. Enormous drops of rain begin to pelt my makeshift canoe shelter, sounding like hoof beats on a plastic roof. Thankfully, almost as quickly as it arrives, the storm moves on—the swamp steaming in the glistening afterglow.

After all these years canoeing the wilderness, storms do not frighten me; although I grant them the respect they are due. An awesome display of natural power, they are given as much to renewal as to destruction. What amazes me about this squall is despite the driving rain, delicate blooms such as pristine white water lilies, yellow and purple swamp iris, pitcher plants and bladderworts with their red-tinged hoods seem to survive the downpour in fine shape, their vibrant colors dappling the endless expanse of greens that form the Okefenokee palette.

Adding to the variety of pigments are the birds that frequent these waters: white ibis with their bright red faces and legs, iridescent purple gallinules tiptoeing the lily pads, pink roseate spoonbills sweeping their bills from side to side to vacuum nutrients from the swamp water, the ubiquitous herons (great blues, little blues, tricolors, black-crowned and yellow-crowned), and, of course, the glossy ibis, with their luminous prism of chromatic color.

Wood storks, black and white outliers in this world of intense hues, swoop from their cypress perches, eyeing a warmouth or crappie for their afternoon repast. Often the precursor of such a scene is the shadow that suddenly and silently passes overhead, causing you to look up and then duck, lest you be the target of this stealthy predator.

Perhaps the most emblematic image of the Okefenokee is the pond cypress, rising slender and tall above the peat-filled tea-stained waters. These ancient spires stand proud and erect—like gateways to new waters—beckoning for exploration. But it's best to resist this temptation and stick to the designated waterways. Otherwise, you could easily look back and find yourself unsure of your entry point. Swamps are notorious invitations to get lost—a fact I had discovered some years back while canoeing the Everglades.

Paddling the Okefenokee can feel like time-traveling, back to the soupy origins of life itself. Though the swamp was formed rather recently in geologic time—some five to seven thousand years ago—the flora and fauna make it seem as if you are part of an ancient biosphere. The plants, many of them carnivorous, seem a reminder of how one false move and the murky waters can close around you, bequeathing your presence to the percolating brew of these verdant wetlands.

Consider, for example, an alligator—the very look of whom harkens back to dinosaur days. As I am canoeing one early afternoon, I spot one that appears to be eight or ten feet in length on a grassy hummock some fifty yards distant. Without warning, it turns and covers that fifty yards in just a few seconds and submerges itself in the very canal in which I am paddling. Such an event serves to remind me that this powerful creature belies its characteristic brooding, lurking presence. Instead, it seems ever poised to lash out suddenly at an unwary prey.

Venerable snakes, including the dreaded water moccasin, silently patrol this seeming paradise. Ubiquitous cypress and mangroves contribute to the sense of ancient enclosure. And, of course, the omnipresent mosquito and their insect cousins—perhaps the most archaic inhabitants aside from the plants themselves—serve to remind that humanness is no guarantee of ultimate survival.

However, I do not wish to create the impression that the Okefenokee is a foreboding environment. My journey through this swamp is, in fact, an inspiration. Being reminded of the origins of life itself, this odyssey deepens my appreciation of the processes that sustain our existence. It is the perfect remedy to recover from my prostate surgery of the previous fall.

The renewed energy I experience from this challenge serves its purpose—whetting my appetite to return to my Alaska explorations this coming autumn. I resume planning a new adventure in a very different venue—paddling the Tanana River through the Tetlin National Wildlife Refuge, backdropped by the rugged mountains of Wrangell-St Elias National Park.

Chapter 9
FALL, 2005 – UP A LAZY RIVER – THE TANANA

"R-r-r-raw-w-l-l-l!"

"That," I think to myself, "sounds like the tiger in our zoo."
But this is no zoo. And that's no tiger.

*   *   *

After a year's hiatus, I have returned to Alaska. My buddy,
John, greets me at Anchorage International just as he did two
years ago, this time with my sat phone in hand.

"Look at you," he enthuses as he gives me a bear hug.
"Prostate surgery and none the worse for it!"

"Actually, I'm pretty lucky," I reply. "They caught it just in
time. Could have turned out much worse. I think they got it
all."

After handing me my sat phone and giving me a quick
refresher on how to use it, John wants to hear all about my
plans for this year's trip.

"I thought I'd try the Tanana," I say.

"A river. Good man, but I thought you were a lakes guy."

"I love the lakes, but I've gotta admit that after this bout
with cancer, I don't feel any younger. You know, I tallied up
all the portaging I did in the Kenai and—since I always had to

make three trips to schlep all the gear—it came to over forty miles! That's a lot of slogging. I decided I'd like to try my hand at a river and see whether I like it."

John looks at me, a bit concerned. "Think you can handle the currents and the rapids by yourself? You want to be careful."

"I've chosen an easy route, so I should be ok. I thought I'd pick up the Tanana near its source and follow it for a week or so through the Tetlin Wildlife Refuge. You've always sung the praises of Tetlin, and from the research I've done, the Tanana should be pretty friendly water at this time of the year. Spectacular country, too. I think it's a pretty safe bet, and I'll see how I take to river paddling."

"You'll probably love it. And you're absolutely right. You'll be in beautiful country with Wrangell-St. Elias at your back. That's one of Alaska's most rugged ranges."

"Yeah, I flew over it once, and believe me, I was astounded. What a wilderness! I've wanted to go there ever since. I got to thinking that since I'm already taking the trouble to travel some four thousand miles from D.C. to Tetlin, I might as well explore the Wrangell too. So I'm going to rent a four-wheel-drive SUV here in Anchorage and drive to Tok."

"It's a great drive," John reassures me. "Let's see. . . Tok's about three hundred miles northeast if you take the Alaska. You can be there in a day or two."

"Actually," I explain, "I've decided to make a real excursion of it and loop up to Denali, then take the Denali Highway from Cantwell to Paxon, and on back down to Tok. At Tok I'll leave my vehicle with my outfitter. Then after my paddling trip, I'll pick it up and come back home by way of the McCarthy Road."

"Wow," John exclaims, with a big grin. "Take me along! 'Course, you know the Denali and the McCarthy are mostly gravel?"

"That's why I'm renting a four-wheeler."

"Guess you've covered all the bases," John shrugs, thinking

over the plan I've just laid out.

"Hope so," I say.

"You know, speaking of taking advantage of flying all the way up here from D.C., next time you come you should plan to stay at my cabin up north of here," John suggests. "I could show you some of the Alaska Range in the Cessna and you could give me some photography tips."

"That sounds like a great idea. It's a plan!" We shake on it.

And with that, I thank John heartily and head for the car rental counter.

*   *   *

In Tok, my outfitters—a Tetlin Wildlife Refuge park ranger and his wife—prove to be just as welcoming as John and extremely helpful. "Is everyone in Alaska like this?" I begin to wonder. She especially takes me under her wing. When she learns that I am solo river canoeing for the first time on such an extended journey, she outlines the various skills I will need to master to enjoy a successful expedition: how to read currents, navigate eddies, avoid the "sweepers" (fallen trees and branches that impede water flow near the riverbanks) and understand the changing flow of water that occurs with each bend in the river.

Naively, I ask, "What should I do if I fall in and the canoe gets away from me?"

Appalled, her husband's reply is succinct: "Don't!"

On our way to drop me off at my launching point on the Chisana River—a small tributary which flows into the Tanana—we stop along the Tanana and she supervises an impromptu but vital lesson: teaching me to use a "bow draw" to carve a sharp turn in order to bring the canoe to a landing with the bow pointed into the river current, thus allowing the craft to hug the shore as you disembark. I practice this maneuver several times until she's satisfied that I've got the hang of it.

Thus armed with this new skill, we drive to my launch point, where she drops me at a patch of exposed riverbank. As she swings back up into the truck cab, we wave our goodbyes. Standing there, watching the taillights of her pickup recede into the distance—as I have so many times before when left in the wilderness—I shudder with the sudden sense of isolation, but quickly shake it off and turn my eyes to the river. Loading my gear, I push off.

"Welcome back to the wilds of Alaska!" I tell myself, feeling the effects of my bout with cancer recede far into the distance.

Remembering other solos I have begun in icy rain and even snow, I'm thankful for this mild, partly cloudy afternoon. Here the Chisana is but a stream, calm and peaceful, and I dip my paddle reverentially, quietly proceeding downstream through this outdoor cathedral. The spires of black spruce reach skyward, even as their reflections plumb the depths of the river.

Onward I paddle at this leisurely pace until I realize that afternoon is quickly heralding evening. As a chill sets in, I begin in earnest to scout for a flat footprint of land on which I can pitch my tent and build a fire.

It's late evening before I am successful in finding the perfect camping spot, on a slightly elevated ledge overlooking the river. Beaching my canoe in the dim light of dusk, I sling my gear onto the ledge—about five feet above the sandbar—secure my canoe, scramble up the bank, and proceed to make camp.

Tired after this first day back in the wilds of Alaska, I cook one of my old standbys, freeze-dried lasagna, and wolf down my evening meal. After cleaning up, I go straight to bed and fall into an exhausted but contented sleep—congratulating myself on my successful return to the wilderness.

It's about 6 AM when I am suddenly brought wide-awake by a ferocious "R-r-r-raw-w-l-l-l!" not more than a foot away from my ear on the other side of my tent wall. I hear snorting and heavy panting. I can almost feel the animal's breath. "This can only mean one thing," I think, "an unhappy grizzly." Still in the stupor of sleep, I lay here for a few seconds contemplating what to do. I have the somewhat absurd notion that I should grab my camera, slink carefully out of the tent, and get a picture. Bad idea! "But am I better off inside the tent or outside?" I wonder, having heard stories of campers being dragged out of their tent by hungry bears. As quietly as possible, I sit up in my sleeping bag to contemplate my next move, and as I do, I hear the grizzly rise up on his hind legs, turn, and trot off into the woods.

Relief does not begin to describe my reaction, having dodged the proverbial bullet.

Fortunately, this time he chose not to confront me—but with his awesome growl he has warned me in no uncertain terms that I am violating his fishing hole and I'd better move. And move *now*. Not wishing a return encounter, I proceed to break camp with impressive efficiency—constantly glancing over my shoulder.

I decide to cook my breakfast on the *other* side of the river. While loading my canoe, I glance down on the riverbank and finally notice the telltale tracks. I can fit my size twelve boot inside the enormous footprints of my visitor—or perhaps I should say my unwilling host.

While making my exit, I feel strangely calm and deliberate. Why am I not shaking like a leaf? Whatever the answer, it seems clear that while the bear was warning me off, he did not wish to have an unnecessary confrontation with this unknown creature in his midst. Unexpectedly, this halo of deliberate calm—no heart pounding, no adrenalin rush—has enveloped me from the moment I was awakened. Turning over the event in my mind, I realize that for some reason, when I sat up in my sleeping bag to assess the situation, rather than feel frightened, I felt alert, cautious and respectful of the possible danger that was at hand. My main desire was to assess the situation and plan my response. Luckily, before I had a chance to act, the bear had the right answer for both of us: leave.

Did my even-tempered reaction to this event contribute to this fortunate outcome? I imagine it couldn't have hurt. I've been told that grizzlies, though they cannot see well at all, have an incredible sense of smell. If I had begun to sweat, and if my brain had released the hormones necessary to raise my adrenaline and cortisol levels, I strongly suspect the bear might have smelled my bodily odors and interpreted their source—me—as prey.

Down a Lazy River

About mid-day I reach the Tanana, which, at this juncture—hundreds of miles before it merges with the Yukon—proves an ideal first river for solo canoeing. Gentle waters complement sunny days and mild temperatures, ushering in Alaska's onset of autumn. I am able to enjoy new sights and experiences while gaining confidence in my paddling. And I don't miss the portaging one bit!

Camping along the shore provides opportunity for exploration. One morning, hiking the flats of the river, I stop after a hundred yards or so to look back to my tiny tent and realize how Lilliputian my presence is—huddled as it is among the surrounding spruce spires in this vast open territory.

Further down the beach I come across one of nature's many fascinating sculptures. The scouring wind and waves have artfully carved the muddy flats into a polished crisscross of rounded ripples. I sit on a nearby deadfall to admire this natural engraving, the breeze gently flapping the hood of my jacket. Finally, I rise with the aid of the walking stick that I have selected from the forest floor, and set out to return to my now-distant campsite. It's time to get back on the water.

Given my previous experience with my grizzly visitor, I am careful to select tonight's campsite in the late afternoon, allowing myself ample light to inspect the shore for telltale tracks and scat. Another advantage of camping before the onset of dusk is that I'm setting up camp at my own leisurely pace, rather than feel pushed by a sense of impending darkness.

After enjoying an unhurried evening meal, I attach my SLR to its tripod and survey my surroundings. Relaxing in the glow of a soothing sunset that lasts for hours, I document the changing light as yellows yield to oranges, reds, and finally purples—the deepening shadows reflected in the Tanana. Finally these silhouettes are swallowed in the late evening dusk.

At times like these, quiet blankets all. The splash of a pike leaping for its supper is instantly muted in the profound stillness. A grebe, etched in shadow, soundlessly paddles across the mirrored river, leaving in its wake an undisturbed V-shaped silver trail. No crickets. No cicadas. No mosquitoes. No bullfrogs. No swamp sounds that were omnipresent in the Okefenokee this previous spring. Only the breathing of the river. Or is that my own breathing?

I look up and the heavens are now full of stars. No moon tonight. I reluctantly rise, douse my fire, bow to my surroundings and whatever creatures might be watching over my night, and retire to the confines of my tent. There I shed my clothes and zip myself into my wonderfully cozy down bag, burrowing my nakedness into its folds to ward off the chill. After mentally inventorying the past day and that to come, I drift off to sleep—a sleep that, this time, does not end abruptly with a bear as my alarm clock.

After an early breakfast of flapjacks and coffee, I'm back out on the water, where life is springing into action. A formation of red-breasted mergansers busies themselves along the shore. As my canoe approaches, in unison they begin to high-step across the water, noisily flapping their wings for take-off. They flock about a hundred yards or so downriver, only to repeat their flight each time I approach.

Farther down as the river bends, a pair of mute swans soars above the treetops. Perhaps I'll see them later this fall at Backwater, my home wildlife refuge on Maryland's Eastern Shore that offers a safe rest stop on their annual migration southward. Joining in the morning cacophony, a flock of ubiquitous Canada geese flee the approach of my craft, rising in unison and flapping furiously to lift their large bodies up and over the reeds. As if on cue, they U-turn in an Escher-like black and white arc and wing their way down the waterway. Like the mergansers, as I advance, they repeat this process, as if being herded downriver.

High overhead, bald eagles challenge each other's air space with acrobatic zeal, talons outstretched and poised to do battle. The Tanana, which had been so silent the previous night, is now a frenzy of activity. As the wind picks up, even the trees join in—the aspens clacking like castanets— announcing the approach of a gathering storm.

Keeping one eye on the darkening clouds as they billow overhead, I proceed on my journey, watchful to see what develops. Eventually, the storm blows past with more bluster than substance, and gradually the afternoon sun reasserts itself.

Given the relatively calm water, I am able to practice my new river skills, executing various strokes and turns with increasing efficiency. I concentrate on the bow draw that my outfitter has taught me—sweeping my paddle from bow to stern to execute a 180 and point the canoe upriver—knowing that this maneuver will prove a vital capability when disembarking in swifter waters. Over and over I swing my canoe into shore, slowly learning to take advantage of the current rather than work against it. Especially revelatory to me is the safe haven that eddies—those whirlpools of backwater in the shallows and along the shoreline—provide to rest and plan my next maneuver.

Another skill that is essential in plying our northern waterways is the ability to read channels. The Tanana, being a glacier-fed, braided river, requires that one keep to the main channel and not be fooled by smaller sister channels that may eventually wander into shallows and sandbars. When seen from aloft, the main channel may appear obvious. However, from a canoe at water level, it can appear as a confusing maze.

I've found it somewhat helpful when I research my trips to Google satellite images of the area I intend to travel. These images give me some sense of the complexities of the river's twists and turns. But one must keep in mind that a sudden torrential rain may redirect the flow of water and render such images obsolete. Ultimately, learning to read the river is your most reliable practice—watching carefully for shifts in the current. Admittedly, sometimes it comes to a leap of faith.

Fortunately, in my future years canoeing Alaskan rivers, only once will I make the wrong choice. In that instance, I come to an island where the river forks. Hanging in an eddy to survey the situation, I carefully examine my alternatives. Either direction seems perfectly viable. The river flow is equally vigorous, though the west fork is choppier. I choose the smoother water on the east side of the island. I proceed about a half-mile down this flow, only to discover that the channel breaks into a number of shallow, unnavigable rivulets. I am forced to backtrack upstream (never a fun exercise) to my decision point and proceed down the west channel.

No such necessity presents itself on the lower Tanana. Most of the river offers clear choices and I paddle without incident.

In all my days of canoeing and camping along this isolated river, not once do I encounter another human presence. Occasionally, the river will bend close enough to the Alcan Highway that I hear distant trucks humming down the road, but then it cuts south and the silence returns.

The weather remains cooperative, sunny and bright with temperatures reaching the fifties during these lazy September days. The warm days and chilly nights combine to bring a change of seasons. As I paddle along, summer literally becomes fall—the birches and aspens adorning themselves with the brilliant colors of autumn.

Finally the day arrives that I am to meet my outfitter. As she stands waiting at a small roadside landing, much to her delight I execute a near-perfect bow draw landing—just as she taught me. She congratulates me on my newfound river skills, and we load my canoe into her pickup.

Off we go. Crossing the Tanana River bridge, I am impressed by what a substantial waterway the Tanana becomes as it flows its way to the Yukon, some five hundred miles distant. I have no more than completed this portion of my journey than I begin to think of possibilities for next year. I do not miss the portaging life.

But at present, I am only halfway through this year's explorations. Bidding my outfitters a heartfelt goodbye—with special thanks for the canoeing lessons—I hop into my four-wheel-drive SUV and head for the depths of the Wrangell-St. Elias wilderness. I find this drive, like many I will embark on in this enormous state, a great pleasure, despite the occasional long stretches of challenging rocky dirt road. Alaska, vast as it is, has only about one-fifth the highway mileage as comparably populated areas of the Lower 48. And since much of the travel centers on population hubs, the outlying motorways feature long stretches barren of traffic.

Thus, although I have stepped out of my canoe and into my SUV, I still enjoy the sense of isolation and adventure that comes with traveling the Alaskan outback. Occasionally, I pass through tiny communities that feature a combination gas station/variety/food store and a few cabins. At one such station, I stop to take a picture of a man and his young son— perhaps eight or nine years old—who are delivering gasoline.

I am captivated by the joy this father and son share as they in pose together for my camera—the rugged, mustached dad in his work cap and dungarees sitting proudly beside his delighted young son, peeking out from under his hoodie.

They remind me of my youthful days in northern Minnesota when my Uncle Claude—also a gas truck driver— would rouse me early on dark frosty mornings to accompany him on his delivery rounds. As a kid, there's nothing quite like the thrill of bouncing down the back roads in the cab of an enormous tanker truck.

Smells of tobacco and old leather surrounded me as Uncle Claude ground the gears through their paces. At little towns like this one I am visiting now, we would stop and I would climb down from the towering cab to help drag the linking hose to the underground storage cap. Then we'd sit and talk while waiting for the tank to fill. Maybe we'd have a Nehi. I felt like a real man.

Eventually I arrive at the Chitina Ranger Station, the western terminus of the McCarthy Road. Like the Denali Highway, this road is a challenging stretch of rugged gravel, winding some sixty miles along the Copper, Chitina, Kuskulana and other rivers into the Wrangell-St. Elias backcountry. Four-wheel drive and a spare tire are highly desirable here.

I cannot help but feel the ghosts along this road. At the turn of the nineteenth century it was a railroad that carried wildcatters, laborers, and equipment to the richest copper vein in the world at that time—the future home of the Kennecott Mines. McCarthy—a wild-west town of that era, which marks the eastern terminus of this road—is now a tourist curiosity. The road meanders by lakes and rivers populated with trout, swans and numerous other fish and fowl.

In the distance, the magnificent mountains of Wrangell-St. Elias beckon. Deep ravines burrow through white and black spruce, interspersed with quaking aspen and paper birch. On the road climbing out of one such ravine, I catch first sight of a structure so incongruous that I cannot at first believe what I am seeing. It's the Kuskulana Bridge, spanning high above its namesake river, a magnificent engineering achievement in the middle of the Alaskan wilderness. A converted railroad bridge, it invites the intrepid driver to cross its single-lane span while the Kuskulana roars in the canyon far below. I can only marvel at this site.

Crossing the span, I proceed cautiously over five hundred feet to the opposite side. There I park my vehicle, dismount, and walk back to the center of the bridge to peer into the gorge nearly 240 feet below. I can only imagine how it must have felt riding the ore trains over this harrowing chasm nearly a century earlier.

Continuing on the McCarthy Road into the late afternoon, I come across another tribute to those who have passed before—a sculpture garden of seemingly hundreds of cairns, similar to those I've seen along mountainous Norwegian roadways and hiking trails. I stop to add my modest contribution to the collection before continuing onward.

Finally, under a brilliant afternoon sun, I reach a parking area at the end of the road. If I want to see the remains of the town of McCarthy, where workers from the Kennecott Mine came to relax, gamble and play, I will have to hike the remaining half-mile. This requires using a footbridge that crosses the Kennicott River, a roiling turmoil of glacier-fed water. The September air is invigorating, and it seems more than appropriate to finish my journey on foot.

McCarthy itself—now boasting only a handful of residents—consists of a collection of buildings that have been restored to maintain the feel of the old town. Saloons, gift shops and a creaky, drafty hotel are the core of what remains. Tours are offered to access the famous Kennicott Glacier, which—much reduced in size since its glory days—is demonstrating the effects of global warming.

In fact, today many of Alaska's magnificent ice fields and glaciers have shrunk dramatically, along with the sea ice that extends from the north slopes to the North Pole. Entire Eskimo villages have had to move inland as the temperatures and—correspondingly—oceans rise, reclaiming lands that have been occupied for centuries.

I decide to spend the night in one of the old hotel rooms. Furnished with minimum comforts, the wind outside serenades me through the night, as well as celebrants in the town's few active bars and cafes. I wake to a brilliant sunrise and walk to the edge of town, where—framed by a golden aspen ablaze in its autumn colors—I find a spectacular view of the Kennicott Glacier awaiting me. It is now, along with most other such snowfields throughout the state, one of Alaska's endangered species. However, given the disturbingly rapid pace of global warming, I feel thankful that I have taken the trouble to navigate this rather demanding road less travelled.

However, it's time for me to return to Anchorage. Reluctantly, I take my leave of McCarthy and its surrounds and stroll the footbridge back to my SUV. I still have well over three hundred miles to travel. It is a spectacular distance. Every mile proves breathtaking, boasting some new feature of the Alaskan landscape. Rivers, glaciers, mountains and waterfalls of every description constantly lure me to stop and linger a bit longer. I do so at every turn. It will take another three days to meander back to Anchorage as I investigate side roads and trails, which offer unique views of nature's marvels.

But now the pull of home and family begins to assert itself powerfully. Whatever new discoveries are to be made, they can wait until next year. Escorted by mountains and glaciers, I make my way back to Anchorage, where I return my sat phone to John, spending my last night as his guest—hosted by his welcoming family. One of these trips, I promise, I will take him up on his offer to visit his wilderness cabin and tour his favorite Alaska haunts in his Cessna.

Late that next evening I catch the red-eye back to Washington, D.C. As I come through the arrivals gate, I spot Janet waving at the far end of the corridor and my heart and my hand wave back. Each of us grinning, we hug our hellos. Home again. It's good to be back!

Chapter 10
2006 – NEW CHALLENGES – WOOD-TIKCHIK

"At nearly 1.6 million acres, Wood-Tikchik State Park is the largest and most remote state park in the nation." So reads a description from the park's website. For me the enticements of Wood-Tikchik are many. A true wilderness preserve situated in remote south-central Alaska—Wood-Tikchik is accessible by foot, plane, boat or canoe. Here, I will be able to combine the river canoeing that I had practiced on my previous trip on the Tanana with paddling some of the largest lakes I have thus far canoed. John—ever a reliable source of Alaska lore—has sung the praises of this wilderness, convincing me that it is well worth hopping a jet from Anchorage to fly some three hundred miles southwest to Dillingham.

In Dillingham, Ric, who will serve as my bush pilot and outfitter, greets me at the airport. After grabbing my gear and loading it into his vehicle, we swing up into the cab and we're off. Arriving at his cabin, I am greeted by Denise, Ric's wife and business partner. Over steaming cups of coffee we discuss sights I shouldn't miss on my sojourn through the mountain-encircled lakes of Wood-Tikchik—such as the magnificent waterfall that forms a year-round cavernous ice palace at its base. My appetite thus further whetted, Ric and I board his four-wheel-drive truck once again and proceed to the lake where his plane is docked.

Anxious as I am to be on my way, Ric has another party to transport. And so, here I sit, hunched in a green plastic chair—alongside three other seasoned-looking Alaskan outdoorsmen—on the lakeside porch of a utility cabin that serves as Ric's wilderness way station. All of us are impatiently awaiting Ric's return.

Immediately to my left is an older man whose bearded, jolly countenance and rotund figure would make Santa jealous. Brown cap pulled over his eyes; he wears a T-shirt that reads, "Alaska Department of Fish and Game." Beside him sits a man in sunglasses, his hat brim pulled low in an attempt to shade the unrelenting Alaskan sun. With his snow-white beard and mustache, he looks like a slightly younger version of myself. On his left sits their colorful companion—a balding man, perhaps the youngest of the three—sporting a purple shirt and holding a bright red sweatshirt that he has shed in the morning heat.

"Where you headed?" asks the one in the middle chair, leaning my way in an attempt to be sociable.

"Up on the north side of Kulik," I reply, referring to one of a series of rather daunting lakes, each some twenty miles long and five miles wide.

"By yourself?" asks the man in purple, his eyebrows raised and his interest now piqued.

"Yep."

They all glance at each other. I'm not sure whether they're impressed or think they've just encountered a fool.

"Ya wanna be careful out there," joins in the Santa look-alike, concern registering on his face.

"I've been doing this for a few years now," I remark casually, trying to establish my *bona fides*.

"No gun?" observes the fellow to my far left, skeptically.

"I'm a photographer," I reply, deflecting the question.

"Where ya been before this?"

"Mostly Canada, but the last couple of years down at Swanson Lakes and then over at Tetlin."

Suddenly they all perk up, interested now.

"Ya gotta go to the Kobuk," two of them remark almost simultaneously. "It's up north of the Arctic Circle about a hundred miles. We were there last year. It's fantastic. Wolves chasing caribou. Grizzlies. You'll really love it."

And so it is that suddenly we are all comrades, trading outdoor stories and swapping information. I eventually find that Ric is flying them to a fishing lodge some distance west. They have always fished together, but unfortunately one of them has recently been diagnosed with cancer. They want to get in another trip together before treatment commences. I felt a stab in my heart. Having recently battled with cancer myself, I was concerned for him. But I also understood the desire not to allow illness to cripple one's determination to live life.

Suddenly, the drone of Ric's plane on the horizon catches our attention. As one, we watch him settle gently on the water and taxi toward the dock. Ric cuts the powerful engine, steers into the dock and hops down from the cockpit to inform me that I'm next man up. I grab my backpacks and stand on the float to heave my gear into the back while Ric straps my canoe to the pontoon of his De Havilland Beaver. As Ric backs the plane away from the dock, my three erstwhile friends wave goodbye and we give each other a thumbs-up.

Soon we're taxiing down the lake, kicking up a plume of spray behind us. Suddenly, with a roar of the engine that thrusts me back in my seat, we are airborne, lifting towards the fast-approaching treetops. I'm tempted to duck. Swinging steeply to the north, we level out and head for the far shores of Lake Kulik.

Once aloft into the bright, crisp and sunny day, I'm captivated by the shadow of our craft moving across on the ground below. Looking up, I catch my reflection in the cockpit window, and realize I'm grinning like a kid. Ahead, a vast expanse of woodland and lakes lies before us, with jagged, tundra-covered mountains beckoning in the distance.

I settle back, cocooned in my headset and listening to the engine thrumming in the background as we swoop over the conifers and lakes below. There isn't a boat or a person to be seen. The sweeping vista seems an endless garden unmolested by modern life. In the back of my mind I am already planning my next trip—to the Kobuk and the Arctic.

Transported

This is only my second floatplane, but already I'm addicted. I think of the many photos I have taken by air, sitting in the window seat of a jetliner at forty thousand feet. This is different. This is like being on my motorcycle, so much a part of the landscape that at times I feel like I can reach out and grab the trees.

The cockpit of the Beaver offers an illuminating perspective when compared with my normal experience of trekking these same mountains and canoeing these lakes. When below, I am swallowed up in my surroundings. From this height I'm part of a blue and green panorama that will eventually morph into my multi-hued destination—the sub-Arctic tundra.

After considerable time flying further and further north, Ric finally noses our aircraft down towards our destination, the waters of Kulik. Passing over the mouth of the Wind River, we glide northwest to the far shore of the lake. Soon we are touching down on gently rolling waves, an impressive wake of spray behind us as we taxi toward a small beach. Cutting the engine, we silently drift toward the shore, anchor down, and begin to unload my gear.

Double-checking our agreement on when and where we will meet for pickup—weather and luck permitting—we say our goodbyes. Ric taxies away and, with a sudden roar of power lifts for home.

Watching the receding aircraft, I slump—the tension and excitement of the plane ride suddenly draining from my body. I've just flown for nearly an hour without viewing another being. Now—surrounded in the quiet of this panoramic landscape—I stand empty. I am truly alone—on my own for the next couple of weeks. It slowly sinks in—the reality of what daunting and invigorating challenges lie ahead.

"Well," I tell myself, shaking out of my stupor, "it's a beautiful September day—not the rain and fog and snow I've had on some trips. Time to take a look around!"

I survey the surrounding landscape. East and west, verdant green peaks embrace the rocky shoreline on which I stand. I stroll some distance up the beach eastward as it winds its way to a rocky point, beyond which the vast expanse of Lake Kulik continues. I adjust the focus on my binoculars and scan the shore of a nearby island for wildlife. All is quiet. Satisfied with this initial investigation, I return and begin the process of setting up camp.

Erecting my tent behind a modest cover of willows populating the shore, I gather wood for the fire, which—nicely shielded from the wind by the nearby trees—I build near a convenient log that can serve as a bench while cooking. I place my coffee cup on a stump, lean my paddles against a nearby tree, and generally go about the business of building a temporary nest.

This accomplished, I step back, hands on hips—pleased with my new home.

I decide to use this first late afternoon to explore my microenvironment. I am learning to look down at what lies right at my feet, even when surrounded by the grandeur of lakes and mountains such as these. This pebble beach where I have set up camp presents a study in still life. Mosaics of subtle beauty, color and form surround me.

Bending low, I discover a flaming red leaf striated with yellow veins. Squatting down for a closer look, I peer at the single crimson leaf. Unable to locate it in my field guide, I'm guessing that I'm looking at a variety of berry leaf, or perhaps bunchberry. Whichever, it is a precocious harbinger of fall—surrounded by a patch of kin still displaying summer green. Soon the entire area will be ablaze with color.

Nearby appears to be yet another kind of berry. Its narrower leaves are a late-summer purple swirling around a cluster of shiny vermillion berries that will soon be harvested by the birds, grizzlies and other critters that frequent this shoreline.

Not to be outdone, a patch of bright pink fireweed attracts my eye. The structure of the stalks and leaves are a wonder of architecture—a graceful symmetry swirling to a height of more than two feet. The delicate pistils that reach out belie the hardiness of this survivor, so-named because it is often the first regeneration of life to follow a forest fire.

Duck-walking over to a feather that appears to be that of a red tail hawk, I can't help but crane my neck to search the skies above for the raptor that might have lost this outlier while soaring overhead. Even more likely, this feather fell loose while the hungry bird was scratching through the gravel underfoot. I glance around for signs of a struggle nearby—but there are no bones or fur or smaller feathers from an intended prey.

Lost in these musing, I finally look up from the world at my feet to discover that the sun has dropped behind the mountains to the west. Its oblique light has washed all color from the sky, and painted the peaks with a brilliant backlit slash of yellows and oranges, while the shadowed lake shimmers metallic silver. The lowering of the sun sends a shiver down my spine.

The contrast of the micro and macro environments reflects my internal and external experience of the wild.

Sometimes when standing tall, surveying the magnificence that surrounds me, breathing deeply of the crisp air, I feel strong, alive—nearly invulnerable—part of a species that in many ways dominates and manipulates its surroundings (or, at least likes to think it does).

But when a cloud covers the sun, chilling the air as now, or the wind picks up, or a threat of rain appears on the horizon, I am quickly reminded that I am also a part of nature's mosaic—weak and vulnerable. As a rational being, I can exercise some control of my surroundings, but that same rationality reminds me that I am a transient bit of flesh in an ever-unfolding evolution. Like the plants, animals and rocks around me, and my ancestors before me, my presence in this world is fleeting—a reed in the river of time.

Suddenly, I am famished, having eaten very little on this day of travel and excitement. It's hard to believe that early this morning I kissed Janet goodbye at Dulles Airport, flew to Seattle, Anchorage, Dillingham, and now here. Soon the rawness of early evening settles in, and I use the remaining light to rummage through my food pack and prepare for tonight's dinner. I select something called "Chili Mac" from my freeze-dry pantry. I figure with a name like that, it's got to be hearty. And indeed, chili lover that I am, I devour every morsel.

Satisfied and sleepy, I sit in a stupor. "Well," I tell myself, "you wanted solitude, and here it is—big time." As the temperatures dip into the low forties, I force myself to get up and add a log to the fire. I dig my trusty down jacket—the one that stuffs neatly into its own zippered pocket—out of my backpack. Lying on my back by the fire—my pack now my pillow—I savor the sub-arctic twilight, the increasingly silhouetted landscape, and the emerging stars. The evening will last well past midnight—far longer than I do.

Exploring Lake Kulik

Next morning, after oatmeal and hot chocolate, I gather my gear and arrange it in my canoe. Dressed in T-shirt, life vest, shorts, Gor-Tex windbreaker and windpants, I strap on my Tevas. Standing up to look out over the seemingly endless expanse of lake that lay before me, the far shoreline is lost to sight.

I turn away from the water and bow in farewell to my campsite—as has become my custom on these solo journeys—grateful for the shelter my surroundings have provided. Turning back to survey the journey awaiting me, I perform one final check to make sure my gear is secure, knowing full well that this is simply procrastination—an excuse to gather the resolve to once again launch myself into the unknown. Finally, inhaling a deep breath, I push off into the icy water.

Excellent weather is still smiling on me, and once the rhythm of paddling reasserts its body memory, I whoop with delight. Every pore seems to be awakening as I bend to my task. My slow, strong, rhythmic strokes liberate my city-bound muscles, and my canoe glides effortlessly in response. Thrusting my torso forward to extend for the next stroke, I dig the paddle deep and then lean back, pulling the blade forcefully through the water. Over and over I repeat the calming cadence until finally—spent in the sheer joy of physical effort, I slump into a resting position—shaking off a year of deskwork much like a dog would shake itself after a fine swim.

Scanning the far distance, my plan is to head for the west end of Kulik over several miles of open water and locate a campsite in that vicinity later this afternoon. There I should find the waterfall and ice cave that Ric and Denise raved about.

It dawns on me that this is my first solo venture across such a huge expanse of water by canoe. Suddenly I feel like a cork on the ocean. As the shore behind me grows more and more distant, I feel increasingly tiny and vulnerable. I must be in a couple of hundred feet of water and more than a mile from land.

"What if I should capsize out here?" I wonder.

"Don't be silly," I tell myself. "Capsizing out here wouldn't be much different than capsizing a couple of hundred yards from shore—either way you're in big trouble!"

My solution is to keep a weather eye on the clouds, but otherwise, I simply tell myself, "Get a grip!"

In fact, a glassy smooth surface greets me throughout the day. Knowing I cannot continue the galloping pace I began with this morning, I now slow down and dip my paddle noiselessly and smoothly, as if not to disturb the quiet reflection of my surroundings.

The lake perfectly mirrors the iridescent green clothing the base of the surrounding mountains, reminding me of pictures I have seen of Ireland. The blue of the sky and the gray-white of the lazy cumulous clouds are duplicated in the water below. Occasionally a lone loon will call for its mate.

Otherwise, the entire landscape is wrapped in silence as I glide lazily, luxuriating in the day—but always aware that the weather can throw me a curve at any time. Throughout the afternoon I alternately paddle and drift, munching on trail mix and fruit. Occasionally I stretch backwards, searching the heavens for birds that might be patrolling high overhead. If they are there, they are beyond my vision.

After some hours, I reach the far west end of Kulik, where I suddenly find myself in the midst of a school of sockeye salmon, their colorful red-gray bodies flashing in the late afternoon sun. Clearly exhausted, some look terribly battered after their journey from their far Pacific feeding grounds. Others lay dying on the nearby beach. I now understand—in a way no nature film can teach—the life struggle they have endured to arrive at this place, lay their eggs, spawn and die.

Looking up from this life and death tableau, I take my bearings, surveying my surroundings. Shading my eyes against the sun-dazzled water, in the southerly distance I can barely make out a waterfall cascading down the lower half of an impressive mountain that rises up steeply out of the sea. At the base of the waterfall, I spy a patch of white, punctuated by a tiny black area. It finally dawns on me that this must be the ice cave.

Checking the position of the late afternoon sun, I gauge that I should have plenty of light left to explore the cave after making camp. Twisting around, I spot a nearby island behind me that seems a likely candidate for a site. Paddling over to investigate, I pull up on a small beach, disembark, and wade through the island's dense shrubbery, searching for a possible spot to set up my tent. Finally, I am able to locate a footprint among the willows that nearly hides my tent from view.

Over the years, I have gone through a process of tent evolution, paying more and more attention to weight, durability, and ease of erection. For this trip, I've settled on a three-season, medium-lightweight, two-person Marmot tent and fly with ripstop nylon seams, highly flexible, collapsible aluminum poles with durable shock cords, and well-engineered airflow. If this choice seems highly specific, it comes from innumerable hard-earned lessons.

There was the time, for example, when I was threading an outside support pole through the tent's attachment loops and the pole bent in half. There is nothing quite like spending the remainder of your trip moving oh-so-carefully when inside your tent, trying to avoid contact with a wet, sagging roof that won't properly shed water due to the bent pole. Each time this necessity slips your mind and you brush against the offended area, moisture inevitably drips through your mesh window and onto your down sleeping bag. Another time, the shock cord—the elastic roping that binds each section of the collapsible pole—broke, thus disabling that particular pole. Needless to say, I began to carry an extra pole.

Tent zippers have proved quite capable of wreaking havoc

on my sleep-seeking psyche in instances where they would stick, break off, rip away from their seam, provide a channel for water to drip through and puddle on the tent floor, or result in numerous other maladies that only revealed themselves through tortured experience. Vestibules (that portion of the fly that forms an entrance chamber) could be unwieldy and impractical—a sagging, questionable shelter for my hiking boots, which were often too muddy to allow inside the tent. Entrances always seem poised to snag my clothing as I try to fold my six-foot-two frame and attempt to carefully crawl inside.

However, to give due credit, the reputable outdoor gear designers and manufacturers constantly listen to their patrons and refine the features of their products. As often as not, the difficulties one wrested with last year are remedied by this year's "new and improved" model, dangling features as alluring as they are expensive.

Thus far, I'm quite happy with my present tent as I quickly and easily construct a shelter that is safer, more comfortable and far easier to erect than the soggy, canvas behemoths that I had struggled with in my early days of camping. My new home now set up, I return to my canoe and head for the ice cave.

Though at first glance the ice cave appears to be reasonably nearby, it is in fact a half-hour paddle—confirming how difficult it is to judge distances in these monumental surroundings, especially given the translucent quality of the air. Though the cave becomes increasingly distinct as I approach, it is not until I set foot inside that I realize how truly enormous it is. It's no exaggeration to say that one could hide a tractor-trailer truck in its bowels.

The cave, on the north slope of the mountain, is formed at the base of the waterfall that is, in turn, a product of the melting winter snowpack. Apparently the ice buildup and the unique local environment is sufficient to keep it from melting in the summer months. With global warming, I wonder about its fate.

Craning my neck, I am again fascinated by nature's architecture. A concave fish-scale pattern forms the ceiling of the cave, about twelve feet overhead. Through the opening at the far end of the bowl-shaped cavern some fifty feet distant, I can see the waterfall that gives birth to this phenomenal cave. Finally, I leave the chill of this natural igloo for the warmth of the afternoon sun.

Carefully picking my way to avoid stepping on the delicate florae, I explore the vicinity adjacent to the waterfall. I am delighted to discover a generous sprinkling of colorful wildflowers. It appears that the tiny blossoms thrive in the spray. I spend the next hour or so with my camera, marveling at the color and variation of these hardy survivors. One appears to be a variety of willow herb, its white petals striated with delicate purple rays. Funnel-shaped blooms of deep purple bend their heads alongside what I believe to be white primrose. Lavender blossoms growing nearby seem to mediate the two extremes.

I am so absorbed in this activity that only the frosty air reminds me that the sun is lowering rapidly. I decide it's best to get back to my campsite. Nearly a half-hour later, dog-tired after a long day in the canoe and exploring along the shore, I approach my island campsite. I marvel at how minuscule its footprint is in this vast wilderness of rugged mountains and endless water. The casual traveler could easily overlook my blue-green tent—nestled in the willow thicket (though there are certainly no such passers-by to prove the point).

A slight breeze ripples the water, but no sounds announce the oncoming evening. The loons, I expect, will begin their raucous calls later. Suddenly, a breeze quickens, bringing additional chill. It reinforces my weariness and the prospect of wrapping up the day's explorations is indeed welcome.

The island proves barren of driftwood, so I set up my

trusty WhisperLite one-burner stove and boil my bag of freeze-dried chicken. Gourmet cooking is not my style in the backcountry—too much extra weight and additional smells to attract the bears and other critters. Better to stay with these tightly sealed packets of freeze-dried nourishment. "Strange," I think, while huddled over the glow of my tiny fire ring, "how something I never cook at home becomes a delicious feast in the wilderness." I eat with great appreciation.

No campfire to sit around tonight—but it's just as well. I crawl into my tent and zip myself inside. I read a bit from Barry Lopez's *Arctic Dreams*, but even this wonderful manuscript cannot allay sleep. I turn off my headlamp, roll over, and drift off. (Interestingly, I will, over the years, share my enthusiasm over Barry Lopez's many wonderful nature essays with my daughter Laurie, an environmental biology professor. She, in one of those serendipitous twists of fate, will later serve as Barry's escort when he is a featured lecturer at her college.)

Next morning, much refreshed and curious about my surroundings on this little spit of land, I begin to explore my perimeter. The island is covered with large, ripe, delicious blueberries. Growing alongside are other large, oblong, blue berries that I have not previously seen. After doing some research on my return home, I decide that these must be "haskap" berries. As is noted on the "Alaska Berries" website, "The flavor has been described as a combination of blueberries, raspberries, and strawberries. It is a multi-flavored fruit with sweetness, tart, tang and a zing all in one." I can personally attest to that description.

Continuing my explorations of my little island home, tiny wildflower blossoms also abound and I spend a leisurely morning hour experimenting with close-up photography, trying each of my lenses to compare their variations. Finally, hunger calls me away and I set about putting my berries to good use. A short while later, I am wolfing down some of the best flapjacks I have ever fixed—at home or in the wild.

Swallowing my last swig of hot chocolate, I stand up, stretch to the sky—legs, arms and fingers spread wide—and breathe in the new day. Bending down as far as I can, I touch my toes, rise up, and do a few yoga twists side to side as well as a long, languorous downward-facing dog. My mind gives a shoutout to Janet, who introduced me to yoga so many years ago. Thus renewed, I decide it's time to pack up my campsite and head down the southeastern shore to access the Wind River. The Wind will connect me to Lake Beverly, my next lake in the Tikchik chain.

As I push off under darkening skies, it is clear that a cold front is moving in, and it looks as if this day on the water could prove a bit choppier than yesterday's glassy glide. Fortunately, the change of weather brings no rain, though it does turn colder. My body, heated by my constant paddling, fails to take much note of this change. Proceeding steadily, rocked equally by the metronome-like movement of my body as I paddle and by the gentle waves, I am able to reach to the mouth of the Wind in a matter of a couple of hours.

It's strange how time collapses out here. The same couple of hours at work might have been filled with meetings and telephone calls and designing computer graphics. When finished, I might have looked up and said, "Where has the time gone?" But I would know the answer. I could reconstruct the events of the day.

Out here, time seems to drift, folding back on itself, and the events of the past couple of hours have become one. It's as if I've stepped—or paddled—into another dimension, a sort of wakeful dreamscape. All this time I've been working hard and hardly working. Drifting back to awareness, I realize I'm hungry, and I break out my daily high protein bar. Absently, I tear the wrapper with my teeth and munch the contents as I look around, alert and yet at ease.

Riding the Wind

An involuntary shudder breaks the spell and I realize a change of current is drawing me to the mouth of the Wind. This change, first felt as a slight shifting in my body, alerts my mind to the unique demands of river canoeing. As I am pulled past the point at which Lake Kulik ends and the Wind River begins, I am immediately on the lookout for rocks, driftwood, and sweepers—obstacles that were of little concern these last two days of lake navigation.

Continuing south down this relatively narrow connection between Kulik and Beverly, I come across a colony of beavers, busily preparing for the colder weather to come. Only about ten yards distant, they glance over at this strange intruder but otherwise ignore me and continue to haul willow sprouts and other vegetation to their dam.

I hang around in a nearby eddy for a half hour or so—my canoe bobbing in the shallows—fascinated by their industrious activity. But if I am to make Beverly by nightfall, I'd best be on my way.

As it meanders south, the Wind River eventually widens to become a small lake called Michalk. Lining the east shore of this lake I come upon rather unexpected company—a group of a half dozen or so fishermen, lined up hip-deep in the waters not ten feet apart from each other, casting for trout. Behind them looms the impressive Golden Horn Lodge—clearly a remote, luxurious-looking outpost that caters to those who want their wilderness experience to be one of well-catered comfort.

Trying not to draw attention, I glide by quietly about forty yards to the west. All of these fishermen appear to be gawking at me as if to say, "where did you come from and where are your buddies?" I might have envied them for their comfort and camaraderie, just as they might have wished for my simplicity and solitude. But the sight makes me appreciate my solo journey all the more, as I realize I would not trade my experience for theirs for any amount. But soon the river spirits me away from all these thoughts.

Unfortunately, the Golden Horn Lodge was hard hit by a winter storm some years later. Sitting as it does in a mountain-lined channel between Kulik and Beverly, the north winds came roaring through and leveled a good deal of the lodge's upper floors. Fortunately, no one was injured.

Continuing south, Lake Michalk empties into the Peace River, the site of a second, more modest fly-in fish camp called Fishing Bear Lodge, featuring rustic cabins. The environmental footprint of this establishment appears modest and draws my curiosity. I am reminded of Forest House, the eco-lodge in Saskatchewan where I had met Rick and Deb that snowy October afternoon so many years ago.

Before continuing downriver to Lake Beverly, I decide to pull over and take a look at this place. Perhaps I might recommend it to friends who want a simpler outdoors experience. Hauling my gear-laden canoe ashore, I am greeted by the proprietor. We shake hands and I sense an instant and easy rapport. Not long into our conversation, we discover a mutual fascination with what the other is doing in such remote country.

"Isn't it tough maintaining this place in the winter?" I ask.

"Actually, I lead photography expeditions in Africa in the winter," he replies. "Perhaps you should come on one."

"I've never been to Africa. I've always thought I might go there someday," I nod. "But I'm not sure I'm an expedition guy. I think I prefer solo."

"You'd love it," he assures me, waving away any doubts.

"You never know. I just might" I admit, shrugging at the possibility.

After exchanging a few stories, we bid each other good fortune and return to our tasks. Pleased as I am to meet a fellow lover of the outdoors, I'm gratified to return to my solitude.

Finally, as the sun flirts with the southwestern horizon, I pull up on a sandbar to stop for the night. The daytime clouds have moved off and the wind has died down, especially in this protective cove that I have selected. Once again, I am aglow in the tranquility of the setting sun as it drops below the distant mountains. A golden halo gilts the wisps of the remaining clouds, reflected in a quiet pool along the shore.

Evening has arrived.

Lake Beverly

Next morning I arise under partly cloudy skies and decide to explore the west end of Lake Beverly for a day or so, before heading some twenty miles down to the southeast end of the lake to take on the rapids of the Agulupak River. The paddle is relatively calm, a slight breeze quivering the water. Mid-day I find an ideal peninsula to make an early camp, featuring a sandy beach and gorgeous views stretching east and west. Its exposed location should allow the gentle winds to sweep away any late-season mosquitoes.

After setting up my tent and securing my belongings inside, I continue on to the west end. There I am greeted with a spectacle of bright green and silver. The surrounding emerald-clad peaks feature an enormous valley carved and scrubbed clean over the millennia by a now-absent glacier—the exposed rock gleaming like a silver beacon as the midday sun breaks through the cloud cover.

I sit in my canoe transfixed, dazzled by the sparkle of the glacier-smoothed rock and the glowing ultra-green of the surrounding tundra. The very air feels scrubbed and clean. As I breathe deeply, I suddenly realize the weight of the environment that I call home in the city-clogged East Coast—the heaviness of the air, the thick mask that overlays my sense of smell, and the coated taste that betrays the price of our industrialized culture. I linger for a number of hours, reluctant to leave this primeval sanctuary.

Fortunately, having already set up my tent and having gathered firewood that afternoon, I can afford to be quite leisurely on my paddle back to a welcoming campsite. As I cook my evening meal, I feel a nip in the air, and the clouds crowd out what remains of the sun. Tired but immensely satisfied, I flop into my tent and immediately drift off to sleep, ready to repeat this fine experience once again tomorrow. However, this is the Alaskan wilderness, and gorgeous weather is only part of what is possible.

Midway through the night, I awake to the steady tap, tap of raindrops on my tent tarp. Fortunately, noticing the gathering dark skies of the late previous evening, I had decided to add the protection of the tarp, knowing that if it should rain, I would otherwise have to stumble sleepily outside in the middle of the night to do so (a lesson learned from previous experience). A bit disappointed in the change of weather, but nonetheless aware that when you wish to live in nature, you accept whatever comes, I turn over to resume my slumbers.

Throughout the night, I occasionally awaken to realize that the rain is now coming down harder. Eventually, it becomes an undeniable downpour—the thunder deafening and lightning strobing my tent walls in a goblin dance. Reluctantly, not wanting to fully wake up, I decide I'd better turn on my headlamp and check the seams of my tent to make sure water isn't leaking through. Rising up on one elbow, I shine my Maglite over all the seams and in the corners. So far so good. No dripping. No puddling. I nestle myself back into my down bag, mindful that I dare not let it get wet. The downpour continues through the night, and my sleep is periodically interrupted to inspect for leaks.

As it turns out, this process continues through the following day, the following night, and late into a second day. Occasionally, I have to contort my body to pull on my rain gear, stick my feet out into the vestibule to lace up my boots, and laboriously crawl out and inspect the tarp—which inevitably sags and pools with pockets of water. I carefully turn out these water pockets in order to keep them from soaking the seams of the tent. Having done this, I have to maneuver myself back inside the tent in such a way as to avoid soaking the inside with my wet apparel.

And so it goes. Day and night blend into one, as I wait out the storm. Yes, I have waterproof jackets, ponchos, socks and shoes. But as most outdoor enthusiasts will tell you, there's waterproof and then there's waterproof. All such garments have their limit. Your clothes inevitably get damp and your skin feels cold and clammy. So, in this circumstance, shedding my clothes, snuggling into my down bag, reading a good book, and munching on trail mix is my solution.

My patience is more than rewarded. Late afternoon on the second day, the storm finally passes. I crawl out of my tent-home bedraggled, both in body and spirit. However, looking up, I am immensely buoyed by what I see — one of the most gorgeous post-storm skies I have ever witnessed. The streaming rays of the afternoon sun bathe the distant mountains in a golden aura, while the nearer hills are silhouetted in black. This entire tableau is reflected in Lake Beverly's waters.

As I gaze at this sight, I recall my childhood fascination with the passage, "I will lift up mine eyes unto the hills: from whence cometh my help." After two and a half days in a rain-soaked tent, the sight of these sun-drenched mountains is doubly inspirational. I spend the remainder of my day basking in this post-storm serenity, occasionally photographing the scene, trying to do it justice.

Next morning, I awake to a blustery wind and a white-capping lake, reminding me of the blow I experienced in Quetico so many years before. Like then, I am more than a little daunted, but this time I have the advantage of previous experience. For one thing, even though I've spent more time than planned hunkering down under the rains of the last couple of days, now I've learned to anticipate such delays and build them into my overall trip plan. Thus, I am in no great hurry, allowing the wind to thoroughly blow-dry my tent and its contents before breaking camp.

But my advantage isn't simply one of being a more flexible traveler. More important, I now know *how to be* in this country. I have learned that the natural world is neither threat nor obstruction to be confronted, but instructor and guide. Pay attention—become its pupil—and you can read its messages, just as one would read a book. With this perspective, I can now stand on the shore of Lake Beverly and survey the particulars of this challenge. It mirrors my Quetico experience in that I am once again standing on a southern shore facing blustery whitecaps driven by winds out of the north.

I close my eyes and invite the smell of Quetico's woods and lakes back into my nostrils. I listen to the howl of that wind, and remember how it felt as it tore at my jacket. Just as I did then, I harbor enormous respect for the spectacle and power of the elements I face. And I remember the paralysis of indecision.

But I also recall the *calm* of joining forces with those elements—how the wind and waves became my cradle. And I smile as I remember the *joy*, the outright *exhilaration*, of this discovery. Just as I did then, I now relax my breathing—seeking once again to collaborate with my surroundings rather than struggle against them. I feel a renewed assurance and familiar sense of tranquility.

Turning my attention to the task at hand, I observe how today's challenge differs from that of Quetico. This time, rather than paddle straight into the whitewater and across the lake, my destination is eastward—down lake—nearly parallel to the breakers that are crashing towards me.

Once again I close my eyes and begin to visualize my intended journey. Breathing deeply, I see myself paddling straight north into the teeth of the wind and waves—adopting the slow and steady rhythm of my breath to the measured strokes of my paddle—conserving energy in order to move out some two or three hundred yards from shore.

Next I envision the flip-turn that I will need to execute in order to attain an eastwardly direction. This is a rather intimidating maneuver that I have had no occasion to attempt before, with one exception—when navigating the rolling waters of the St Lawrence River by motorboat. At that time, my young son Geoff was in the boat with me, and when executing the delicate turn, the boat abruptly reared up in a nearly vertical aspect while navigating the deep trough between the white-capping crests. Suddenly, hanging on for dear life, a wide-eyed Geoff was staring down at me from high in the bow—looking into my eyes for reassurance. "Hang on, I called to him over the wind and the roar of the complaining outboard, "We'll be just fine!" And we were.

Now—eyes still closed—I see myself gauging the point at which my canoe arrives at the very crest of a wave. At that point, I will need to dig my paddle deep on the port side in order to suddenly pivot eastward—all the while shifting my weight forward like a bicycle racer bent over his handlebars— and decisively execute the flip-turn that will head me down the lake, somewhat parallel to the waves, but sufficiently turned southward to avoid being rolled over in their trough.

After rehearsing this procedure in my mind several times—eyes closed and nodding my head at the point of each maneuver—I turn to gather my gear and canoe. Holding my heavily loaded craft against the incoming breakers, I set out. Not unlike Quetico, when I try to hop into my canoe against the tumult of Lake Beverly's winds and the force of the rollers, the breakers turn me back more than once. But, unlike Quetico, I feel sure of the ultimate outcome. It proves much less harrowing to launch into the froth and paddle out to sea, the bracing whitewater leaping the bow and spraying my face.

When it comes time to execute the critical turn—having

implanted in my mind's eye that vision of myself waiting patiently to ride the longest, largest breaker to its crest—I dig in my paddle forcibly and swing the canoe eastward—shouting enthusiastically at the success of my gambit—and proceed east-southeasterly down the shoreline. Remarkably, it is just as I had envisioned.

As expected, the rolling action of the deep swells eventually bears me back to shore. But each time that happens, I rest a while to regain my strength and my focus, reclining on a rock to enjoy a power snack while contemplating nature's display and envisioning my next foray. Thus renewed, I launch back into the wind-driven waves. My journey becomes a series of triangular mini-trips northward out from the shoreline, and then eastward as far as I can go until the winds inevitably beach me. After being blown to shore for the third time, I take a photo of this majestic sea.

My destination is some twelve miles distant—but in the late evening I arrive, paddling through an enormous school of spawning salmon, which, like me, are circling the swirling headwaters of the Agulupak River. Exhausted after hours of wrestling with the wind-driven lake, I wearily haul my canoe to shore and prepare camp. Tomorrow I will test my skills in the rapids of the Agulupak, but tonight I'm content to watch the late-setting sun over the now becalmed waters. I listen to the distant lullaby of the wolves, and marvel that—more than ever—I feel so at home in this untamed country.

The Agulupak

At the headwaters of the Agulupak, there sits a small cabin, the unlikely outpost of a lone park employee whose job it is to survey the activity of the salmon spawn. Otherwise retired, he spends three lonely summer months here each year manning his post—and he loves it.

"Couldn't believe my eyes when I saw ya out there last night," he remarks after inviting me for a cup of morning coffee. "Never seen nobody take on Beverly in that kind of weather."

"That was quite a blow," I agree, inwardly proud of the fact that I had mastered yesterday's chop. It's good to hear that my paddling skills have impressed a seasoned observer.

"Where ya headed?"

"Just working my way down the lakes as far as I can for the next week or so."

"Where ya from?"

"Takoma Park, Maryland," I reply. "It's just outside Washington, D.C."

He whistles. "Long way from home. I guess today yur headed down to Nerka?"

"Lookee down there," he interrupts himself before I can answer, jumping up from his chair and reaching for his binoculars. "There's a big ol' silvertip comin' up the far side," pointing far down the west shore of the Agulupak. All during our conversation his eyes are constantly scanning the outdoors.

"Where? I don't see him" I respond, craning my head in the direction he's pointing. Like a kid, I never tire of the sight of one of these magnificent animals lumbering through the wild.

"Right down there," he says, pointing again. "Jist beyond that tall pine. Here. Try the binocs."

Sure enough, the grizzly, a couple of hundred yards down the far side of the river, is ambling our way, its great head sweeping from side to side—stopping every few steps to lift its nose and sniff the air. We both watch wordlessly, fascinated, while it heads up the riverbank. Finally, the creature decides to take to the woods and moves out of our vision. Excited by the interruption, but resigned that the show is over, we return to our coffee.

"Any suggestions about how to tackle the rapids?" I ask tentatively, still aware of what a novice I am at river canoeing.

"I've only been on the Tanana, and that was a pretty smooth ride."

"See where the river divides at that island?" he asks, handing me the binoculars again.

"Yeah."

"Best to take the right fork. The left one peters out in about a half-mile."

"But that looks like a lot of whitewater on the right," I observe.

"Yeah. It's pretty tricky. But ya see those two boulders?"

Focusing in, I look carefully and spot the two boulders sticking up prominently like a five-foot-wide gateway with water rushing through.

"Ya wanna head between those two boulders and hit the sluice."

"The sluice?"

"Yeah. It drops about three or four feet there, but once you pass that drop, you're home free."

"Appreciate the info," I say, trying to sound casual while thinking, "Three or four feet!"

"No problem. Jist stay away from those rapids and hit the sluice."

And with that I thank him for his hospitality and head for my canoe.

Once underway, I proceed down river towards the whitewater. The air is crisp and cold as the wind whistles down the channel, echoing between the surrounding mountains. The rumble of the rapids, which only a moment ago seemed so distant and removed, now permeates my ears. I approach the churning froth, my eyes glued on the gateway boulders that appear to be the only passage that isn't blockaded by large rocks and cascading, swirling whitewater. I fight the tendency of the insistent current to push me too far to the right and hold steady for the sluice.

Clearly, there's no room for error. If I hit the gap dead

center, my canoe level and straight, I can navigate the opening without scraping against one of the boulders. If not—well, there is no "if not." Holding the craft steady, I speed toward the opening. At the last second, I hunch forward—straining to see through the cold spray—and split the gap perfectly. Immediately, the canoe bucks downward over the cascade, diving into the churning cauldron below and righting itself as the stern completes the passage.

"Yeowee!" I whoop as I shoot through the sluice, my adrenaline high and my spirits higher—the scariness behind me. Now that I know I can do it, I wish I could repeat it over and over again. What a rush! Briefly, I look over my shoulder upriver where I catch a glimpse of my recent companion, standing on the front deck of his cabin, waving his approval. Before I can wave back I'm swept even further down river, riding the swift current.

About ten feet over on my left, huddled on a large boulder and facing into the wind, are a covey of red-breasted mergansers. As I zip by in my canoe, I fumble for my camera and take a quick shot—holding the camera with one hand while steering with the other—hoping that they won't simply look like a blur. Somehow, their presence reassures me, as if to say, "Yeah, we do this all the time."

Later that day, the Agulupak behind me, I safely emerge onto Lake Nerka. It has been a fun ride. I feel that I've added a bit of whitewater canoeing to my river skills.

But for now, I enjoy the calmer waters of Lake Nerka. Almost immediately on entering the lake, I hear the unmistakable clump of a moose moving through the woods along the north shore. As the day draws to a close, I proceed lackadaisically and begin my daily search for a suitable campsite.

Native Land

I often describe the wilderness as vast. One feature of that description is the vast silence. A mantel of silence no urban dweller can truly know or perhaps even imagine. A silence only occasionally broken by the piercing whistle of a falcon on the hunt circling high above, the fretful cry of an owl in the murky evening, the soulful howling of a distant wolf late at night, or the early-morning cacophony of a loon calling for its mate. A silence made for openheartedness, meditation, and mindfulness.

Yesterday evening, satisfied that no grizzly tracks were apparent and glad for a flat surface for my tent, I had selected a pebbly sandbar on Nerka's shores as my home for the night. It had been well over a week since Ric, my bush pilot, had left me to fend for myself on the north shore of Lake Kulik. Since that time I had made my way over these challenging lakes with silence my trustworthy companion.

Thus it is especially surprising to be woken at about six in the morning by the foreign, but unmistakable, drone of an outboard motor propelling its craft swiftly by my campsite. I wonder who can be navigating these waters so far from civilization. Perhaps they wonder the same about me as they pass by my campsite. Whatever the answer, the activity is sufficient to rouse me from the warmth of my sleeping bag, and, emerging from my tent to another spectacular crisp autumn morning, begin my breakfast preparations.

Just as I am about to add the last of my wild-picked blueberries to my pancake mix, the boat returns. After we exchange friendly waves, the motorman swings his craft around in an arc and heads for my campsite, cutting the motor and letting the boat drift toward shore.

This is my first encounter with a Native Alaskan Yup'ik Eskimo. A grizzled, near toothless man—likely my own age—but wearing the leathery, sunbaked skin of a seasoned outdoorsman, he stands erect behind the steering wheel in the stern of his open craft while his Adonis-like son—whose handsome, muscular frame reminds me of my own son—hops obediently into the shallows, head bent down and smiling shyly, and pulls the boat to shore.

The irony does not escape me that while his father is piloting a craft powered by a sleek, eighty-horsepower Evinrude, I am plying the waters of his ancestors in their more archaic mode of conveyance—the canoe. I walk over from my campfire to greet them, and—as is the way with those who meet in such far-flung areas—each of us asks the other where they are coming from and where they are heading.

I explain that I have paddled some sixty miles or so from the lakes to the north. He, in turn, informs me that he has motored up from his home far to the south, where, he proclaims, he is the head man of his village. As to my destination, I am making my way some days hence to a prearranged lake where my bush pilot will pluck me out of my wild sanctuary and I will return, eventually, to my community in the Lower 48. He and his son are hunting moose, stocking up during these late autumn days on winter provisions for their village.

He describes, with a demeanor of infectious jocularity, how the previous winter the snow had come up to his shoulders, and thus, he laughs, there was certainly no opportunity to hunt in those conditions! Enquiring if I have seen any moose, I point up the shoreline to where I had heard one tramping through the woods the previous evening. He relates that others in his hunting party on the south end of the lake are, as we speak, dressing a fresh kill. Then, beaming with pride, he bends down and reaches into the boat's holding tank. Lifting up an enormous silver sockeye that he caught earlier this morning, he displays it proudly—raising it high with his right arm to match the entire length of his chunky stature.

Addressing his still shy and silent son—who all this time has remained outside the boat holding the mooring rope—I ask him his name. The son gives an embarrassed smile, but continues to keep his head down and eyes averted. His father laughs heartily and answers for him, and in that instant I wonder if I have possibly been indiscrete by asking the young man a direct question. However, if I have committed such an indiscretion, each is too polite to inform me.

After wishing each other a good journey, the son bends to the task of pushing the craft away from the sandy shore and nimbly hops aboard. As they swing their boat around and motor up-lake, I grab my camera and take a photo of the boat's receding wake—the photo that I had been too tentative to request during our actual visit.

I watch them disappear as the silence once again envelops me. I stand here filled with a sense of dignity about this meeting. I imagine each of our cultures standing like ghosts behind us, an unbroken ancestry witnessing this timid, early-morning introduction as we gaze at each other without wariness or guile. I had instantly felt respect for the jocular father and his shy son. In turn, it seemed as if I was the recipient of a similar regard. It was as if the simple discovery of each other in this remote place and at this time, was sufficient credential to evoke mutual admiration.

As I stand here, I realize I am romanticizing this event. After all, I tell myself, one chance meeting does not describe an entire people. Nonetheless, so struck am I with this encounter that I am inspired to plan a time when I can return and perhaps come to better know Alaska's Native people.

Around the Bend

The Wood-Tikchik wilderness is an ever-changing environment. Not only do the surrounding mountains, lakes and rivers seem to shift shape and color depending on time of day, weather, and perspective, but they can appear ominous, welcoming, or indifferent depending on one's mindset. Trepidation invites timidity, wariness and outright fear. Bravado may beget accident, shock, or even catastrophe. Acceptance opens one to a much more complete experience, especially when combined with patience and common sense. Inspired by my morning visitors, I proceed through the day with my mind flung open to any possibility. Surprises, I have discovered, are frequently just around the next bend.

After spending the next couple of days canoeing the choppy expanse of Nerka's waters, early that next evening I find myself in a quiet lagoon at the west end of the lake, gazing into water so clear it feels as if I can reach out and touch bottom. Suddenly, not eight or ten feet below, I spot an enormous northern pike, almost as long as my canoe, lying lazily beneath me. The fisherman in me leaps with excitement. I'm tempted to lower a hook and line.

But why? What use have I for such an enormous creature? To eat? To mount as a trophy on my wall? To tell a whopping story about battling to catch him? Whereas in the past I might have seen this pike as trophy or prey, now he simply seems like a fellow living being. I feel like a guest in his territory. At the very least, I should not disturb him. Better yet, I should thank him for sharing these waters. Perhaps I would feel differently if I were a Native hunter like my morning visitor and needed this fish to help my village survive the upcoming winter. But I am not a Native hunter. And so, I simply continue to gaze and admire. Eventually, he moves on, and so do I.

Looking up, the evening shadows are silhouetting the surrounding mountains. It's time once again to make camp. My day has been full and I am suddenly dead tired. I search my campsite for kindling to build a fire beside which I can sit quietly and reflect on the day's events.

Afterward, as I lie down in my tent, the lake quietly lapping at my doorstep, I think about what I had said a few weeks ago in response to a question my friend Rich had posed concerning my far-flung expeditions.

"Why do you go there?" he, a homebody, asked.

"To see what happens," I had replied.

I think about how simple, but how true, my answer was.

And today, a lot has happened.

I fall asleep.

Swimming with the Fishes

As it turns out, that next morning my adventures with fish will resume. Yesterday I had marveled at one lone, regal-looking northern pike. Today, it's thousands of salmon.

I return to the shallows at the west end of the lake, because my topo map indicates a stream located there will connect me with Little Togiak, the next lake on my Wood-Tikchik journey. Initially the shallows are about ten feet deep and easy to canoe. But as I proceed the water eventually drops to a depth of only one or two feet and is choked with reeds. I struggle to paddle forward until the bottom of my canoe begins to scrape the sandy lake bottom, and I am barely able to sustain momentum.

Finally, reluctant to do so because the water is ice-cold, I pull on my waterproof zip-on pants and try out, for the first time, my neoprene diver's socks and booties. Carefully, I spread out my body and lower myself over the side of the canoe, trying not to roll it over atop me. Once in the water, to my amazement, my feet and legs feel warm and dry—a confirmation that some gear really functions as advertised and is worth the investment.

Grabbing the bow rope and hitching it over my right shoulder, I begin to haul my gear-laden canoe through the slough, feeling for all the world like a Volga Boatman—"Yo-ho heave-ho! Yo-ho heave-ho!" Getting into the spirit of the old Russian barge chant, I sing at the top of my lungs as I strain to pull what seems to become an increasingly heavy load. And no wonder. The stream is widening and the oncoming current is becoming fairly rapid, splashing directly against my canoe and me. The slog upstream is becoming annoyingly onerous.

However, bent to my task, I am committed. There's no jumping into the canoe now, lest I be swept back to my starting point and have to begin anew. Meanwhile, concentrating on my task, only now do I notice the increasingly noisy decibel level of what is becoming a shallow, small river beneath my feet. Then I realize the noise is not only from the slapping of the waves against my boat and me. It's the sound of thousands—perhaps tens of thousands—of salmon headed upstream all around me. I look around and realize I am in the middle of a huge migration. All around, sockeye salmon are struggling desperately up this small river.

Finally, after hauling my craft against the current for about a hundred yards, I (we, thousands of us) reach the lake. The salmon determinedly swim on. I pull my canoe to the shore and flop on the rocks, thoroughly spent. The whole experience gives new meaning to the term "fellow traveler."

Of course, my journey is nothing compared to these sockeyes. They have traveled hundreds, even thousands of miles from their Pacific feeding grounds to return to their birthplace. The price they pay for traveling upstream through often-torrential currents, scraping against sharp rocks, boulders and branches is evident in the injuries and scars they display. One cannot but admire the resilience and determination of this species as they seek to propagate. Their surviving offspring will spend the next year or two here in their sub-Arctic waters before heading out to the far Pacific—only to eventually repeat the homing cycle.

As the day progresses, the salmon and I are never far apart. I have inadvertently—but literally—stumbled upon their spawning grounds. In these clear waters, I can lean over the side of my canoe and watch as the males spray clouds of sperm over the beds of newly ejected eggs.

From this time forward, I have no desire to resume my fishing activities. Too bad—I have some colorful hand-carved lures that I really love. But I have quite simply lost the desire, and certainly the thrill, of landing the big one. I will take my pole, lures, and tackle box with me on a couple of future trips, but they fall into disuse. I feel no need to make this a moral crusade. But for me, the strange camaraderie of my upstream journey with the salmon seems to have ended my career as a fisherman.

From Fish to Fowl

I quietly guide my canoe into a little harbor of rocks near the lakeshore to rest. Perched overhead, in a copse of leafy trees, is a bald eagle. Jerking his head from side to side, his eagle eye is ever alert for an afternoon snack. Now and then, he appears to spot something and tenses his powerful body for takeoff—only to abort upon changing his mind and settle back onto his perch. His indecision gives me a moment to change lenses and try my telephoto. I have chosen an Olympus E-300 camera for this trip because its hi-powered compact lenses are easier to backpack—both lighter in weight and only two-thirds the length of other well-known field cameras. Thus I am able to rapidly swing my less bulky telephoto lens into action without the aid of a tripod.

My luck holds and the eagle is more than accommodating, remaining on his perch long enough for me to quietly and quickly snap a number of stills. Finally, spotting a possible meal, he once again hunches his body and this time takes off, leaping into the air, his powerful wings flapping with increasing intensity until he glides forward, intent on his prey. I take his portrait mid-flight.

And so the theme for the day switches from fish to fowl—from ichthyology to ornithology. The hungry eagle reminds me that it's time to break out the trail mix and M&Ms. Munching until satiated, I resume my own journey. (As one might imagine, each year I lose about fifteen to twenty pounds on these vigorous and demanding journeys. And despite my vows to keep the weight off, I regain it over the winter, like a hibernating bear.)

Gently wafting on the chilly breezes of the late afternoon,

I hear the unmistakable cries of several loons. Lured by their cacophony of tremolos reverberating around the bowl of the lake—I paddle nearly to the far shore until I reach the edge of their small flock.

If you asked me to encapsulate the call of the wild, my candidate might be the loon. With its elegant black head and beak, its striking green neck ring and its black and white checkerboard back, the voice of this graceful, princely-looking bird seems perfectly designed to express the myriad variations of the wilderness experience. At sunset when the wind gentles and the forest quiets, it is the loon's haunting wail, echoing across the waters, that announces the arrival of evening. As you sit fireside and the first stars usher in the canopy of night, that desolate call redounds in your very soul—which can't help but echo its own wistful reply—"Here I am. Where are you?"

How to compare the loon's song? A clarinet? An ocarina? A Peruvian pan flute? A bit of each perhaps—but none can truly duplicate the rising and falling "o-o-o-o-ah-ah-ah-ah-o-o-o" as the loon calls out to its mate. It is the sound of sunset; of peaceful invitation to the close of day; the return to the nest; the welcoming of night.

How, then, is it that the creature which utters this haunting cry can, at other times of day, convey such a variety of cacophonous, even daffy, babble? There is nothing else that mimics this "loony" laugh, except perhaps an ocarina wavering rapidly between the high and mid-ranges of a musical scale.

The Loon Preservation Committee, which makes it a point to study these calls, tells us that this "crazy" tremolo is most often heard in the daytime, and, in fact, is the loon's alarm signal. That I can confirm. Many times, as is the case on this Wood-Tikchik afternoon, when my canoe first noses into their waters, this warning cry is issued over and over. Strangely, as I creep carefully closer, the alarm dissipates, and the loons and I co-habit the space from that point forward in peaceful coexistence.

Alarm or no, this sudden raucous intrusion into the quiet of the wilderness seems so primitive, so wacky, that I find the whole scene infectious, and eventually my own crazy laughter joins the echoes across the lake. Caught up in this spirit, I am compelled to share it. I fish my sat phone out of my dry bag and phone Janet in order to share the madness. As it turns out, Janet is at that moment driving through the bustling streets of Washington, D.C. Answering her car speaker phone, she is suddenly surrounded by the infectious quavering tones of this loony chorus, broadcast over thousands of miles from my canoe in the Alaskan wilderness. Captivated by this momentary wildlife serenade—so opposite to the urban traffic she is then negotiating—Janet laughs delightedly.

If the fish and the birds are reliable daytime companions, the moon frequently commands the night. Sometimes I find it hard to sleep when, on a clear night, the moon backlights my tent and invites me outside to sit under its spell. More than once I accept the invitation. The moon is the chaperone of night, shedding its irrespective light on all of us—flocks of sandhill cranes that make these northern climes their summer home, caribou migrating to their winter grazing, grizzlies patrolling the lakeshores and riverbanks, wolves howling their lament, and the human family trying to make sense of it all— each of us moving to our own rhythms and purposes.

Moon Magic

For me—and I imagine for humankind since our beginnings—the moon is a source of contemplation and beauty, and sometimes a cold reminder of the finite nature of existence. For other denizens of the night, it is perhaps a hunter's moon. For still others, it undoubtedly serves as a compass and guide for movement and migration.

Sitting outside my tent on this particular Wood-Tikchik night, warmed by a rekindled fire, the moonlit night sky serves as a conduit to an ancestral past, far beyond memory, but not beyond imagination. I think back to the land bridge that once connected Native Alaskans to their Siberian villages—how intrepid women and men relied on these same stars and moon to guide them and give them comfort in the vast expanse that lay before them, following the footprints of great bears, mastodons and other creatures large and small upon which they depended for sustenance.

I feel beholden to them for making it possible for me to sit here tonight. I am a guest in their land. Though I possess only a sad glimmer of their incredible skills, knowledge and determination to survive, I am grateful to visit these native lands now so admirably inhabited by their progeny—the Aleut, Yup'ik, Inupiat and Athabascans, the Tlingit, Haida and Tsimshians—and all of those cultures and tribes lost to Western historical record.

*   *   *

A couple of days later, my Wood-Tikchik adventure draws to a close. I spend these days marveling at the jagged peaks that surround me, while, along the shore a riot of orange-red berries spangle the greenery, inviting the ravens to eat their fill. My last evening is spent trying to find a campsite that will serve as a proper pickup spot for the bush plane. Ric had cautioned me that it was important that he be able to bring his plane close in order to load my gear and canoe without the pontoons being thrown against rocks by wind or waves. This means locating an accommodating site to pitch my tent and await my pickup.

However, no matter how far I search up and down the shore, no such site even remotely presents itself. Instead, the surrounding mountains drop sharply into the lake, leaving no footprint even for my small tent. I am reminded of the trouble I had locating a campsite in Saskatchewan. Night is approaching, and after a gorgeous, clear day, the clouds move in. Even though the weather is shifting, I am treated on my last night to a glorious sunset.

Eventually, as darkness approaches, I am forced to set up camp on a series of boulders that will allow me to pitch my tent on a sharp slope and spend my last night trying to get some sleep at a most precarious angle. I know Ric will not be happy with my choice, but, try as I might to fulfill his instructions, I now have to hope that somehow we will adjust to the situation—not an unusual circumstance in negotiating wild country.

This next morning I step out of my tent into a fog that throws my pickup plans into doubt. I call Ric on my sat phone, warning him of my precarious perch and the uncooperative weather. Seasoned guide and pilot that he is, Ric has seen it all before. He suggests we wait out the weather and hope the fog will lift. Some hours later I begin to see blue sky above the heavy patches of fog that nestle in the valleys. Finally, the lake clears, and we seem to have a go.

Soon I hear the drone of Ric's Beaver in the far distance. I watch as he touches down on the water, sending up the familiar rooster tail of spray as the pontoons skid along the lake's surface. Eventually the nose of the plane dips to a gentle stop. A rather disgruntled Ric steps out onto a pontoon to survey the pickup site, then slowly paddles the plane to a safe docking. We load my gear and canoe and, in less than twenty minutes, we are airborne.

As I survey Wood-Tikchik from aloft, I feel the familiar pang of wishing I could stay. But my time here is over, and, quite satisfied, I am ready to return to hearth and home. But I know that about this time next year, I will be back. My journey has only begun.

Chapter 11
2007 – A MONTH IN THE ARCTIC – THE KOBUK

When I was a child growing up in the Midwest, the arctic was intriguing, alluring, and foreboding—a distant land that was the province of polar bears, Eskimos and National Geographic. I never dreamed I'd go there. As a man, I had come to love canoeing the wilds of Alaska, and its northern expanses now sang a siren song. I felt impelled to go there and witness its beauty for myself before the entire ecosystem was lost to global warming—not the global warming of endless debates in Congress, but the climate change that had already begun to engulf Native Yup´ik villages in the melting ice.

Now I am headed for the Kobuk, a river that flows above the Arctic Circle some 280 miles from Walker Lake to the fabled Chukchi Sea. Why the Kobuk? Initially, I was intrigued by the wholehearted recommendation I received last year from three outdoorsmen I met on my expedition to Wood-Tikchik.

"You've got to go to the Kobuk," they had agreed excitedly. "The sheefish are enormous! It's wild! Wolves chasing caribou downriver. You'll get some great photos!" Before that, I hadn't even heard of the Kobuk or sheefish, but I was struck by the enthusiasm of these erstwhile companions and filed their advice in my memory.

Upon my return home, I begin to look into the region. My research reveals that upstream the Kobuk features challenging rapids and flows through a seldom-traveled wilderness of deep woods bordered by rugged mountains. I also learn that downstream, the Kobuk is home to a rich Native Inupiaq Eskimo culture (the name "Kobuk" itself is Inupiaq, meaning "big river"). If I start at the source and follow it to the mouth, I will pass by a number of Inupiaq villages, for which the river is a source of transport and sustenance.

Then I stumble across some exciting information. I discover that Alaska's Western Arctic caribou herd crosses the Kobuk at a location with the peculiar name of "Onion Portage" while migrating from their summer to their winter feeding grounds.

I am hooked.

This great migration, repeated annually for thousands of years, has been the subject of countless documentaries. In the past, I have seen these impressive migrating herds featured on TV wildlife programs. I am now determined to witness and photograph this phenomenon in person.

Up to now, my goal each year has been to travel in solitude. But this year the possibility of interacting with Native Alaskan Eskimos is also alluring. Why not, I ask myself, arrange a trip allowing for both experiences? By my calculations, if I start my journey at Walker Lake—the source of the Kobuk—it will take me a couple of weeks of wilderness paddling to reach Kobuk, the first of three Native Eskimo villages along my route. During that time I will be entirely alone. I will then need to pass through the villages of Shungnak and Ambler to reach Onion Portage. All in all, most of the two hundred plus miles of paddling will still entail being alone in the wilds.

My task now becomes to guesstimate when this year's crossings will most likely occur. Each year the exact time varies, depending on weather conditions and related factors. I decide to take the direct approach. Locating a phone number from their website, I call the Ranger Station at Gates of the Arctic National Wildlife Refuge.

"That's hard to say," replies a Ranger to my request for information about when the migration will cross the Kobuk this coming fall. "You might want to contact a fellow named Scott Jones who lives in Ambler. He's about fifteen to twenty miles upstream from Onion Portage and might be able to give you a better guess about when the main herd will be crossing this year."

Thanking him for the referral, with growing anticipation I call Scott, who, along with his wife Piquk, are two of Ambler's three hundred or so inhabitants. "Hard to say," Scott replies after I explain who I am and describe my plan to camp at Onion Portage. "My best guess is the main group might cross in early September, but you can't know for sure." Then he adds, "If you do decide to come, be sure and stop by on your way. We'd be happy to show you around."

North by Northwest

And so in late August of 2007, I head for the arctic. The journey requires a twelve-hour flight from Dulles International to my jumping-off point—the outpost of Bettles at the southeast corner of Gates of the Arctic National Park and Preserve—by way of Seattle, Anchorage, and Fairbanks. I have arranged a swap on this particular trip—my outfitter in Bettles will supply me with an inflatable canoe and a bush-plane ride of some two hundred miles to the remote waters of Walker Lake (headwaters of the Kobuk) in exchange for aerial photos of Walker Lake and its environs.

After arriving at Fairbanks, I check into the Alpine Lodge, just across the highway from the airport. The desk clerk—a fellow named Larry—greets me warmly.

"Anyplace decent to eat around here?" I enquire, as I sign the register.

"All kinds," says Larry with surprising enthusiasm. "Our restaurant's got a great breakfast, but you shouldn't miss Pike's Landing while you're here. Everyone goes there."

"What's the draw?"

"Good food. Great bar. And it's right on the water. When the weather's like today, everyone sits outside and takes in the river and the sunset."

"Sounds perfect. How do I get there?"

"Just go out the door you came in, turn left, and walk down along the riverbank 'bout a half-mile. You can't miss it."

Later that evening, the northland sun lazily riding the horizon, I return singing the praises of Pike's. Larry is still behind the desk, and we strike up another conversation.

"You live here in Fairbanks?" I ask.

"Yep. I've got a great little cabin I'm building out on the edge of town, near the university. Wanna see it? I get off in about an hour and I'd be glad to show you some of the town."

Before I know it, we're in Larry's car, touring Fairbanks. Shades of my experience with John. Does everyone in Alaska have time to just drop whatever they're doing and give a stranger a tour? I wonder. Larry proudly shows me the downtown, the university, the nearby wildlife sanctuaries, and his cabin on the outskirts of Fairbanks. The cabin is rustic, yet just right for a bachelor.

"'Scuse the mess," Larry says as we walk through a maze of insulation, boards and carpentry tools on our way to the front door. "I'm winterin' the place."

"Your first winter?" I ask.

"Nope. My second," Larry replies. "But I learnt my lesson last year."

"Not many people last too long here," he says, with more than a hint of pride that he had made it through his first winter. "Too cold. Too dark. People get lonesome or depressed. But I love it. I mean to stick it out."

I never cease to wonder at the open hospitality with which

I am greeted throughout my wanderings in this state. Only hours ago Larry was my desk clerk checking me into his motel. Now it feels like I've known him for years.

*   *   *

Next morning, after a typical Alaskan breakfast of sausages, bacon, eggs, potatoes, hot cakes and coffee at the Alpine, I join a half-dozen other intrepid souls on an early-morning feeder flight from Fairbanks to Bettles. Once aloft, we bounce through leaden skies, short on visibility and heavy with the threat of rain.

Finally arriving at Bettles, we run through the rain for the lodge, where I meet my outfitter. "Looks like we're socked in for a few days," my host observes, using his sleeve to rub the steam off a window and gauging the surrounding fog outside. "I'll let ya know when we can take off for Walker. Meanwhile, ya might as well make yourself ta home. There's a room upstairs ya can have."

The low-hanging fog, blustery winds and intermittent rain squalls threaten to keep me grounded indefinitely. But by now, something of an Alaska veteran, I have learned to flex with the weather—understanding that the best-laid plans are made with a hope and a prayer and a willingness to postpone. I end up hanging around Bettles for a couple of days, swapping stories with the locals around cups of steaming coffee, exploring the town's half-dozen buildings, and checking in at the Gates of the Arctic ranger station.

Finally one morning, a small breach in the clouds reveals a patch of blue—a welcome sight, tentative though it is. My pilot—a young man named Kyle—and I decide to take advantage of this momentary break in the rain. We grab my gear and load it onto Kyle's floatplane, which he keeps moored at a nearby waterway. After he pumps the excess water out of the pontoons, I hop aboard.

For me, lift-off never loses its excitement. Sitting in my co-pilot's seat, Kyle hands me a pair of headphones so we can talk to each other above the clamor of the engine. Checks are made, switches are flipped, levers are adjusted; then suddenly I am thrust against the back of my seat as the powerful engine roars into duty and the water rushes toward us, throwing up a curtain of spray from the pontoons as they skate over the surface. Slowly the aircraft gains sufficient speed to escape the water and soon we are skimming the tops the spruces, circling round and tilting at a steep angle until I am looking straight down into the forest. I lean over, straining to see if I can spot a moose or a grizzly. Finally, we level off, gain altitude and settle into the flight.

During the morning we negotiate our way between rain squalls that hug the mountains on either side of our flight path. I occasionally lift up the handle to open my passenger window and try to focus my camera on a distant storm.

"Careful!" Kyle yells over the engine. "Grip that window tight, or the wind'll rip it right out of your hands." I follow his instructions and resist the mighty rush of outside air as the small plane tosses and swerves at the mercy of the elements. Fortunately, I've come to feel at home riding small planes as if they were bucking broncos—relaxing my body and letting it sway and jerk in harmony with the air currents that buffet our craft.

And so, as we carom our way toward Walker Lake, I feel secure. I've heard and read horror stories of pilots who lost their way, got caught in storms, and took chances that the wilderness will not forgive. Fortunately, aviators I've flown with have been knowledgeable of their terrain, experienced, and—most of all—safety-minded. Though still in his twenties, Kyle has accumulated more flying hours than men twice his age. He has been rigorous about his pre-flight safety checks. He is alert, friendly and relaxed. He's no cowboy. He will get us to our destination.

Approached from the air, Walker Lake is a surprising emerald swath cut in the midst of the remote interior of Alaska's arctic landscape. On a clear day its sun-spackled waters would dazzle against the undulating umbers, reds and purples of the surrounding mountains and tundra. However, on this dank, grey, overcast day, Walker's beauty broods.

Kyle—once he touches down and delivers me to the grizzly-tracked shoreline—is anxious to embark on his return flight, as the first drops of a new, chilling rain splatter our windbreakers. We unload my gear and shake hands, bidding each other safe journey. Kyle grabs a wing strut, swings into the pilot seat, and lifts off into the gathering mist, the deafening roar of the engine receding until it is muffled—then engulfed—by silence.

I am alone.

Wild Thoughts

Shoulders slumped, head bowed, the adrenaline rush of the plane ride drains from my body. Being left behind in this boundless expanse of the wilderness is sobering. As I stand here, watching the clouds swallow up Kyle's plane, the familiar doubts that come every year when I am left to fend for myself in the wild niggle their way into my consciousness. "What have I gotten myself into? It's freezing out here!" I recall Saskatchewan, when it was actually snowing, and I am flooded with negative thoughts. "I could be in a cabin by a warm fire. Did I remember matches? The water filter? My stove? Of course I did! But it wouldn't hurt to check again!"

But I will not allow these thoughts to gain a foothold. "You've done this before!" I tell myself. "Don't obsess! Get busy and put up your shelter before everything gets soaked. All you need is hypothermia!" Shoving that despairing notion aside and flapping my arms to keep warm, I reboot my attitude and review my list of chores: survey the land; select a footprint for the tent that will assure the most comfort and safety; put up the tent; store my gear; gather fuel; forage for berries and prepare to cook dinner—all in the drizzle of the dimming arctic evening. Once these tasks are accomplished, I can allow myself to stop and feel the quiet exhilaration of returning to my wilderness home.

After dinner, hands in pockets, shoulders hunched against the cold, I amble down and stand quietly beside Walker Lake. My diaphragm feels alive with nervous energy and I have to remember to breathe deeply, let my chest expand and slowly exhale. Gazing out from the silvery arctic shoreline with the sun lowering behind a gauze of misty clouds, I realize that it is now nearly eleven in the evening. Grey light rims the mountains. In another hour the light will be nearly gone, allowing for three or four hours of darkness before a new day emerges.

As I stand—breathing deeply and drinking in my surroundings—I turn up my palms and face to feel the rain, giving myself over to whatever nature has in store for me. I allow my shoulders to droop, and gradually relax my muscles; consciously repeating the process until all tension melts away and calmness inhabits my very cells.

Sighing involuntarily, I silently give thanks. I thank myself for making the effort to travel to this place, and I thank this place for accepting my presence. Truly grateful to be able-bodied and alive, I anticipate the journey on which I am about to embark—visualizing the days ahead, estimating the time it will require to reach my destination, and mentally preparing for the physical effort to come.

I know that morning will bring an early challenge—a stretch of churning whitewater that continues for about a half-mile. Before dropping me off, Kyle had generously flown over the headwaters of the Kobuk, following them southward out of Walker Lake, giving me an opportunity to scout its characteristics from 200 feet above—the rapids, the twists and turns of the river, and the choices that I will face when the river branches, divides and rejoins. With these images in mind, I climb into my tent and close my eyes.

* * *

Now it is morning, and after a breakfast of picked berries and oatmeal—the rain having subsided—I gather my gear into my Incept inflatable canoe under still threatening skies. Though the same length as the Kevlar canoes that I have normally used, the Incept's bulbous sides intrude on cargo space, and I find myself squeezed into and surrounded by what I have determined to be unquestioned necessities for the weeks to come: camera bag at my feet, Duluth bag doubling as a backrest, and an assortment of dry bags stuffed with tent, dehydrated food, clothes, stove, and water filter. I inspect my campsite to make sure I leave no trace. Satisfied, I wade into the chilly waters of Walker Lake, push off, and begin my sojourn eastward from Walker's south shore to the headwaters of the Kobuk—the river I will call home for the next three weeks.

Not long after leaving Walker Lake and paddling into the small estuary that will eventually broaden into the Kobuk, the headwaters became a roaring torrent. These are the very same rapids I saw yesterday from two hundred feet above in Kyle's bush plane. From that view, they appeared as peaceful ripples along the river. Here below, the "ripples" are almost deafening and I gauge the whitewater cascading through the boulder-strewn torrent to be Class IV—perhaps even, at some points, Class V.

Alone in the wilds, I have always chosen caution over bravado. Though I am traveling in an inflatable canoe, which is far more forgiving in these conditions (I would never even consider taking a hard-sided canoe through this churn by myself), I have not yet had an opportunity to become accustomed to its behavior. And so—though I am sorely tempted to take on the challenge—I reluctantly pull over to the shore to unload my gear, deflate the canoe, and portage over the next half-mile until I am beyond the rapids.

The portage, as I feared, is no simple task. Initially, there is a steep, bramble-entangled embankment to climb, overgrown with saplings and slick with mud. I scramble the fifteen feet or so to the top—grabbing the saplings for handholds and footholds, returning for my canoe and gear. At the top, an old portage path is barely visible. Trekking up and down this water-soaked, undulating trail, forging small creeks and tramping over roots and under low-hanging branches, I am gasping for breath by the time I reach a suitable input— and this is just the first leg of my portage! It has taken me nearly an hour and I am yet to bring the remainder of my gear and the canoe (which will then have to be re-inflated)—a minimum of two more trips.

Some two hours later, I stumble into the clearing where I have stashed my portaged gear, wheezing and disheartened. I am already significantly behind schedule. "Wait a minute!" I admonish myself. "What is this so-called 'schedule'? It is entirely of your own making! You can just as easily alter it. You're not in the city anymore! So adjust!" I sit down, take several long breaths, and continue my silent conversation with myself.

"Perhaps," I suggest, "instead of doggedly paddling on until ten or eleven this evening when dusk forces you to look for a campsite, you could simply stop here and regroup—'ya think?" Looking behind me, I notice the top of a rise some twenty yards distant where I could pitch my tent and command a view of the river. Though schlepping my gear up the steep slope demands one last effort that I don't really feel like making, the reward of a gorgeous view proves commensurate to the task.

True, compared to the more than two hundred miles that lie ahead before reaching my destination of Onion Portage, the mile or two that I have traveled today is a pittance. However, by slowing down to a stop and making camp early, I am able to recoup my energy and, for the first time today, really take in my surroundings.

I unpack my tripod and begin to focus (quite literally) on the delicate, exquisitely charming and colorful flora and fungi that carpet the arctic floor—juicy bright red-orange-capped Amanita muscaria mushrooms—unfortunately poisonous—spring up like stubby sentinels from the spongy moss. Miniature villages of innocuous orange mycena huddle together under the protection of deadfalls, and pale green lichen cling to the glacier-scrubbed bedrock. The time I have gained by deciding to make an early camp in the soft bathing of the late afternoon light becomes a precious gift as I photograph the minuscule world at my feet.

In my reverie, my senses have inured themselves to the constant roar of the nearby rapids. Finally reawakened to the thundering sound—camera in hand and carefully parting thorny brambles—I fend my way through the dense thicket along the riverbank until I manage to crawl out on a boulder jutting into the midst of the churning water. Lifting my gaze, it is only now that I realize that the sky has cleared and become a deep azure expanse sharing a smattering of fluffy white clouds with a dazzling sun—a most welcome change from days of grey overcast.

I point my SLR upriver to capture the exuberant cascade that cuts a swath through the now-bright August afternoon. Balancing myself precariously on the slick boulder, the icy, brilliant downrush sweeps towards me, spraying my face in a pine-scented blast. Finally, I turn away, suddenly exhausted from this long day of portaging and exploration. I scramble on all fours back up to my tent site, my body tired but my spirit invigorated.

Stowing my camera equipment, I begin my evening routine—priming my stove and preparing my dinner.

Tonight's freeze-dried special will be beef stroganoff with noodles, a carb-loaded favorite after the exertions of the past sixteen hours. I spend the late evening gazing down at the river, pleased with my decision to stop and rest in this place. Tomorrow, I will start afresh.

Parlez-vous Francais?

Putting in early the next morning just beyond the rapids, I can appreciate the decision to abandon a hard-sided canoe for my inflatable Incept. I know there are more rapids to come, and this isolated wilderness is no place to take unnecessary risks when traveling solo. But for now, I enjoy a relatively peaceful Kobuk and a leisurely paddle, giving myself an opportunity to familiarize myself with my new craft.

As the morning progresses, the river broadens, the backdrop of the purple mountains my constant companion. As I gain familiarity with my inflatable canoe, I glide peacefully, a welcome release from the tension of yesterday's rapids. Mile after mile I proceed through the calm waters, drifting farther and farther from shore.

Later that afternoon, while paddling mid-river, my peace and quiet is interrupted by a barely audible "ps-s-s-s"— like air leaking from an inner tube. Leaning over anxiously to inspect the canoe, I try to locate the source of this ominous sound. My confusion lasts only a moment as I realize that the right side of my canoe is rapidly losing air. Digging my paddle vigorously, I head for the shore, now about thirty yards distant—my canoe sinking lower and lower into the Kobuk. Finally, by the time I get to shore, the right side of my craft is flaccid, threatening to swamp my gear. I quickly hop out, fearing that I have sprung a leak and will have to patch it here and now.

My inspection does not reveal a leak and I let out a not inconsiderable sigh of relief. Instead, I discover I have accidentally sprung open the stopper cap on one of the air valves, apparently dragging the heel of my Tevas against it, accounting for the rapid deflation. For a moment I allow myself to feel just how vulnerable my conveyance is and how far away from civilization I have travelled. I quickly put these thoughts aside, get out my air pump, and re-inflate the canoe. Soon I am again on my way with the self-reminder to double- and triple-check my gear—and be careful where I put my feet.

Several miles downriver I have another unexpected occurrence. On most of my trips, I have quite deliberately sought solitude, often going for days or even weeks without meeting another soul. On this particular trip, I know that several days downriver I will come across a number of Inupiat villages. However, paddling later this afternoon, I already hear the unmistakable sound of voices—and they seem to be speaking French. As I round the next bend in the river, I come across an encampment of three men and two women, obviously on an expedition of their own.

As surprised to see me as I am to see them, they wave me ashore to share a bottle of French wine—a hospitality I can hardly refuse. Amazed to come across each other, we exchange stories about our adventures. As it turns out, one of the women is a professional guide from Anchorage. The group she is guiding has come all the way from France to fish the Kobuk. I am amazed to see the amount of gear they have flown in. They obviously are here to enjoy their stay, and their guide is providing them with a complete camping experience. Before bidding each other bon voyage, we snap photos of each other.

Continuing downriver, warmed by the wine and the glow of camaraderie I have enjoyed with the French adventurers and their guide, I keep my camera handy for more possible surprises. As I glance overhead, the birds display their daily routine. Alerted by a high-pitched whistle, I am treated to the aerial gymnastics of a peregrine falcon, repeatedly diving down from its cliff-top perch, patrolling the river for its next meal. Soon after, a clamor high above draws my attention to the acrobatics of three bald eagles battling for territorial supremacy. As I crane my neck to witness this spectacle, they dive at each other relentlessly, talons extended. Later that afternoon I am scolded by an osprey, whose shrill cry warns me away from her nest, high atop a spruce tree. Ospreys add to their nests year after year, and this nest appears large enough to cradle me.

As evening approaches, I spot a large seagull nesting high in a tree along the south side of the river. Though I am a seasoned bird-watcher, I never realized that seagulls are to be found so deep in the interior. Apparently she has the same reaction to me. She wastes no time leaping out of her nest and swooping to the attack. With talons exposed, she zeroes in directly for my scalp, brushing menacingly against my cap as I duck to avoid the sharp claws. Never before or since have I experienced a seagull as aggressive, but I quickly conclude that all species, when sensing danger, will defend their nests vigorously.

Now, beginning to lose the light of the long arctic day, I search for a suitable site to spend the night. After dinner and cleanup, I tumble into my tent, too tired to build a campfire. It has been about twenty hours since I launched my canoe this morning, and I am more than ready to mull over today's events and mentally prepare for tomorrow. If my calculations are correct, I should soon arrive at Kobuk Canyon.

Kobuk Canyon

As I approach a bend in the river, I catch a glimpse of what appears to be swirling whitewater. Craning sideways as far as I can to better hear, the waters of Kobuk Canyon don't sound too menacing. But as I grow closer, I realize that the bend in the river has muffled the sound and the challenge will be substantial. With towering cliffs lining both sides and plunging straight into the churn, the possibility of portage is erased. I have no choice but to take on the churning water.

Before doing so, I brace my paddle against the current and pull over to the shore. Disembarking, I stand on the riverbank, shading my eyes with my hand to cut the glare of the sun on the water, and carefully scout a possible passage through the intimidating flow. Sweeping my gaze over the water, I notice a swirling eddy on the north side of the river about halfway through the cascade. That eddy, I decide, might serve as a resting point for further reconnaissance. From there I can better determine the best route through the remaining stretch of rapids.

Closing my eyes and breathing deeply to calm myself, I envision my path through the churning water. Initially, I see myself paddling vigorously through the froth until I reached the protective eddy. There, I can rest, evaluate my progress, and chart the remainder of my course.

Opening my eyes, I push off and jump into my craft—committing to the vision and leaving all doubts and hesitation on shore—keeping the eddy firmly in sight. Straining with powerful, swift strokes to avoid being swept by the current to the middle of the river, I urge the inflatable in the direction of the whirling pocket of water. I whoop with relief as I achieve the eddy. Stopping to rest, I'm already panting from the excitement and exertion—but feeling much more confident because I have navigated this first part of the rapids as planned.

From my new vantage point, it becomes clear that my best route is to head back across river toward a large boulder that occupies the middle channel, swerve around it to the left, and drop through a small cascade. This maneuver should be sufficient to reach the quieter waters of the lower rapids.

I rehearse the idea several times in my mind. It will be no mean trick to go across the force of the surging current. Cautiously, I paddle back into the whitewater and, leaning upriver with deep, sweeping strokes to allay the current, head as best I can for the middle passage, trying to avoid the menacing boulders, whirlpools, and cascading sluices that lie between my goal and me. I almost attain the mid-river boulder when, instead of successfully working my way to the left of it, I glance into its port side, sending me into a spin.

Had I been in a rigid canoe, I would have capsized. As it is, the relentless current turns me sideways and fills my canoe half full of frigid water. However, rather than capsize, the forgiving air-filled craft bends around the enormous rock and releases me back into the current. True, at this point I am swept down the river facing *backwards*, but as I had calculated from the eddy, the rapids are milder here and I am able to swing back around to a forward-facing position and float the last quarter mile to calmer water.

Drenched, but excited, and grateful to be afloat with all my gear intact (this is no place to be swamped, a hundred-plus miles from the nearest village), I make my way toward the safety of shore to set up camp. Surveying the shoreline carefully, I notice grizzly tracks and decide to move on. However, I soon discover that the entire shoreline on both sides of the river is covered with such tracks.

Eventually—soaked to the bone from my confrontation with the rapids—I decide to pitch my tent on a small islet near the south shore of the river. This piece of land—about ten yards wide and a hundred yards long, deflects the main stream of the Kobuk northward and forms a smaller rivulet about ten yards wide on its south side.

Even though it's the arctic, it is still late summer hot, and I strip off my soaked clothes and lay them on my overturned canoe to dry. Then, wading into the chilly water, I take a bath—sitting on a convenient rock in the middle of the rivulet to wash my hair, laze in the late-afternoon sun, and savor my latest exploits with whitewater.

Ursus Not So Horribilis?

Seeing all the grizzly tracks, I think about my decision to

move through these environs unarmed. Traveling solo in the Alaskan wilderness without a gun is not generally recommended procedure. It seems everyone has their story about the infamous grizzly bear (Ursus arctos horribilis) and the price to be paid when encountering this magnificent animal unprepared. And I'm not about to disagree with that caution—one *must* be prepared for such an eventuality.

However, I long ago decided that carrying a gun is not a good way for me to be prepared. For one thing, I have no experience as a marksman, and if a grizzly is slung low, pawing the ground and clacking its teeth (as happened to my friend John), you'd better know how to handle your firearm. As I sit on my rock I remember how, at John's insistence, I fired a weapon designed to stop a grizzly—his pump-action Winchester shotgun with three-inch slugs.

"Aim in front of the feet," advised John. "You're just trying to scare him."

"Good luck with that!" I thought, as I pointed the gun at my imaginary foe, squeezed the trigger, and managed to kick up a bit of dirt. Mostly, what I got from my lesson was a large shoulder bruise.

As a compromise, I decided to take pepper spray on my trip to the Kenai in 2003. I dutifully followed a ranger's recommendation to make as much noise as possible while moving through the woods and sang at the top of my lungs. But soon I concluded that this was defeating the very reason I had come to the wilderness. Truth be told, I really had no desire to shoot a grizzly, whether it be with a gun or a can of bear spray. A camera would have to suffice.

Using my own common sense, I now move through bear country with caution and respect during times of year where berries and salmon are plentiful. When possible, I hang my food out of reach, although on treeless stretches of river such as this, there is no such option. That's why I choose to take nearly odorless freeze-dried food packets. Ultimately, if I should happen upon a grizzly—like that time I was awakened on the Chisana River a couple of years ago—I'll behave in as non-threatening a manner as possible and hope for the best.

But enough about bears, and speaking of food, it's near time to eat. Finding a dry pair of shorts and a T-shirt in my dry bag, I pull them on and slip on my Tevas. Before breaking out my cooking gear, I go to the riverbank to stretch and breathe in the late afternoon fragrance. Closing my eyes, I let the events of the day wash over me. Finally, I open my eyes and glance downriver.

I can hardly believe what I see. I had just been thinking about grizzlies and now, lumbering up the riverbank, are not one, but two of them walking abreast as if out for an evening stroll—about a hundred yards distant. They are both good-sized adults, one a "blondie" with dark-brown legs, and the other a dark chocolate silvertip.

I grab my tripod and camera and, trying to stay calm, start snapping photos. This is exactly what I had always hoped for—an opportunity to photograph grizzlies in the wild. Not the nearly-tame creatures that tourists crowd on platforms to see—eagerly taking photos of salmon leaping into the bears' waiting, gaping maws—but magnificent animals such as these roaming their natural habitat—wild, unfamiliar with bipeds, and hundreds of miles from the nearest tour guide.

However, now—of all times—my camera seems to be malfunctioning. Is my battery dead? I quickly fumble through my bag and find a replacement battery. The camera still won't work. No time. I grab my older, simpler, point-and-shoot Camedia and am finally able to capture some successful shots.

All this time—likely no more than a half-minute—the bears amble their way up the riverbank closer and closer until, looking up, they notice me, now some fifty yards away. They halt and sniff the air to determine what this unfamiliar odor is, and then they continue their approach. They stop a second time. Even with their poor eyesight, now they can make me out, and they have a decision to make—retreat, or come closer to investigate this new presence.

Interestingly, each bear makes its own decision. The blondie chooses caution—turns around and begins to walk back upriver. The darker bear, however, decides to satisfy his curiosity, and advances downriver until he stands just opposite me, on the other side of the small channel that separates my island from the shore. "That's far enough," I think, hoping he'll agree.

However, undeterred, he starts across the rivulet towards me—the same stream in which I had been bathing just an hour or so before. Halfway across, this magnificent creature climbs up on the very rock on which I had sat to wash my hair. "Great!" I think, "It's probably his favorite fishing rock." He stands there, balancing on all fours, bending his head down repeatedly to sniff the rock and then looking up at me. It's as if he's saying, "You've been sitting on my rock!"

Clearly, he's now trying to decide whether to continue on towards me. At this point he is no more than ten yards from me—eye to eye—and I tell myself, "Well, I guess all these years of deciding not to carry a weapon is being put to the test."

Slowly, calmly, never breaking eye contact with the bear, I step from behind my tripod, bend down to pick up both of my canoe paddles, and lift them high above my head, holding the shafts with both hands—legs splayed apart—trying to take up as much space as possible. I must have looked somewhat like da Vinci's Vitruvian Man. "Maybe he'll think I'm a moose," I hope, as I stretch myself to my full six feet two-and-a-half inches.

We stand here, thus linked, for maybe ten or twenty seconds. Clearly, he is gauging whether his curiosity is worth the risk of a confrontation. Finally, he pivots around on the rock, displaying his hindquarters. It is not lost on me that he feels comfortable enough to turn his back on what might have at first seemed to him a potential foe. He casually recrosses the stream, and slowly meanders into the willows on the other side. I feel grateful, and spend the next few minutes collecting my thoughts and deciding on my next move—canoe paddles now lowered to my side.

Once again, I sense that same halo of calm that had enveloped me during my previous experience with the grizzly on the Chisana. I feel good—as in cautiously validated. I now know that when put to the test, I am willing to accept the consequences of my decision to journey in this wilderness unarmed and alone. Ursus horribilis and I have greeted each other warily—but with curiosity—each exercising our own instincts. We had held each other in a questioning gaze, and each of us had, ultimately, rejected the idea of threat.

Had I been holding a weapon he might have smelled the gun oil—or the powder—and sensed danger. Had I raised such a gun to take aim, his sense of threat might have increased. As it was, satisfied that he was not in danger, he turned his back and ambled away to rejoin his mate.

As for me, I decide to stay in my campsite on the island. I am in bear country, and given the evidence of footprints along the river, everywhere I set foot on the Kobuk will prove to be bear territory. In this case, since such a meeting has already occurred, it seems best to stay where I am—a known entity.

Now I feel I can relax and be curious, and I pick up my SLR to ascertain why it has malfunctioned. After a thorough inspection, I notice that one of the settings has slipped and caused the photos to underexpose. Relieved that the problem is easily solvable, but disappointed that I was unable to get just the shot I wanted, I reset the camera and it functions properly.

Later, as I cook my supper, I look up from my campfire and see the two grizzlies about fifty yards downriver. They are sitting on their haunches, as if patiently waiting to see if I will leave. I eye them for some time, but they do not move. Rather, they lick their fur coats and sit with heads bowed, occasionally looking my way.

Finally, it is time for me to crawl into my tent and go to sleep. It's dark enough now that I can't make out whether they are still there. No matter. I feel safe—or at least as safe as one can feel with two such sentinels nearby. I lie in my sleeping bag, listening for any telltale sound. But the night is peaceful, and the peace descends on me.

I fall asleep.

*   *   *

Next morning, I crawl out of my tent and, first thing, check to see if my two visitors are still there.

Gone.

I'm crestfallen. I kind of liked the idea of them being around and now I miss them. Oh well, it's a new day and who knows what or who is around the next bend in the river. I tear open a packet of oatmeal and mix it in a cup of boiling water, adding a few blueberries I'd picked a couple of days before. Staring into a steaming cup of hot chocolate, I sit quietly. Finally, I rummage through my daypack and find one of the maps I've printed from the web. Kobuk, the first of the Inupiat villages, still looks to be a couple of days paddle.

Putting my map back in its waterproof pouch, I struggle to my feet and begin the process of breaking camp. First I empty my tent, repacking my sleeping bag into its protective dry sack, stashing my headlamp and my copy of *Arctic Dreams*. My tent is super light polyester, a space-age miracle compared to the old canvas one I started out with some fifty years ago. I grab the tent by the door poles and lift it high overhead to shake it vigorously, thus cleaning it of any sand and mud that I may have tracked in. Next I collapse and fold the tent and, along with the stakes and poles, repack it into its waterproof sleeve.

After packing my gear into my canoe, I look around wistfully for one last glimpse of my grizzly visitors. No dice.

Wading into the chilly water, I push off, hop into the stern, and head downstream for another day on the Kobuk. For several hours I travel in peaceful oblivion—quite a change from the challenging whitewater of the previous afternoon. However, my reverie is broken when I spot a young man standing on a rise along the otherwise deserted south shore. We wave to each other and he beckons me to join him.

Once I disembark, we greet each other warmly, each of us smiling as we express our surprise and delight at discovering the other in such a remote location. As it turns out, this young Inupiat Eskimo—perhaps in his early twenties—is tracking caribou. Upon finding out that I carry no weapon, the first thing he wants to show me is his Remington 700 rifle, which fires three-inch hollow-point shells that look like they can stop most anything. He insists I fire it, wanting me to appreciate the beauty of such a well-crafted instrument. It is indeed a masterful piece of craftsmanship.

I sling the weapon to my shoulder, take careful aim at a tree root some fifty yards across the river that he suggests can serve as my target, and carefully squeeze off a round. Before I can observe the result of my effort, I find myself sitting flat on my backside from the unexpected violence of the kickback. My newfound friend laughs heartily and proceeds to instruct me on how to fire his weapon *and* keep my feet. Eventually I manage to fire a few rounds that kick up the dirt reasonably near the root.

Our conversation turns to hunting, and he proceeds to tell me his grizzly story (no Alaskan worth his salt is without one). It seems his uncle and aunt were out picnicking on the riverbank about a year previous when they spotted a large silvertip meandering through the brush. His uncle took aim at the animal and succeeded only in angering it by inflicting a flesh wound. The grizzly turned on a dime and charged toward the two now-frightened souls. They barely managed to leap into their motorboat and skedaddle, leaving the picnic behind.

The purpose of this narrative is clearly to illustrate just how dangerous a grizzly can be. However, I am tempted to think that the story equally illustrates just how dangerous a *human* can be to a grizzly that was simply minding its own business.

"I had quite an experience a few years ago," I tell him. "I was camped on a small ledge on the banks of the Chisana and was awakened about six in the morning by the roar of a grizzly right outside my tent."

"That sounds pretty scary," he says.

"You know it. When I was setting up camp the night before, I hadn't noticed his tracks, and he sounded pretty angry. But he didn't seem to want a confrontation. He left after warning me off."

"You were lucky," my companion observes.

"Maybe," I go on, "but maybe the grizzly sensed my lack of fear and decided I wasn't prey."

He smiles politely, looking skeptical.

Then I tell him what happened just last night, here along the Kobuk. "Actually, there were two of them this time."

I describe how the second grizzly and I ended up standing there only a few yards apart, each of us looking at the other for maybe ten or twenty seconds."

"Must have felt like a lifetime," he says.

"You know it! But the way I figure it, maybe the bear was gauging whether his curiosity was worth the risk of a closer encounter. Whatever was going through his mind, he finally turned around on the rock, and left."

"That's surprising. You were really lucky," concludes my companion.

"True, but the funny thing is," I add, "later, when I'm eating supper, I look up and there they are again—the same two grizzlies—about fifty yards downriver. They're just sitting there on their haunches, as if they are waiting to see if I'm gonna leave."

"Just sitting there?"

"Yep. I keep glancing at them for some time, but they don't move. They just sit."

"How long did they stay there?" he asks, totally intrigued.

"I'm not sure. Finally, I crawled into my tent to go to sleep."

"Must have been hard to sleep," he observes.

"You'd think so," I say, trying to recall just how I was feeling. "But I figured if they were going to do something, they'd have done it by then. I actually felt pretty safe—or at least as safe as you can feel in that situation. I kept listening to see if they were crossing the stream. Long story short, I fell asleep. They were gone the next morning."

After hearing all this, my Inupiaq listener could only shake his head and laugh.

Wishing each other well, we say our goodbyes.

The People of the Kobuk

On my previous wilderness voyages, I seldom—if ever—met another human being. With the exception of the French fishing party and my new Inupiaq acquaintance, this is also true for the first hundred miles or so of my Kobuk expedition. Otherwise, I am occupied with the vicissitudes of the river, its currents, rapids, and occasional obstacles, along with the birds and animals who make their nests and homes along its banks—among them the aforementioned grizzlies, and even a reclusive wolf, who, while patrolling the riverbank, stops to take my measure. Such encounters awaken in me a profound sense of connection with these animals—who seem as fascinated with me as I with them.

However, I know that eventually I will come across three Inupiat villages before I arrive at Onion Portage. Early on, still far upriver from the first village of Kobuk, I paddle by a smattering of isolated, seemingly unoccupied, summer cabins, high on the knolls above the river.

In short order, I come upon Josephine's fish camp, which is situated on the otherwise deserted river flats. Josephine, I discover, is well over seventy-five years old. But like most of her Inupiat contemporaries, Josephine embraces an arduous lifestyle—no retirement plans on the Kobuk.

Surrounded by tin washtubs, blue tarps and white buckets, Josephine and her daughter busy themselves cleaning the salmon that they have seined from the river early that morning. A huge pile of discarded entrails lay before them, swarming with flies. Some yards away are the peeled poplar poles of the drying rack with their triangular supports, their crossbars laden with salmon and whitefish filets.

Behind her, peeking shyly out from the canvas back of a director's chair is Josephine's namesake, her four-year-old granddaughter. I marvel at the wildness of the scene. The fish camp is situated on a rock-strewn shoreline, seemingly in the middle of nowhere. Some hundred yards distant, copses of scraggly willows line the perimeter of the camp, while the far horizon is torn by the jagged outline of purple mountains.

While her granddaughter plays peek-a-boo with me, Josephine explains (all the Inupiat I meet are fluent in English as well as their Native tongue) that her camp is three bends of the river (twenty-five miles in this case) from Kobuk, her village. She, her daughter and her son-in-law Melvin spend their arctic summers on this isolated shoreline harvesting fish for their village.

Melvin walks over from his labors and immediately insists I sample the whitefish he is drying and join him in their shelter for a breakfast of moose meat and coffee. I soon discover that every Native Alaskan I meet will try to fatten me up!

I step into the family home, a rough-hewn frame of poplar poles covered with polyethylene plastic sheets to ward off the wind and weather. The floor beneath our feet is pebbly dirt. Melvin, dressed in a baseball cap, plaid shirt, and blue jeans, sits on a cooler and offers me the solitary chair available—a three-legged campstool.

Thus hunkered down, we are surrounded by the necessities of a summer fish camp: mattresses and bedding atop wooden platforms; clothes hanging from the center support pole alongside a handy shotgun; a clock resting against the far wall; and utensils on a plastic cloth covering a low wooden platform that serves as the dining area.

Melvin offers me coffee accompanied by chunks of quite tasty moose. I ask him how, cooking moose and drying salmon and whitefish, they manage to keep the grizzlies at bay. Melvin directs my attention to a smudge pot that burns day and night, and replies, "They don't like the smoke." After swapping stories about our experiences on the river, it's time for me to push off. A gift of dried whitefish stuffed in my food bag, I step into the canoe and bid them a good day, aglow with the satisfaction of a filled belly and an appreciation of their hearty lifestyle.

I haven't proceeded more than mile downriver before I am waved ashore by a young Eskimo couple that is enjoying a day of camping with their toddler son. They are standing in front of a small shack that is situated on a rise in the riverbank about forty yards from the water. They beckon me to join them, and I am more than happy to do so. Protesting that I have only just eaten, they will have none of it, and insist that I partake of a particular delicacy they are fixing that morning—seal in oil. They laugh as I grimace at the slimy tidbit—doing my best to appreciate their offering—and they admit that perhaps it takes some getting used to.

We exchange farewells and I continue downriver. Later this same day, I meet yet another Inupiat couple, picnicking with their nephew and two children on the sands of the riverbank. As we chat, I mention Josephine's fish camp, and the young woman tells me that her mother, Rosaline—who raised her along with thirteen siblings—also has a fish camp some days' journey downriver. She asks me to be sure and look in on her mother when I reach that bend in the river, and I promise I will do so.

After a long day's paddle, I proceed downriver until I come to a large bend, where an accommodating sandbar seems the perfect place to halt for the night. Erecting my tent and preparing to bed down for the evening, I look up from my labors to admire the setting sun. It is now nearly 11 PM, and the clouds are painted with soft, yet bright pastels of yellow, orange, red and purple. I set up my tripod and begin to capture these late evening colors.

Absorbed in the nuances of the changing lightscape, it is nearly a half-hour later when, as I bend down to reach for another lens, I glance behind me. To my surprise, there, on the southeastern horizon rises a perfect full moon, adorning a sky still tinted pink by the glow of the setting sun. Alternating sunset with moonrise, I continue photographing first one, then the other. Finally, as midnight approaches, I put down my camera and, exhausted from the day's excitements, crawl into the protective cocoon of my tent.

Next morning I break camp, pack up my gear, and prepared to shove off. However, just before getting underway, I notice a sudden drop in temperature, and the unmistakable smell of moisture in the air. I scan the sky. Sure enough, on the near southern horizon, dark cumulus are billowing and moving rapidly in my direction.

"Should I just chance it and get on my way?" I wonder. "Don't be stupid!" I tell myself, and quickly unpack my tent and tarp and begin a race with the onrushing storm to erect shelter. Unloading my gear from the canoe and throwing it in the tent for ballast, I duck in and zip the fly just as the first gigantic drops of rain start to pelt the walls. The downpour lasts about twenty minutes. Then, quickly as it arrives, it blows over and I repeat the process of breaking camp—this time with a wet tent. Such are the capricious dictates of traveling in Alaska.

Later that next afternoon, I check in with Janet on the sat phone. I tell her about the full moon and she asks excitedly, "Did you see the lunar eclipse?"

"What lunar eclipse?" I reply.

"The one last night," she says. "It was incredible!"

I'm astounded that I missed my one chance to photograph a lunar eclipse on a perfectly clear night in the wild. I had stayed up well past midnight photographing that very moonrise. But the eclipse began a few hours later, and I had slept right through it!

The Villages

Resuming my journey, I paddle towards Kobuk, Josephine's family home and the first Inupiat village on my wilderness itinerary. A flock of sandhill cranes passes overhead, noisily clacking their way downriver. This is my first sighting of these strikingly beautiful birds since I last saw them in the Okefenokee Swamp three years ago.

Thinking back to that time, I marvel how far I have come since my prostate surgery some months before my Okefenokee sojourn. Remembering those who helped me navigate that health crisis—doctors, family and friends—I realize that thanks to them, I am here now, following the sandhills over the thousands of miles of their migratory wanderings.

Now, in the late afternoon, I approach Kobuk, my first sighting of a Native Alaskan village. Nestled at the foot of a green mountain and behind a wide, sandy beachfront, this gathering of less than two hundred souls seems to blend with the magnificent wilderness that dwarfs it. Half a dozen flat-bottomed boats equipped with hefty Yamahas and Evinrudes—outboard motors designed to ply these waters for salmon and sheefish, as well as transport families up and down the river—line the shore.

Paddling up alongside, I jump into the water, pull my

modest inflatable ashore and introduce myself. Only a couple of men are down on the beach when I arrive, one bent over his outboard and the other tending a tin-roofed drying shack—its racks laden with salmon curing in the sun. We strike up a conversation and soon they are giving me directions concerning the best place to camp that evening, just up the shoreline a mile or so.

Thanking them, I head downriver and, in the dying light, set up camp for the night. As most always in the arctic, the day is climaxed by a spectacular sunset—one that lasts for hours. The deeply silhouetted horizon evolves from silver to gold to deep purple, colors that are echoed in the now stilled waters of the Kobuk.

Next morning, I resume paddling west toward Shungnak— the second of three Inupiat villages along my river route to Onion Portage and beyond. Shungnak lies on the protected north side of a fork in the Kobuk River. If you are not aware of its location in advance, you will likely take the south fork and bypass it. Fortunately, I had learned this valuable piece of information from Melvin the other morning, back at Josephine's fish camp.

In fact, that conversation with Melvin altered my plans considerably. As I chewed on the breakfast of fresh-cooked moose meat he had prepared, I mentioned that I was headed for a village called Ambler to meet Scott and Piquk, whom I had contacted some months ago to speculate when the caribou herd might be crossing Onion Portage. The Portage was beyond Ambler by about twenty-five miles, and—given the pace of my paddling thus far—I was beginning to grow nervous about whether I would get to my destination in time to witness the migration.

Melvin thought for a moment.

"The river from Shungnak to Ambler has many bends," he observed. "You could save a lot of time if you took the plane from Shungnak to Ambler."

"I had no idea Shungnak had an airport," I said, surprised that there would be air service between villages that had such small populations.

"My brother lives in Shungnak. He could pick you up in his four-wheeler and take you to the airstrip," Melvin suggested. "It's a long walk with all your gear—about a mile uphill." (I learn that there are three main modes of transportation in the arctic summer along the Kobuk: motorboat, four-wheeler ATV, and airplane.)

Now, I stop along the river for a late lunch. While I'm sitting on the sandy riverbank munching a power bar, a man in a motorboat comes along. Upon spotting me, he swings his craft into shore. Wearing a black ball cap, white cotton over-shirt, and blue jeans, and carrying a can of soda, he hops out, walks over, and introduces himself as Frank, Melvin's brother. After Frank makes sure I understand how to locate his secluded village, we make arrangements to meet on the beach at Shungnak the next day. He also gives me the name and number of the village's air dispatcher so I can use my satellite phone to arrange for a flight to Ambler.

Shungnak is an Eskimo term referring to the jade stone of the surrounding area. It was originally the old village of Kobuk, situated about ten miles upstream. When old Kobuk experienced severe flooding, most of the residents resettled in this more protected area on a north offshoot of the main river. Even though Melvin and Frank have forewarned me to keep an eye out for the divide in the river and take the north fork, I proceed with some apprehension.

Like most wilderness rivers, the Kobuk has several offshoots and tributaries, and thus it is a challenge to make sure that I take the correct fork, lest I paddle for miles in the wrong direction. Tense and unsure, I scrutinize every tributary until I reach what I believe to be the divide I'm looking for. Rechecking my compass for what seems like the hundredth time, I cautiously proceed up the north fork. After traveling a considerable distance, I still do not see the village ahead. But my years of navigating the wild have taught me to trust my compass readings and stay the course—even when it seems doubtful. Finally, I spot Shungnak in the distance, and I breathe a sigh of satisfaction.

With a population of about 250, Shungnak overlooks a broad, extended beach from the heights along the river plain. As in Kobuk village, several flat-bottomed motorboats are beached along the river, and a few villagers are out preparing for a morning of seining and fishing. I climb out of my gear-laden canoe, pull it well onto the sandy shore and proceed to deflate my canoe, folding and stacking it alongside my gear.

While waiting for Frank to get word of my arrival, I strike up a conversation with Grover Cleveland (yes, the former president's namesake), a septuagenarian clad in an army jacket, a cap with the message "No Pebble Mine," and hip waders. Grover informs me that "No Pebble Mine" refers to a mining operation upriver that some residents believe threatens the natural and wildlife environment of Alaska's Bristol Bay and its associated waters. Others are not so sure. They point out that the mine, which provides employment, is a boon to the local economy.

"Korea," Grover proudly answers when I ask where he had performed his army service.

Grover is helping his wife—a robust, weathered woman wearing a lavender cloth jacket with a pink bandana protecting her head from the already-hot arctic sun—prepare for a day working the river. Their flat-bottomed metal boat is filled with nets and a large corrugated tub.

I tell him about my visit to Josephine's fish camp and discover that he is related to many of the folks I have encountered downriver. The topic then turns to the unusually warm weather.

"I can't believe I'm in the arctic in September and it's eighty degrees," I comment. "Have you seen any effects of global warming up here?"

"A great many," he replies. "Look over there," he says, shading his eyes and pointing beyond the far shore. "The river used to flow way over there before it started getting so hot in the last ten years or so. We're losing precious tundra. And, the growing season is a lot longer now."

While we talk, a woman with an infectious, jolly smile walks up, dressed in a T-shirt and waders with a blue coat tied around her hips. After wading into the Kobuk she volunteers for a photo. Then, joining Grover's wife, the two women head upriver for a day of seining.

Not too much later, up motors Frank in his four-wheeler. We pile my gear, my deflated canoe, and myself into the small open cart he is pulling. Hanging on precariously, off we go on a careening, bumpy ride up the dusty, potted hillside road that leads through the village of Shungnak. At my request, we stop briefly at a small wood and tin structure that features a crooked sign that reads, "General Merchandise." I leap off the cart, go inside, and buy a Coke—a sort of luxury in these parts where groceries have to be flown in, often hundreds of miles. Then we resume lurching our way up to the airstrip, some half-mile or so beyond the village outskirts.

I thank Frank, pay him for his services, and off he goes, leaving me sitting in the midst of my disarrayed pile of gear. The arctic sun beats down, and I settle in for a two- to three-hour wait. An iridescent, ebony raven tilts his head and eyes me from its perch in a nearby tree. Lying down, using one of my packs for a pillow, I doze in the warm sun.

Upon waking, I stand up to survey the open country that surrounds this isolated airstrip, feeling a bit like Cary Grant waiting at the deserted crossroads in *North by Northwest*. The airstrip is on a slight rise and affords a panoramic view. To pass the time, I dig out my camera to record the immediate stretch of scrubby grassland, the azure blue pond beyond, a few well-kept tin-roofed buildings and houses scattered about, and the backdrop of spruces, willows, and the distant mountains.

There is a hanger-like garage abutting the airstrip, and I notice electrical outlets on the outside walls. Each village generates its own electricity, and I take this opportunity to recharge the many batteries that always accompany my trips. While I'm engaged in this activity, several people begin to gather at the airstrip, some walking up from the village, some driving their ATVs.

Soon, the unmistakable buzz of a small aircraft draws my attention to the eastern horizon—then another, and yet another. Eventually, three small planes swoop out of the placid blue skies to land in succession on this tiny airstrip, raising a cacophony of noise and dust. It is as if bees have suddenly been drawn to honey. As the airplanes land, the villagers swing into action, unloading the planes' contents and hauling them back to town. I am the only passenger to actually board one of the craft. The pilot climbs down to help me stow my canoe and gear in the cargo hold. Shaking hands, we introduce ourselves and soon are winging our way toward Ambler, the next village along the river.

Leaning forward to look out the tiny passenger window, it is fascinating to see the Kobuk snake its way below me. I can almost envision myself paddling its waters. Having canoed nearly two weeks, most of that time spent in isolation, I am ready for a break, especially since the river's current has slowed at this point to a crawl. Ambler, some thirty miles upriver from Shungnak, is only a few minutes by plane, but given the many bends of the river, this ride will easily save me a couple of days paddling.

Once we touch down in Ambler, I walk up to one of the villagers who is unloading cargo. He agrees to come back for me once he has delivered his load. Sure enough, about a half-hour later he returns, his two young daughters in tow. I tell him I'm headed for Scott and Piquk's house. It's all the direction he needs. We load my gear into the small open trailer behind his ATV, which seems to be the cargo carrier of choice in these parts. I step into the trailer and another careening ride commences.

Scott and Piquk

Scott and Piquk prove to be welcoming and generous hosts, as well as a source of invaluable information. Scott has lived in Ambler, the village of his wife's birth, for over twenty-five years. Piquk has just returned from a day of gathering berries, an important activity in the economy of the Kobuk. Both are intimately familiar with arctic Alaska and generously share their knowledge and experience.

That evening, Scott and Piquk—astride one four-wheeler, while I command a second—lead me out to tour the off-river backcountry. Though they are old hands at negotiating the extremely rough trail, I find it quite challenging. Seeing what a novice I am with an ATV, Scott politely suggests that I let Piquk take the wheel. Switching places, Piquk easily guides the machine up the steeply rutted terrain. We halt at the top, stopping to admire the golden evening sun and to survey a magnificent view of grasslands, meadows, tundra, forests, and mountains stretching as far as the eye will allow. We savor this view, drinking in its crisp beauty, and scan the horizon for game.

Scott soon spots some caribou grazing in the far distance, and helps my untrained eye locate them. The spot we have stopped at, Scott explains, is where he shot a moose the previous year. He had gone back to the village to get some help dressing the animal, but when he and his friends returned, they were too late—a grizzly was running off with their 1500-pound kill clenched between his jaws. Scott could hardly believe it. It was as if the grizzly had picked up the equivalent of their four-wheeler and absconded with it!

As dusk approaches, we return to the village for an

evening of exchanging stories. Finally, I thank Scott and Piquk for their incredible hospitality and retire outside to set up my tent on a patch of grass. After this long, eventful day, in a short time I am asleep.

Come morning, after sharing a breakfast of oatmeal and coffee, Scott helps me load my gear onto the ubiquitous cart behind his four-wheeler.

"You really ought to come here in the winter. I could take you on a snowmobile tour," Scott offers.

"Sounds tempting," I say, and file the possibility away in my memory.

We bump our way down to the banks of the Kobuk, and Scott gives me some last pointers about what to look for when I get to Onion Portage. He also suggests that instead of returning upriver to Ambler as I had planned, I continue paddling down the Kobuk to the village of Kiana. From there I can take the local flight from the Kiana airstrip to Kotzebue, where I'll be able to catch a jet to Anchorage.

Shaking hands, Scott and I wish each other well. He pushes my canoe off, and I resume my paddle down the river. Scott stands on the riverbank, waving goodbye, receding from my view with each stroke, until, remarkably, I am once again alone on the Kobuk.

A Dream Come True

Toward the end of the day, I notice that the south bank of the Kobuk is gradually broadening into a wide, pebbly sand flat. Suddenly, it dawns on me that after some 200 miles, I've arrived at Onion Portage.

I can't believe it!

What a beautiful sight. Here I am at the crossing point of a caribou migration that has taken place for thousands of years. On this late August afternoon, Onion Portage sparkles with breathtaking colors that only nature can boast—a rusty, sandy shoreline abutting the deep blue-green waters of the

Kobuk, overhung by brilliant skies. Across the river, beyond the north shore, stands the magnificent azure purple range of the Jade Mountains. Billowy white cumulus clouds sail the breezes, adorning the mountaintops. The broad, flat expanse of red, sandy beach on the south shore extends for hundreds of yards.

Suddenly feeling worn out from my labors, I stop paddling and slump onto my seat to tearfully take in the view and briefly celebrate my accomplishment. Finally, I turn and slowly paddle ashore, still finding it hard to believe that I've reached my destination. Dragging my canoe onto the beach, I stand in the quiet, letting my shoulders slump and breathing deeply. A stiff breeze whips the flaps of my jacket as I survey the area for the best location to make my camp. Looking far up and down the beach, I had expected I might find hunters camped here as well. To my surprise, I am completely alone, without a person—or caribou—in sight.

Where is everybody? Am I too early? Too late?

I walk the expanse of beach. Looking down, my heart leaps excitedly as I finally register the thousands of fresh caribou tracks right there beneath my feet. They're here! I made it! Now the feeling really hits home. Three weeks of canoeing through canyons and rapids, whitewater and becalmed doldrums, and I have finally arrived. I hug myself with satisfaction, and then get busy setting up camp.

I plan to spend two nights here. What a luxury—to stop, take a breath, and become a part of my surroundings. It feels like a kind of homecoming, as if I've been in this place before. The quiet is palpable. The scrunch of my footsteps is the only sound as I stroll over to my dry bags, retrieve my binoculars and focus up and down the beach.

I decide to explore my new home, walking up the beach some two or three hundred yards, and then down the other way about the same distance. The late afternoon sun paints the sky end of day colors. Back at my campsite, I stop and listen.

Nothing.

I'm impatient to see the caribou and still a bit worried that I've missed the bulk of the migration. I remind myself to put aside my expectations, though it's hard to do when my entire trip has been pointed at this destination. "Worrying won't change the outcome," I tell myself as I prepare a celebratory dinner of mac and cheese, still congratulating myself on having made it this far.

Finally, hearing and seeing nothing remarkable, I enter my tent and settle into the comfort of my down bag. Using my headlamp, I read for a couple of hours, too excited to close my eyes. But soon I have read myself to sleep.

I awake slowly in the middle of the chilly arctic night, sleepily trying to determine the source of the continuous splashing that resembles breakers crashing on the riverbank, one after the other. But no, that isn't quite the right sound. Now—completely awake—I feel my adrenalin rise. I recognize what has to be making that sound, and hope against hope that I am right.

I unzip my tent door and poke out my head. Adjusting my eyes to the surreal darkness, I can just barely see the wraith-like outline of the caribou and clearly hear the splashing of their hooves as the herd dashes across the river. I want to whoop with joy, but restrain myself—not wanting to startle the herd.

The ghostly forms recede and stillness returns. Reluctantly, I crawl back into my sleeping bag. I can't hope to get any photos of the crossing in this darkness. I'll have to wait until dawn, which now can't come soon enough. Throughout the remainder of the night I am awakened occasionally by the splashing, sometimes so close that the herd must be coming ashore just yards from my campsite. After each awakening, I return to sleep with a smile of satisfaction. This journey down the Kobuk is proving to be a totally unique experience.

As I wake to my first dawn at Onion Portage—after a night of splashing hooves that confirm that the caribou are indeed still migrating south in groups of twenty or so—I exit my tent and realize that I am still totally alone. I had expected to come across Native hunters who would be harvesting meat for their village's upcoming winter food supply.

"Perhaps." I surmise, "the main migration has come through and the hunters have moved on." However, I am not alone for long. Soon the splashing resumes, echoing down the Kobuk. Looking up, I see a group of about twenty caribou dashing through the waters—sending up an enormous spray in their wake—headed for the south shore.

Excitedly, I run for my camera.

Once ashore, the caribou stop to regroup as if they're engaged in a family reunion—and for all I know, they are. Among this family are three stags, the lead one an old bull with a magnificent rack. Some two hundred yards downriver to the west of me, they all stand quietly—turned my way—looking intently in my direction.

Slowly, carefully, I begin to walk closer, cutting our distance in half in order to get a clearer photo of the group. Still they stand, staring, as if trying to gauge my intentions. I am struck by their lack of intimidation and the curiosity they exhibit as they allow me to approach closer and closer. Finally, they turn, gallop up a nearby sand dune, and disappear into the willows.

Not long after, another group comes dashing across the river about 150 yards upriver to the east of my tent. Again, I grab my camera. This time, once they assemble on the riverbank, the group begins to approach me. Remarkably, they approach cautiously, rather than aggressively—that is, rather than have their head downs, antlers at the ready, they are elegantly upright, walking with poise—like models on a runway. Of course, I am delighted because this means that I will get closer shots of the herd. They circle behind me on the broad beach, continue downriver to where the first group had come ashore, and then disappear into the willow scrub.

Soon again, another group crosses downriver and assembles where the first group had. However, this time, instead of disappearing into the willows, they begin to approach me. Closer and closer they come. I am both elated and confused. Having come all this way, I am snapping photos that I had only dreamed might be possible. However, why are they continuing to come directly at me, now closing the gap to no more than twenty-five yards?

It doesn't take long to get my answer. Suddenly, directly behind me the river bursts with churning water. Coming ashore no more than fifteen feet behind me are three caribou—a buck, a doe and their calf—wide eyes flashing, as startled to see me as I am to see them. I click off photos as rapidly as I can as they cautiously move ashore and circle around me to join the rest of their group—giving me a wide berth. Now it's apparent why the herd is approaching me—they are coming back to pick up the stragglers! Even my presence is not going to deter them from making sure these three late crossers are safely able to rejoin their group.

The following day, I witness an even more impressive display of this protective behavior. Another group of about fifteen caribou are crossing about a hundred yards downriver, assembling on the beach in the same approximate location as their predecessors. Usually, once the herd has assembled, they spend as little time as possible on the beach, where they are exposed to the predatory wolves. However, this time, instead of dashing off into the bushes and the protective tree line beyond, they wait. And wait.

What are they waiting for, I wonder? They all stand stock still, facing the river they have just crossed, and seem to be looking back intently toward the other side. Grabbing my binoculars, I scan the far bank, and then I spot them—a mother and her calf. Clearly, they are refusing to cross. I think surely the herd will leave them behind to fend for themselves. To wait much longer will put the entire group at risk.

Suddenly, much to my amazement, the entire herd dashes back into the river, and, plunging and splashing headlong through the waters, returns to the side from which they have just come, rejoining the doe and her calf. Together once again, the group proceeds further downriver, obviously hunting for a crossing point that all can agree on. After proceeding another hundred yards, they re-cross to the other side, including the balky doe and calf, and disappear into the safety of the bush.

The following morning, I pack my provisions into my canoe—giving Onion Portage one last fond gaze before dipping my paddle reluctantly into the current and proceeding on my way. The very beach I have inhabited for the last few days feels hallowed. I have shared this time with the caribou, and can envision—almost feel—the ghostly trek of their ancestors as these descendants repeat a pilgrimage of ten thousand years.

I have come to witness their journey. I leave with an appreciation for the way they protect each other, and for how vulnerable they appear when crossing the Kobuk, exposing themselves to the possibility of prowling wolves and the gun-sights of Native hunters. Each time a new group came ashore from their river crossing, they were immediately aware of me as a strange presence on the beach. They would stop and gaze at me for minutes at a time, displaying unabashed curiosity. Just as the grizzly had done some days previous, they seemed to assess that I was no danger.

I ponder these events as I paddle along the shore of Onion Portage. Then I look up from my thoughts and notice another small herd that has come back out of the bush up ahead, walking down the beach directly toward me. As they continue steadily in my direction, closing the gap, I realize what their seemingly counterintuitive behavior implies—I am the straggler! Seeing me moving through the water along the shoreline, they are coming back to get me. Soon they are no more than twenty-five yards from the canoe and I can no longer resist—I reach for my camera and bring it up to my eye to focus. The moment they see this movement, they turn tail and run back into the bush.

"Of course," I admonish myself, "I've just made the same movement as aiming a gun."

The Hunters

Later this same day I happen across three Inupiat hunters who invite me to join them for coffee. Thomas, George and Derrick introduce themselves. They have just dressed a fresh caribou kill—its bloody scalped antlers lay on the sand to be picked clean in a day or two by the ravens. The river runs red from the slaughter. Wearing shirts proudly emblazoned with the name of their village—Noorvik, about sixty miles downriver—they are harvesting caribou for the coming winter.

We talk of many things, including the behavior of the caribou. I describe to them what I had witnessed—how the caribou had re-crossed the river to retrieve the reluctant doe and the calf. "I was really surprised to see how they are willing to put the entire group at risk in order to include the more vulnerable ones."

Apparently, they are surprised as well. They listen intently, fascinated to learn of this behavior, having never seen such a thing themselves. Thomas says, "We are hunters. They would never allow us to come that close. The instant they smell or see us, they run."

We talk about the other animals I have observed in the past three weeks. About the differing demeanor of the two grizzlies I had encountered upriver—how one had ambled away while the other had approached me, displaying great curiosity about my presence. And about how they eventually rejoined later on and sat patiently while I cooked my dinner some fifty yards away. I told them of the wolf who came loping up the beach one afternoon. When he saw me in my canoe only five yards or so from the shoreline, he paused for fully a minute, staring at me with that same look of curiosity.

"Maybe fight, flight and freeze aren't the only instinctual reactions an animal exhibits," I suggest. "Maybe, like humans, curiosity is another reaction." Nodding thoughtfully, my newfound acquaintances are inclined to accept this premise, even though—in their experience—wildlife always flee their presence. "Do you suppose they can tell intent?" I wonder. "Maybe they can smell or sense the presence of a gun."

They shrug.

I ask them about village life, and if they ever have a desire to travel the wider world. "Oh, we've done quite a bit of traveling," they tell me. "We've worked the oil fields up on the North Slope and just last year we fought wildfires down in Nevada and California. We have to do this to get money to buy fuel for our motors and other supplies." However, each of them makes it emphatically clear that, whenever possible, they prefer to stay in their village and continue their life of hunting and fishing.

Finishing the coffee, we all shake hands and pose for pictures. They share some dried whitefish with me to take along on my journey. I thank them, wish them good hunting and resume my paddling. Having decided to follow Scott's recommendation, Kiana—about twenty-five miles downriver—is now my destination. I should be there in two or three days.

After a long afternoon of paddling, I again make camp.

Family Reunion

The next morning is wet and overcast. I break camp in a cold drizzle and proceed downriver pelted by recurring rain squalls. I cover my gear with a tarp and paddle head down, hunkered under my poncho. It's pretty miserable, but I count myself fortunate to have traveled most of these last three weeks in generally dry and sunny weather. In fact, I can only remember three rainy days on this entire trip—one of them at the very beginning when Kyle dropped me at Walker Lake.

Later, as if in response to my musings, the weather begins to clear and the sun reasserts itself. As is often the case in today's arctic summer, it turns hot and steamy, so I throw off the tarp and poncho to let my body and my spirits—and my gear—dry out. Soon, as I approach a large bend in the river, I say to myself, "Are those voices?"

Rounding the bend, I see several families gathered down on the south riverbank and up on a promontory above, upon which a small cabin is perched. When the gathering spots me, a woman breaks away, comes to the edge of the river, and calls out, "Come and join us. We have some caribou stew for you!"

Surprised—unaware that word of my approach has preceded me downriver—I beach my canoe and climb up the steep slope to where a number of folks are drinking coffee, laughing, and generally enjoying each other's company. The woman who invited me to come ashore is named Tessie (her Inupiaq name is Tuvingan) and she explains that her sister had sent word downriver that I was coming and had insisted, "they should feed me."

"Of course!" I replied, "Now I remember. You are Rosaline's children!"

I am immediately ushered into the cabin where the caribou stew is cooking and country music is playing from a speaker hanging on a nail on the back wall. A bowl is thrust into my hands and filled with the hot, aromatic stew. It's delicious.

As I mingle with my hosts, I learn that the rough-hewn cabin belongs to Jim, one of Rosaline's sons, and that I have stumbled onto a family reunion of Rosaline's children, grandchildren and great-grandchildren. Boys and younger men with rifles come and go, hunting in the pines behind the cabin. Younger children are trying their hand at fishing along the shoreline, and—as at any such reunion—clusters of family members are talking animatedly.

Rosaline herself, an octogenarian, stands about five feet four and is wearing a multicolored parka, jeans and rubber boots—standard dress in this part of the world. Her face is weathered by years of outdoor life, yet she appears hale and hearty. She tells me her fish camp is six bends downriver and invites me to drop in when I come by. Wanting to return the hospitality that is thrust upon me, I offer to document the family reunion with photos. A number of the family line up and—standing on the edge of the rise—smile for the camera. I promise to email the photos.

Many of those gathered for this reunion have come upriver from Kotzebue, a town of some thirty-two hundred, huddled on an exposed peninsula near the Bering and Chukchi Seas. However, the camp here on the Kobuk is clearly home—the center of a life in which Rosaline's family has grown up catching salmon, whitefish, and sheefish, hunting caribou, and picking berries.

Employment in Alaska's larger towns and cities—though sometimes necessary in order to obtain the cash for boats, motors, gas and supplemental food—holds little fascination for most of those I speak with. I think of the trio of hunters I had met just the day before, who, as much as they had seen of the world outside, always returned to their village along the Kobuk—obviously the choice of their hearts.

The fact that village life would maintain such appeal in today's world initially surprises me. I think of how difficult it is in my home state of Iowa for young folks to remain on family farms, given the relentless competition and consolidation caused by big agribusiness. Towns and small cities are suffering population loss as well. However, as I witness the pace of day-to-day Native life and the powerful emotional bonds of family and community—set amidst, and integral to, an ecosystem of natural flow and beauty—I can appreciate why the Inupiat might prefer their ancestral home to the lure of distant locales.

Even so, this world I am paddling through is a world on the cusp, and the desire to maintain traditional village life is complicated by the demands of a larger society based on modern conveniences procured by the exchange of money. I come to learn that a heavy toll is exacted, especially on the younger men of the Kobuk, who—once proud to assume their traditional roles of hunter and provider—now frequently feel despondent about how difficult it is to maintain such a function in present-day village life.

As the afternoon lengthens, the reunion begins to break up and the families head for their boats. Rosaline and her family pile into their craft, and—amid the roar of the fifty-horsepower motors—wave their goodbyes as I return to my canoe. No sooner have they proceeded beyond the next bend in the river than I am once again alone, free to investigate the cliffs where the old gold mine used to be—across the river from Jim's cabin—and free to resume my own unhurried pace.

This pattern—contact followed by isolation—repeats itself with daily frequency. The next evening, after a long day of paddling, I finally pull into a thin patch of shoreline and haul my canoe and gear up a steep embankment to higher ground. I have no more than settled myself than along come two motorboats occupied by three women and two men who are curious to discover who this stranger is that is camping on their shores.

Soon we are introducing ourselves and conversing like long-lost friends catching up. Just as I, they are headed for Kiana, where two of them work in the local health clinic. After I explain that I am a photographer and a sometime writer, one of the women asks me, "Have you ever read *Authentic Alaska*? It's a book that features Native writers."

"I've never heard of it," I confess.

"You really ought to read it!" she advises me enthusiastically.

I promise to look it up when I get back home. (It turns out

to be an incredibly poignant and informative collection of essays and biographies detailing the challenges of past and present life along the Kobuk. I wholeheartedly recommend it.)

As we talk, the weather grows chillier and we stand here, hands in our pockets and stamping our feet to stay warm. Only a few days ago, we were baking under the sun, and I am reminded of the extremes this country presents. Reluctant as we are to say goodbye, they turn to resume their journey to Kiana, and I turn to build a fire.

Afternoon Tea

The next day is gorgeous—bright blue skies, billowy clouds sailing briskly, and a return to summer-warm weather. Kiana is now only a couple of days away. On occasion, I pass a modest cabin perched high on the steep rises above the riverbank. At one point a window of one of those cabins is thrown open and a man leans out and calls to me, "Where 'ya comin' from?"

"Walker Lake," I yell back.

"Walker Lake?" he says. "Come on up and have a cup of tea!"

Thus it is that I meet Verna and Jerry.

Jerry and Verna, I discover, have recently married and are dividing their year between Verna's cabin on the Kobuk and her home in her Native village of Kiana, and Jerry's ranch in Montana. Verna describes herself as an Alaskan Native with one foot firmly planted in her Inupiat Eskimo culture and the other in the world outside. She knows and appreciates the demands that are increasingly made by modern society on traditional Inupiat life. To help bridge the transactions and transitions that such demands require, she is engaged in proposing and writing grants for tribal organizations, schools, and governments.

They share a love of hunting, fishing and the outdoor life. "We saw a white wolf this morning along the river," they tell me excitedly. "Did you happen to see it?"

"I'm afraid not. I would really love to have seen that!" I reply, shaking my head. "I did run across a tricolor just a couple of days ago."

"You came all the way from Walker," Jerry says. "That's about two hundred miles. Obviously, you came through the rapids at Kobuk Canyon."

"Yep," I say proudly, not bothering to describe how during the last portion of the rapids my canoe was going backwards. "I was soaked to the bone, and that evening, I had a run-in with two grizzlies." Of course, I have to explain. They shake their heads as I relate the experience.

As we drink our tea, Verna describes how she and Jerry angle for sheefish on the Kobuk. "Jerry catches the fish. I sit at the back of the boat and gut it, clean it, and grill it on a Coleman camp stove."

"A Coleman?" I ask. "You cook it right there on the river?"

"That's the best way to eat it," says Verna. "Really fresh. Have you ever had sheefish? It's delicious, it's my favorite fish, I like it more than salmon and I love salmon. Its meat is thick white flakes like halibut, but halibut is bland compared to shee. Shee has a flavor that's hard to describe. You just have to try it."

"First I ever heard of it was last year from some guys down in Dillingham," I reply.

Eventually, after discussing our immediate plans, we compare schedules, and discover that Verna and Jerry are returning from their two weeks at the cabin on the very day I plan to arrive at Kiana.

"You've got to stay with us," they say without hesitation. "You stay the night and we'll help you arrange a flight from Kiana to Kotzebue.

"That way," says Verna, "I can cook up some sheefish for you. All we have at the house right now is frozen—not as good as river-fresh—but it's still delicious."

Who can refuse such a generous offer? With these plans in mind, I prepare to return to my canoe. We walk outside and stand on their front landing, sharing it with a dressed side of caribou that is hanging by the door. Taking out his knife, Jerry asks if he can cut me a slice to take for my dinner. I politely refuse, not wanting the smell of fresh meat to encourage another meeting with a grizzly.

Standing there together, we admire the view from their cabin porch, perched as it is among the pines, high above the Kobuk. I make my way back down the steep path I had ascended about an hour earlier, and once again, continue downriver.

As I paddle along, I relax in the late afternoon sun, as well as in the good feeling that I wear like a protective cloak. After a couple of hours, I select a place to camp at the end of a mile-long sandbar, and go about my evening routine. This will be my next to last night on the Kobuk. Including tomorrow night, I will have spent twenty-three days on the river.

That next day, my paddling brings me to Rosaline's fish camp, which—like Josephine's—is easily identified by racks of salmon drying in the arctic sun. Rosaline's swift motorboat had carried her downriver far in advance of my paddling. Remembering her invitation to stop by, I beach my gear-laden canoe and—waving up to Rosaline who has stepped out to welcome me—climb the steep bank up to her camp cabin. She greets me with a cup of coffee, and I meet yet another of her daughters and her son-in-law. Another daughter whom I had met at the family reunion is also here with her two young boys. We talk animatedly and take pictures again—the boys posing proudly with their fishing gear.

The cabin is cozy, a fire going in the stove even though today's weather is quite mild. I feel very much at home and am reminded of my days as a boy in Iowa, visiting my grandparents, aunts, uncles and cousins. Rosaline allows me to take one last portrait of her marvelous features before leaving. The gray of her hair and the lines in her face tell the story of a remarkably vigorous and lively woman—still operating a fish camp in the wild at a time when most of the older folks I know are long retired. Finishing the coffee, we smile our goodbyes and I resume my journey to Kiana.

Late that afternoon, I select a final campsite, where the river bends north towards Kiana—now no more than ten miles distant. As I pitch my tent for one last time, I look across the river and see Rosaline and her daughters and grandchildren motoring by on the other side of the broad expanse. They will reach Kiana tonight, but it will take me another full day.

Tonight my peripheral neuropathy pain asserts itself with a vengeance, and I find sleep difficult. Usually, my time in the wild is helpful in alleviating this malady because at the end of the day I am so weary that I am able to ignore the pain and sleep comes relatively quickly. But every few days, the pain has its way, and sleep comes grudgingly—if at all. I slather Aspercreme on my feet and ankles, but it still feels like someone is jabbing needles into them.

Actually, in all these years, I've been pretty lucky on these journeys. Aside from the occasional annoying cold, I've not been sick while in the wilderness. My blood pressure pills have done their job and I haven't sustained any serious injuries. All in all, I count myself fortunate. But all that isn't helping me sleep tonight.

Finally, it is morning. After dragging myself from my tent, washing down a high-protein bar with some hot chocolate, and cramming my gear for one last time into my canoe, I push off for the village. It proves to be a somewhat difficult slog, as a headwind decides to remind me of how strenuous the paddling can be.

Weather-wise, I can't complain on this trip: only a few rainy days, not too many doldrums—where a lack of breeze and current conspired to nearly halt my progress—and precious few headwinds to match the one that opposes me today. I am within a couple miles of Kiana when Verna and Jerry come motoring by, their boat laden with coolers, backpacks and duffle bags.

"Want us to toss you a line and tow you?" Verna calls out over the drone of the motor.

"Of course he doesn't," Jerry replies for me. "You don't think he came all this way just to be towed in the last two miles!"

Jerry's right of course, but I have to admit I am sorely tempted. There is nothing romantic about the effort that is required at this point to maintain forward progress—and the late afternoon winds have picked up even more.

"Meet you on the beach," Jerry yells, and revs the motor. Soon they are out of sight.

It seems serendipitous that as the river quiets, I can now hear the unmistakable clacking of sandhill cranes. These ancient-looking birds with the distinctive patch of red adorning their heads migrate yearly all the way from the Texas Gulf Coast. I have run across them three or four times on my journey down the Kobuk, but have never managed to get close enough to take a clear photo.

Now, only hours before I will step ashore at Kiana, they swoop in for a flailing landing and begin strutting down a mud flat across the river from me. Resisting the temptation to give in to my growing exhaustion and continue on to my destination, I swing my canoe around and cross the broad expanse of river to where they are busily foraging.

I draw closer and closer, inching my canoe into position, determined not to flush these skittish birds from their intent combing of the mudflats. Not unlike chickens, their heads bob fitfully as they step one foot forward, and then the other, carefully proceeding in unison as if synchronized to some internal harmony. Amazingly, they take no notice of me. And so, in the very last hour of my expedition—after weeks of trying to photograph these illusive creatures—they give me this one parting gift.

I mean to take only a few minutes, but I spend nearly an hour watching these fascinating avians, feeling privileged to have one last opportunity to enjoy a truly rare experience. Finally, I abandon my prone position across the bow of my canoe, stow my camera, and begin the last of my paddle down the Kobuk. The gusting wind reminds me that nothing good comes easily, and I dig deep with all my strength.

The beach at Kiana is in sight, about a half-mile distant. Above lies the village, with roads cut out by the ATVs that track from the beach up the hill to the protective high ground. Keeping a weather eye on my goal, I bend into my paddle, slowly but painstakingly honing in on the shore ahead.

It is now that I see him—Jerry is lurching down the rutted road from the heights above in his red four-wheeler. What a welcome sight! Arms akimbo, he stands on the beach patiently awaiting my arrival—ready to help me deflate the canoe for one last time, pack my gear and enjoy the inviting warmth of their Kiana home. Sheefish. Talk. Laughter. More sheefish (it is, by the way, as delicious as advertised, especially when prepared by Verna). And eventually sleep on an air mattress in the loft, too tired to pay any mind to shooting pains in my feet.

Goodbye to the Kobuk

These past few years, mindfulness has been a much-discussed topic. Once the province of Eastern spiritual practice, the more we in the West have learned about our changing brain, mirror neurons, and about the impact of our relatedness, the more mindfulness has come to assert itself in our vocabulary. My expeditions to the northern wilds have always felt, for me, like journeys into mindfulness; stepping into a vast and silent expanse of space and time that invites— almost demands—contemplation, reflection, and an expansion of relatedness beyond the human realm to include all of nature's manifestations.

If mindfulness is a journey into an unknown country where expectation drops away and possibility becomes your companion, then perhaps the expeditions I have recounted in these pages can be called an exercise in mindfulness. And if stepping into this country represents the opportunity to—like a newborn—hear anew, see anew, smell anew, and feel anew— then perhaps this wilderness of silence is the space of mindfulness. If a flight to unknown shores where you are dropped into aloneness—where the familiar is dreamlike and the dreamlike is strangely familiar—then perhaps that aloneness is the replenishing solitude of mindfulness.

Finally, if mindfulness is standing beside yourself in silent witness, emptied of the constant editorial content with which you normally filter your life—devoid of judgment and absent of analysis—where you quietly gaze into the eyes of the other and see that gaze reflected back at you, and where you discover with each inhalation an unexpected expansion of your perception—then perhaps these happenings that I have described here are the happenings of mindful awareness.

Lying in Verna and Jerry's darkened loft this last night in Kiana, silently resonating to the foreign yet familiar sounds of the house, with the wind outside blending with the breathing of those sleeping below, I think about these things. I think about drifting down the Kobuk under silent clouds, beckoned to shore by welcoming strangers who—one after the other— invite me into their hearths and hearts, feed me their food, and share their heritage.

They are giving me the gift of their wilderness, a treasure I can take home—expanding my spirit and opening my heart— so that when I return to my life of cars and buildings and television and internet, and possessions that seek to capture and define, I can carry this experience with me.

A Bird's-Eye View of Alaska

Today, I return to the air for the final leg of my Kobuk journey. The flight from Kiana to Kotzebue gives me a special opportunity to appreciate the challenge that would have presented itself had I made this same journey by canoe. Seen from aloft, the Kobuk delta becomes a warren of rivers, tributaries, streams and lakes as it approaches Kotzebue. It would have required some skillful map and compass navigation to keep to the main course.

The villages along the Kobuk appear fragile, huddled as they are in the remote arctic expanse—Kotzebue perhaps even more so because it borders on the vast Bering Sea in an era of rising waters. However, the hardy and inventive Eskimo culture has shown us that one cannot merely survive over thousands of years, but thrive in what those of us from warmer climes might consider a hostile environment. I do not wish to overly romanticize those who live along the Kobuk, but to acknowledge what they repeatedly showed me—that they are a resilient people who truly love and care for their land and the life it provides for them.

Upon landing in Kotzebue, I gather my gear and make arrangements to return my deflated canoe as cargo on the next commuter flight back to Bettles. I myself will continue on to Anchorage, by way of Nome.

Kotzebue at this time is home to a mostly Native population of just over three thousand (compared to nearly two hundred eighty thousand in Anchorage). I am surprised to find jumbo jets flying in and out of this small community, but later discover that—calling itself the "Gateway to the Arctic"—Kotzebue is the jumping-off point for a variety of outdoor adventurers the world over. Even more so, I am surprised and delighted to see the attention Kotzebue garners when President Obama visits eight years later, employing this setting to illustrate the urgency of addressing the change in climate with which these Eskimo villages are contending daily.

I am now waiting for the jet plane that will take me from Kotzebue to Nome. I walk the streets of this community during my brief layover, but all too soon I have to return to the airstrip and bid my final farewells to arctic Alaska.

My late afternoon flight to Nome turns out to be a perfect time to see the Alaskan coast and the untamed Bering Land Bridge Natural Preserve. As the sun lowers over the landscape, the tundra and mountains glow the color of the ancient lava flows that used to scorch this land. In the early evening we touch down on Nome's landing strip.

We disembark onto the tarmac, and those of us who are continuing to Anchorage take our places waiting in the small terminal. Nome is widely known as the terminus of the renowned Iditarod dog sled race. I am surprised to discover that for all its world renown, it is only slightly larger than Kotzebue.

Later that night we ascend once again and are treated to a Cheshire cat moon floating over a seemingly endless bank of clouds. I sit back in my seat, happy to replay the last three weeks in my mind before returning to the bustle of the city. Though Anchorage is, compared to my East Coast environs, a modest urban center, its freewheeling zoning has resulted in a sprawl, resplendent with strip malls and suburbs—although most American suburbs do not feature the occasional bear wandering into the streets.

Alighting in Anchorage at last, I proceed to a nearby motel, take my first shower since I bathed on the fishing rock back on the Kobuk, and fall into bed. My thoughts turn from the Kobuk to the remainder of my visit. Tomorrow morning I will meet John and return the sat phone. Then I will join him for a special tour of the Alaska mountain range in his Cessna, followed by an overnight stay at his wilderness cabin.

Next morning, John picks me up and we drive to the Lake Hood Seaplane Base (the largest such base in the world) to pack our gear into John's Cessna. Hopping into the cockpit,

John hands me my headgear and goes through his safety check. Seatbelts? Check. Headphones? Check. Ignition? Check. Fuel? Nav system? Check. Flaps? Check. Soon we are aloft and winging our way north towards the Alaska range, my camera at the ready.

Gliding low over the forests, we keep an eye out for moose and grizzly, pointing excitedly at possible sightings. Occasionally we see farmland below, interspersed with meandering rivers fed by runoff from the mountains in the far distance. Eventually, John points to the horizon and announces, "There's the Alaska range."

Gaining elevation, we see the great glaciers—endless fields of ice snaking through the distant landscape, surrounded by magnificent cliffs topped with fields of tundra—yellow, orange, rust, and bright green. The land is pristine, untamed wilderness—desolate, cold, forbidding, awe-inspiring and—for the most part—uninhabited.

Banking sharply, we swoop down over these rivers of ice, laughing out of sheer joy, Dire Straits blaring "Dashboard Lights" through our headphones.

"Can you lift the wing slightly so I can get a better camera angle?" I ask more than once. Each time John accommodates my request. "What a photographer's dream," I exclaim, thanking him profusely over the music and the roar of the engine for providing this unique opportunity to capture images that I would only have dreamed of just a few years before.

"You can teach me to use one of those," John replies, nodding towards my camera. "I've been thinking of getting an SLR myself."

"Glad to do it," I say. "Any time. It's the least I can do."

"I want to show you an incredible glacier cliff," John exclaims with his usual enthusiasm. "Then we'll head for a place where I always find black bears feeding."

"Onward," I respond, catching his buoyant spirit.

Soon we're banking again and plunging downward to get a better look at a glacier that towers hundreds of feet and abuts a surprisingly mint-green glacier lake.

"Can you tilt the wing one more time?" I ask. John obliges as I attempt to a capture how it feels to look down at this surreal, glossy ice massif.

Swinging the Cessna around in an aerial U-turn, we now head east to locate John's black bear site. Along the way, as the mountains recede in the background, rivers and tundra stretch as far as the eye can see, bespeckled in delta-like waters that reflect the overarching sky.

About a half-hour later, during which John explains some of the techniques of flying the Cessna, we circle over a quiet lake and spot two black bears on the distant rocky shore. John cuts back the engine, almost whisper-like, and gently lands near the shoreline where the bears are feeding. Each of us exits the plane to stand on our respective pontoons, gently rocking as the lake laps at our feet, and watch the bears tear apart their salmon catch while seagulls wait patiently for the leavings.

We stay at our bear observation post for at least a half hour. John, delighted to share this scene with me, patiently waits while I try out different lenses and camera angles while balancing on the float of the rhythmically swaying plane—occasionally grabbing the strut for support.

"'Bout time we left," John finally suggests—tactful as ever—and I reluctantly agree. If we want to reach his wilderness cabin in the light, now is the time to go.

We climb back into the Cessna, secure our headsets and gear, and head north to John's cabin in the woods. Upon reaching the skies over the cabin, I am amazed at the beauty and appeal of the scene below. Sitting in its own patch of green on the shores of a sparkling lake is the modest abode, footsteps away from a dock and boathouse. As we glide smoothly onto John's lake and motor our way to the dock, I feel a sense of serenity.

Just as the Inupiat had so generously shared their lives with me, John is doing the same.

Chapter 12
2008 – THE GREAT CIRCLE ROUTE – THE YUKON

Then

It's 1949. I'm eight years old, lying on my stomach in our Midwestern living room, head cupped in my hands atop the pyramid of my arms, feet absently waving akimbo. My ear is glued to the old Zenith as the speaker booms, "On King! On you huskies!"—the deep baritone of Sergeant Preston urging his team forward into the storm. The excited dogs strain in their harnesses, yapping noisily as their leader—the "wonder dog" Yukon King—leaps forward. Classical music swells in the background, and we're off to catch the bad guys in the days of the gold rush.

Nothing quite fired my imagination as a child like the adventures of old-time radio. More-so than TV, a luxury which none of us could afford at the time, radio invited you to set the scene, envision the characters, and participate in the journey—then go outside and reenact these stories with the neighborhood gang, always adding your own embellishments.

"I get to be Sergeant Preston! No, it's my turn! You're the bad guy! I don't wanna be the bad guy. I wanna be Yukon King. You can't be a dog! Who sez I can't! Anyway, he's not just a dog, he's part wolf!"

Now

Now, it's September 2008. I'm sixty-seven years old and I'm winging my way from Dulles to SeaTac on a sleek jetliner—beyond imagination in my youth—looking down 40,000 feet at the Heartland. Below me is a checkerboard of corn, wheat, soybean and alfalfa fields—the same fields that cradled me as I lay listening to Sergeant Preston so long ago.

My destination? The Yukon. After all these years, I'm off to see the land of my childhood fantasies. "What is the Yukon really like?" I want to know. To find out, I'll fly on from Seattle to Fairbanks, by way of Anchorage. In Fairbanks I'll rent a car and drive a 2000-mile loop through the vast Yukon Territory.

That's right—on this trip I'm renting a car. After last year's long paddle down the Kobuk, I want to take a break from canoeing, from the work of schlepping my gear, and from being confined to the vicissitudes of the river. Perhaps I'm feeling my age. But adventuring by auto is nothing new for me. All my life I've loved to explore by car—to have the freedom to choose destinations that are tucked away, off the beaten path, accessible only by remote gravel roads and little-used blacktop highways. If I want to pull over and hike a mountain trail along the way, I'll do it. If I want to stop and camp—day or night—I'll stop and camp. Perhaps I'll decide to stay in some rustic, out-of-the-way cabin for a couple of nights. And if the weather turns bad, or there's no place to spread out for the night, I'll just sleep in the car.

I know I'll miss the challenges of canoeing, but I promise myself to get back to them in a year or two. Right now I'm excited to do my solo exploring this way—following Sergeant Preston's footprints from Dawson City to Whitehorse and Skagway and back through the vast Yukon Territory.

Anchorage Rendezvous

As has become my annual ritual, I arrange to meet John at the Anchorage airport, catch up on the past year and pick up a satellite phone. Disembarking, I spot John waiting outside the security area. Each of us grinning, I walk over and am swallowed in a huge bear hug.

"How're you doing?" John wants to know. "No new scares?"

"I'm fine," I reassure him. I think my prostate cancer surgery the year after we first met caused him as much concern as it did me. "PSA still reading zero."

"You don't look a day older," he lies, hefting one of my fifty-pound backpacks over his shoulder like it weighs nothing.

"Back at ya," I reply truthfully. To me, it's as if we just talked yesterday.

We leave baggage claim, recheck my gear for my connecting flight to Fairbanks, and stroll over to the gate.

"We still on for the Kenai?" asks John.

"Wouldn't miss it," I reply. We'd arranged to meet again at the end of my trip to reprise last year's Cessna flight over the mountains and glaciers—this time flying over some of John's favorite haunts to the south of Cook's Inlet. These aerial excursions with John seem like a grown-up version of my youthful wanderings, when I would borrow my dad's '56 Pontiac and investigate the surrounding environs for hours on end.

"See you in a couple of weeks," I say, before heading for my plane.

"You're welcome to stay with the Mrs. and me when you get back," John suggests, in what has now become an annual invitation.

"Looking forward to it," I respond warmly.

John's unending generosity continually amazes me. Ever since our first meeting some five years ago—when he gave me that whirlwind tour of Anchorage—he's been showing me his Alaska. More than once, I've overnighted at his house on the outskirts of the Anchorage when arriving for or departing from one of my visits. I've enjoyed long conversations in his wilderness cabin and rode shotgun in his Cessna as he shared with me his favorite discoveries—always accommodating my efforts to capture those experiences with my camera.

During these times, John regaled me with stories of the Iditarod Air Force—a group of bush pilot volunteers who stand ready to transport mushers, dogs and vets. One such story in particular comes to mind. John—captain of this group of volunteers, and the subject of a film documenting their exploits—recalled one of their rescue training exercises:

"So there we are. Right? Out in the middle of nowhere, and we're supposed to dig this snow cave and spend the night. You know—survival training. Well, that night it's like -38° below. So we're digging, making an airshaft for breathing and all that, and we begin to wonder when George is gonna to show up. George Murphy is this old-timer who everybody knows. He must be in his seventies. I reckon he's logged more bush time than all of us put together."

"So anyway, it gets late and we figure he must not be coming. Right? Later, we're all huddled in our cave half freezing, and we hear this engine droning in the distance. Well, we figure it must be George."

"Sure enough, I peek out and see George's plane gliding in smooth as you could want, his skis hardly kicking up any snow. George taxis to a stop. Without missing a beat, he hops out of his plane, digs out a small impression in the snow, lays down in it, throws a tarp over himself—and goes to sleep for the night without so much as a how d'ya do."

"You're pulling my leg," I say.

"I kid you not," laughs John, shaking his head. "I kid you not."

Considering the stories of hardship, resilience, bravery and tomfoolery that I've heard during my years in Alaska, I'm inclined to believe it.

"Time to go," I say, though I'm tempted to just sit here and trade stories, even if I do miss my flight. Reluctantly bidding John farewell as he crushes me in another bear hug, I board my plane for Fairbanks.

Lift Off

It's beautiful weather for flying. A yellow-gold sky overhangs the distant snowcapped mountains of Chugach State Park. The mid-morning sun is a white disk backlighting the clouds. Soon we're aloft. In less than an hour, majestic Denali towers above the clouds that skirt its base. As is my custom when flying to Fairbanks, I have grabbed a window seat on the left side of the plane, just in case the weather allows me to photograph this icon of Alaska. Gazing out the window I can only marvel as the magnificent mountain comes into view—a great pyramid that spawns a hundred lesser foothills, would-be Denalis in the making.

Soon we are touching down in Fairbanks, one of my favorite cities, partly because of its untamed feel and setting, and partly because last year it was my jumping-off point to the Gates of the Arctic National Park—which, in turn, was the base of operations for my Kobuk River adventure.

As I did last year on my Kobuk trip, I check in at the Alpine Lodge. I was so taken with the hospitality of the lodge during that experience, that we bartered a deal: I would create an ad for them on my website in exchange for staying there whenever I'm in Fairbanks. Both the lodge manager and I felt we'd made a good exchange.

Hitting the Open Road

Now, after an evening relaxing at Pike's Landing at the end of a long day in the air, I return to the Alpine to review my strategy for this trip. From Fairbanks, I'll head for Alaska's remote Top of the World Highway and on to historic Dawson City in Canada's Yukon Territory. Proceeding along the fabled Yukon River past Whitehorse, I'll travel through the magnificent White Pass to Skagway—and finally head back to Fairbanks by way of the Haines and Alaska highways. All in all, this loop should introduce me to some of the most storied, remote and scenic areas of Alaska, the Yukon and British Columbia.

After a breakfast of flapjacks, bacon, sausage, eggs, orange juice and coffee, I throw my gear into my SUV rental and start out. As I leave Fairbanks, it feels strange not to be headed for a canoe launching site, since canoeing has been central to my previous expeditions. But the fact is, long before I discovered solo canoeing, I was crisscrossing the continent on solo car trips. By now I've traveled in all fifty states, Canada and Mexico—mostly by car.

Many times, in my younger days, I drove across the Lower 48 from Washington, D.C. to Moscow, Idaho, to visit my Iowa-transplanted family. On those trips, I frequently disdained the shorter route through Chicago and instead choose to go over the Great Lakes—admittedly longer, but more suited to my temperament as I escaped the urban hubbub to navigate the isolated lakes, rivers, forests and towns of Canada's imposing pre-Cambrian shield.

Often I would get out, stretch my legs, and enjoy the many waterfalls, lakes and rivers that marked my journey. Lake Superior was a favorite. I'd stand, hands in pockets, on the northern shores of Longfellow's "Gitche Gumee," leaning into the wind and gazing over the "Big-Sea-Water" as the waves lashed the rocky beach.

I embarked on my first extensive driving exploration when I was just nineteen—no more than a kid—driving from Iowa to Mexico on my winter break from Grinnell College. Grinnell boasted a Spanish House, and I was intrigued to see for myself the Mexico described by friends who resided in that house. With their help, I plotted a course from Nuevo Laredo to Acapulco, and made the trip on a shoestring budget in a Ford Falcon I borrowed from my mom.

One commonality links that trip with the one I'm beginning today. Then, in Mexico, as now, in Alaska, I was welcomed—even though I was a stranger. Even the police were helpful.

"Where is Insurgents Street?" I recall asking an officer, having pulled to the side of the road.

"I am sorry Señor," he responds in his most polite English, accommodating yet another confused Yanqui, "but I have never heard of such a street."

"But it's printed right here," I protest, thrusting a map out the driver's side window, pointing for him to see.

"Aaah, you mean In-soo-hen-tes," he laughs, correcting my pronunciation—my "g" being his "h." And with that he patiently explains how to reach my destination. I am attempting to keep a promise to a college friend to say "hola" (now the "h" is silent!) to the Pontones family, who had hosted her when she was an American Friends Services Committee exchange student in Mexico City.

Finally, with the guidance of my accommodating policeman, I am ringing the bell on the gated wall of the Pontones villa. A maid comes out to answer my ring and, speaking no English, returns to the house. Soon out run siblings Sarita, Yolanda, Mani and the entire Pontones family.

"Welcome, welcome. Any friend of Ellen's is ours as well. You'll be staying with us, of course!"

And with that, I am taken in. I eat their meals, sleep in their beds, attend their posadas, tour their beloved city, stay in their guest house in Acapulco, and join them to watch incredibly audacious divers leap more than a hundred feet from the La Quebrada cliffs into the crest of a wave as it crashes into a small gulch jutting into the Pacific Ocean beach far below.

All unplanned. All spontaneous. All hard to believe as I think about it. I still have to pinch myself.

Snapping back from Mexican highways to the one I am

presently traveling, it registers that I haven't seen another car for some time. The further I travel southeast from Fairbanks, the smaller the towns and villages that populate my drive.

As I proceed down a particularly deserted stretch of highway, I spot a moose cow and her calf about a hundred yards ahead, grazing the edge of a marsh along the roadside. I slow down, and quietly pull over to watch. No matter how often I come across this ungainly-looking behemoth (an animal who, in fact, combines strength, grace, speed and agility), I cannot help but stop to admire—lingering as if it were the first time I have witnessed such a sight.

Like all mothers in the wild, this moose keeps a weather eye on her calf, even when stopping to quench her thirst. The calf—like most all youngsters—never grazes too far from mama's gaze. As I watch, the moose—having eaten and drunk her fill—wanders back into the protective forest, followed dutifully by her offspring. Resigned that the show is over, I put aside my camera, start up my vehicle, and continue down the road. It feels like a nice omen to have come across this moose family so early in my journey.

I drive towards Tok, where, three years ago I had spent the night in a cabin that looked like a gingerbread cottage in the woods. Tok brings back pleasant memories of my first Alaska river trip, though I still feel fortunate that my first encounter with a grizzly turned out as well as it did. Since my hope is to get to Dawson—site of my initial Yukon campsite—by nightfall, I resist the temptation to stop and say hello to my old outfitters.

Crossing the Tok River Bridge, I pass along the north side of the Tanana. If I look with the eyes of memory, I see myself paddling downriver, practicing sweep turns and reveling in the same autumn colors I am seeing now. But soon the road veers away, and with it my shadow self.

In a short while I see a small sign pointing north to the backcountry towns of Chicken and Eagle, my only confirmation that I'm at the intersection leading to the Top of the World Highway. Making an abrupt left, I head north, my heart racing a bit as I now enter new territory.

But my high spirits are soon dampened as I witness a disheartening panorama—mile after mile of devastation wreaked by the Taylor Complex fire of 2004, one of the most destructive wildfires in Alaskan and U.S. history. Hundreds of thousands of charred tree skeletons blanket the hills and mountains, reaching eerily into the air, as if in supplication. Fireweed and willow struggle to take root in the cindered understory, hinting at the possibility of renewal for this desolate landscape.

I can't help but think about the moose and her calf that I saw only a couple of hours before—grazing a peaceful meadow adjoining a protective forest. Their cousins and myriad other wildlife would have been incinerated by this roaring inferno. Even today—after more than three years—I am told the temperature on this desolate ground has not cooled to normal. I realize that such fires are necessary in the natural order of things, but I still hope that this devastation is not the result of a careless camper.

Continuing north, I come to the Fortymile, a designated Wild River and destination of many prospectors during the days of the gold rush. I pull off the road to read a plaque commemorating the hardships they endured. Back when I first elected to try river canoeing, Fortymile was highly recommended as a marvelous wilderness experience. Now, gazing down at a portion of this creek—whitewater churning and cascading over the boulders—I realize what a challenge parts of the river would have presented and feel relieved that I chose the gentler Tanana. Now, given my experience on other Alaskan waters, I might be tempted to take it on.

Soon, I come to a fork in the road. If I turn north and west, after a couple of hours of rough driving, I will reach the community of Eagle, an Alaskan outpost on the Yukon River whose hardy residents are given voice in John McPhee's *Coming Into the Country*—a fascinating read for those who might wish to better understand the challenges of moving through and settling in this often difficult land and climate. Much as I would like to see Eagle for myself, I decide to stay on plan and continue on to Dawson so I can arrive before dusk.

I take the right fork.

Later, as I approach the border with Canada, the scene changes dramatically.

"Now I know why it's called the Top of the World Highway," I say to no one in particular.

The road has reached an elevation of more than four thousand feet. The view from here to the far horizon is an endless palette of orange, rust, yellow and purple tundra. I exit my SUV, careful not to tread on the delicate ecosystem of lichen, heather, wildflowers and mushrooms—remembering that footprints on the tundra can last for years. I choose a place to sit beside the road and immerse myself in this reverie of color.

The alpine air is crisp and clean, and I breathe deeply. Losing track of time, I finally rouse myself. I've been sitting so long—lost in this incredible landscape—that my legs feel locked. I can hardly get up. Struggling, I finally attain a standing position. Bending over, hands on knees, I shake my head in disbelief.

Boy, are you getting creaky! Don't remember having this much trouble simply getting to my feet back when I first started these trips. Now wait a minute, you're not that much older now, or are you? Got to get back in shape. Skyline with Geoff is only a month away. Promise you'll get on your bike every day when you get home. Yeah, I will. No, really, promise! Ok, ok!

Still hobbling, I climb into my vehicle, vowing to do more than a little hiking on this trip. It's true—my annual autumn leaf-viewing bike ride with Geoff is next month. It's a tough ride—some forty miles up and down the mountains of Skyline Drive in Shenandoah National Park—but worth every ache and pain.

Clear as yesterday, I can feel the wind rushing by as we raced down that mountainside last year in the late afternoon shadows and suddenly burst out of the darkness into a brilliant and blinding sunset. Like *The Wizard of Oz*, it was as if the whole world instantly changed from black and white to Technicolor. Whooping it up, we pulled into an overlook and Geoff hopped up on a boulder—assuming his best "Rocky" pose while I snapped his picture.

Fast on the heels of this memory, my mind flashes back even further to when Laurie and Geoff and I were climbing out of Yosemite Valley, slogging up a slippery path past a rainbow-bedecked waterfall, to a mountain lake. It was early spring—snow still melting—and the water spray was icy cold and bracing. Despite the typical spring mountain weather—toasty warm in the bright sunlight and shivering cold in the shade—we climbed higher and higher, our body heat sufficient to stay comfortable in shorts and T-shirts.

Seeing me puffing like a steam engine under the weight of my forty-pound pack, Laurie feared I was going to have a heart attack. But, truth be told, I was simply out of shape. Running my own graphics design business, I hadn't found time to prepare properly. So this trip itself became my training. Laurie had joined us for that first week before returning to the U of Colorado to pursue her doctorate.

Geoff and I went on to climb Cloud's Rest and the rear approach to Half Dome. As we neared the top, I was quite proud of my accomplishment until I realized that the person hauling himself up the rope trail behind me had no use of his legs! A policeman who was shot on duty, he had half the use of his lower body and twice my determination. I remember and salute him still.

After spending Father's Day in backcountry Yosemite

cooking a special treat in our campsite (pita pizza) and sharing our celebration with a lone and homesick father camped nearby, Geoff and I decided to take on the Grand Canyon on our drive back home. But upon arriving at the canyon, we found that we should have secured a reservation a year prior to hike the popular Bright Angel Trail to the Colorado River. Luckily, impressed with our recent Yosemite credentials, the rangers allowed us to strike out to the river on a nearly abandoned back route that featured no signs, little evidence of a trail, and zero hikers.

As it turned out, we enjoyed an adventure-filled hike on that gorgeous descent through geologic time—occasionally nearly losing our way. Trying to wade across a rushing river pouring out of a high cliff waterfall, I was almost swept down the roaring stream until Geoff pulled me to safety. That night we lost most of our food cache to chipmunks (of all creatures!), and we were forced to share a single bag of ramen over the next couple of days.

But it was worth it. The following night we slept under a full moon that bathed the cliffs with shimmering light, and woke to a sunrise that painted the canyon walls a rainbow of reds.

I emerged from our month of challenge—hiking through both high and low altitudes—twenty pounds lighter and perhaps in the best shape of my life. Still fully energized, I couldn't wait to take my first bike ride upon my return home. I drove out to my favorite cycling route that snakes through the hills around Poolesville, Maryland. However, it began to rain and the roads turned slick. I decided to run instead. To my amazement and delight, I found myself running like a deer—light, effortless, and joyful—on a natural high. Finally, I made myself stop, realizing I had run far faster and longer than ever before.

But that, I remind myself, was twenty years ago.

The Top of the World

This cascade of memories dissolves as I approach the customs station at Poker Creek, the highest point on the Top of the World Highway and the northernmost of U.S. customs outposts. A short distance beyond I pull over at its Canadian equivalent—Little Gold Creek. These remote stations will soon close for the winter, as the roads will become impassable. Clearing customs, I proceed down the now unpaved highway. Topping a rise, the winding Yukon River comes into view far below. I spot the tiny George Black Ferry crossing—the northern terminus of the Klondike Loop Highway, a 325-mile stretch linking Dawson City to Whitehorse.

This is my first glimpse of the mighty Yukon in all these years I've been exploring Alaska. A storied river, the Yukon has carried Native Alaskans and Canadians, prospectors and settlers for hundreds—likely thousands—of years. Why am I not canoeing it right now, I'm tempted to wonder. But I know that my planned route will take me more than a hundred miles south along this north-flowing river.

"Oh well," I tell myself, "Can't canoe 'em all!"

By now I have descended the mountain to the riverbank. The ferry arrives and its gangplank clanks open. I am the sole passenger. We chug slowly across while the Yukon rolls gently beneath. A few minutes later, the ferry deposits me just north of Dawson City, destination of so many eager prospectors during the Klondike gold rush years in the late 1890s when nearly 100,000 hopeful adventurers endured incredible hardship in an effort to reach the gold fields.

I stroll down historic Front Street, impressed with its replicas of saloons, dance halls and other establishments that seem to echo with the rowdy and desperate voices of the "stampeders" who came here so long ago expecting to find riches—but more often spent far more than they acquired. At the south end of the street, I stand by the statue that has been erected to commemorate these hardy prospectors, upon whose legend so much of present-day Dawson City's economy seems to depend.

Days later in Skagway, some 430 miles to the south, where this trek for riches began—I would find a similar dedication to retelling the Klondike stories. Much as I came to this area inspired by my childhood radio adventures depicting these tales, I feel somewhat ambivalent to see Dawson and Skagway now so seemingly dependent on reliving past glory.

I find the souvenir shops and other tourist attractions are of little interest to me. I'd rather get back to the wide-open spaces. With one last farewell to the Dawson of old, I leave the gold fever nostalgia behind and head south for nearby Mt. Dome, where, I'm told, one can enjoy a panorama of the town, the Yukon River, and the surrounding territory.

Summiting Mt. Dome, I find the view from this pinnacle is indeed breathtaking. Spread out at my feet, Dawson City—its 1500 souls now a mere fraction of its boom days—nestles beside the great river, which winds into a horizon buttressed by distant mountain ranges. I can see my route stretched out before me in a way no map could possibly capture, and I feel a surge of excitement as I envision my journey in the days to come.

There is a sign as you enter Canada's Yukon Territory which boasts, "Yukon—Larger Than Life." As I stand here, the slogan feels like no exaggeration. I feel my smallness, not simply in stature or space taken, but in the brief passage of my lifetime compared to the physical and temporal landscape that stretches out before me. Even today, this boundless wilderness is sparsely populated, and no doubt I am seeing it as human beings have seen it for centuries—no, millennia.

Standing here, I am reminded of the lyrics from "Ghosts":

> *My ghost sits up there,*
> *watching me stare,*
> *down through the spaces of time.*

When I wrote those words more than thirty years ago,

sitting under a starlit sky at the base of Virginia's Old Rag Mountain, I was staring up at the summit where I had stood earlier that same day. Now, staring down at the landscape and river below, these events feel linked—a bit like *déjà vu*, but even more like a confluence of time and space.

Overlooking this vast plateau, I'm reminded of how the song continues:

> *My soul jumps the cliff*
> *my memory goes stiff,*
> *freezing some past I can't know.*

Something about standing at the edge a precipice elicits an atavistic temptation to hurl oneself out into the void. Perhaps it's about taking wing. Perhaps about defying human limitations, as if by soaring down, following the bends of the Yukon all the way to its source in British Columbia, one could leap beyond the present into another dimension of experience.

More likely, it's just a crazy notion—the human mind, ever-churning. Smiling at these thoughts, I close my eyes and breathe deeply, allowing them to drift away.

Opening my eyes, I trace each bend of the river and visualize my day's journey. Today the Yukon flows peaceful and serene—a royal blue ribbon—patiently carving its way through shimmering limestone cliffs that dwarf the neighboring aspen- and spruce-clad foothills. However, locals tell stories of how capricious this same river can be as it winds its way through arctic Alaska to the Bering Sea—especially in the early spring during ice-out when you can hear it crackling like gunfire echoing up and down the frozen waterway.

In geologic time, this river is but a recent visitor. Many thousands of years ago, this land was a sheet of ice, a hostile barrier to those early ancestors who crossed the land bridge from eastern Siberia into what was then the milder climate of northern Alaska. Only when the ice receded could they venture down through the territory which my gaze now encompasses: the native lands of the Dene—Northern and Southern Tutchone First Nations—whose Athabaskan cultural and linguistic heritage reaches back to those ancient passages.

Lost in my historical time warp, and captivated by the grandeur of this scene, I almost forget to look down at my feet. A carpet of color surrounds me—a delightful minimalist world of vibrant wildflowers. Carefully kneeling down for a closer look, I marvel at their robust beauty. All exhibit an amazing symmetry—arctic lupine, their petals and leaves arranged in perfect swirls of geometric precision, and first-year lodgepole pines, their leaves a whirl of Christmas green. Far from delicate, they are true survivors, staking their claim in a climate where only the hearty endure.

I am reluctant to abandon my perch. However, taking one last look to implant this marvelous scene in my memory, I step into my vehicle and return to the plateau below. With the river as my guide—I head for Whitehorse, Skagway, and beyond. Proceeding mile after mile without passing another vehicle, the vast, primitive, untouched landscape surrounds me—as if this land that has now known human presence over the past few centuries has nonetheless remained unaffected.

Eventually, the traffic picks up as I approach Whitehorse—another name that frequents the *Sergeant Preston* stories. However, I am delighted to discover that Whitehorse has moved beyond themes of Klondike gold to create a thriving art community. Diversity reigns, with shops containing paintings, photographs, pots and other artistic creations. I make a note to return to this city, hoping someday to perhaps display the very photos I am taking now. After poking around for some time in the shops and local museums, I'm ready to head back to the open road.

Midday becomes late afternoon, and again the traffic reduces to a trickle. Now I find myself traveling by an endless expanse of lake, shimmering metallic silver in the cloud-hazed sunlight, soft ripples dappling the surface. The ever-present mountains provide a silhouetted backdrop. This otherworldly canvas reinforces the sense of timelessness this landscape conveys, and I pull over to the side of the road.

Quietly exiting my vehicle—as if I might disturb the scene—I locate a comfortable boulder, and sit in the chilling breeze. Not a sound. Not a bird. Nothing but serene expanse—and my thoughts—which soon recede and join the stillness. I'm in no hurry. I lie back, and using a suitable rock for my pillow, I close my eyes and start to drift away.

My memory flows like the river, and I now see myself driving through Idaho's Sawtooth National Forest, taking a shortcut on my way to Sun Valley. As is true of many of my shortcuts, it actually takes longer than it would had I used the interstates. Not unlike today's journey, the drive offers inspiring views, solitude, and quiet—on a nearly deserted road that follows a meandering river.

Unlike today, the weather is quite hot, and after pulling to the side of the road, I strip off my clothes and jump into the inviting water. For a time I splash around like I did as a twelve-year-old, frolicking in the Cedar River with Grandpa Miller's terrier, Poochie. But unlike the Cedar, the water in this Idaho mountain stream—despite the hot weather—is freezing cold. I soon get out and flop on the shore—arms and legs spread, inviting the sun.

Then, like now, I drift off to sleep.

Waking, I find myself back beside my Yukon lake, feeling the chill of the late afternoon breeze. Grudgingly, not wanting to leave this idyllic setting, I rise, stretch, and resume my journey toward Skagway. Soon I will be following the Klondike Highway into British Columbia and through the White Pass, famed as a passage through the rugged mountains in the days of the gold rush. At the four thousand foot summit of the pass, I gaze down at an enormous valley, sparkling with waterfalls, through which a river meanders its way toward Skagway.

Descending the serpentine pass on a highway that is a marvel of modern engineering, one can only try to imagine the tens of thousands of prospectors—their pack mules burdened with months of supplies—struggling up the nearby Dead Horse Trail through the mud and the cold to find their way north to Whitehorse. Hundreds of pack animals died along this arduous route. However, the stampeders remained undeterred—even though upon reaching the fields of their dreams, those dreams were seldom realized.

I stop frequently to photograph the cascading falls that hurtle down the imposing cliffs. Across the valley I make out what seems like a tiny toy train (actually the famous White Pass & Yukon Railroad) crossing a trestle while precariously hugging the mountain cliffs. Four locomotives are employed to push the rolling stock up the slope. I presume the view for the passengers is both spectacular and harrowing.

Finally, my descent through the pass levels off, and no more than an hour later I am walking the streets of Skagway, Alaska—a city born of the Klondike Gold Rush. Surrounded by historic plaques and monuments commemorating those bygone times, Skagway today is a bustling port, ferrying locals and tourists alike on glacier and whale viewing expeditions, or linking them to other ports such as Juneau—Alaska's capital city—and Haines, where I am headed to continue my loop back to Fairbanks via the Haines and Al-Can Highways.

It's strange. At other times—for example, when traveling with Janet—I truly enjoy being the tourist. My people-person personality is in ascendency. But when I am on a solo wilderness trip, I am poor company. Clearly, I seek solitude, anxious to be on my way and connect with those parts of the land where the business of modern commerce rarely intrudes. I am ambivalent, because I know I would love to return here with Janet—to ride the White Pass Railroad, to wander through the gift shops of Whitehorse, and to visit with local artisans and residents.

But on this visit, the bustle grates on me, even as I try to appreciate—at least for one night—the many unique venues of Skagway. After some time meandering the town, I check into a weathered, historic hotel (most everything in Skagway seems connected to some piece of gold rush history) near the docks.

Restless, I walk down to observe the ferries coming in and out of port. Long lines of sightseers wait to board the excursion boats for an evening of watching whales fluke and glaciers calve. A mother runs after her excited youngster, trying not to lose their place in line. Two lovers gaze into each other's eyes, unaware of the hubbub around them. Older couples on retirement cruises stand patiently, hand in hand, perhaps checking off one more item on their bucket lists. The scene mellows me. As the line begins to board ship, I get up to take my own leave.

I wander back to my bare-bones hotel room, furnished quite simply with a bed and bath on rough-hewn wooden plank floors. The sounds of the evening drift through the thin walls. A jukebox plays in a bar down the street. Footsteps echo down the sidewalk outside and seep into my room—the conversations of those strolling by muffled just enough to be unintelligible. No modern soundproofing here. It feels as if this establishment has preserved not only the memory, but the ambiance, surrounding those who long ago spent the night anticipating the following morning—waiting to strike out for the north.

Back at the harbor the following morning, I locate the Haines Ferry and join the queue of cars waiting to board. Soon we are embarked and on our way to Haines, a small town about an hour and a half distant, where I will pick up the Haines Highway and travel north from this southeastern tip of Alaska, back through British Columbia, and again through the Yukon Territory. Haines, a picturesque town of about two thousand, neighbors Glacier Bay National Park, and boasts some of the most scenic territory in the Alaskan Panhandle.

I walk to the stern deck of the ferry, where I lean over the railing to follow the wake as it patterns off into the distance. The wind backwashes spray into my face—cold but invigorating. The captain comes on the horn and points out a whale pod about two hundred yards off the port bow. I squint against the silvered reflection of the morning sun on the water, and perhaps can make out the outline of two—maybe three—humps moving slowing through the chop. Soon they are gone, if they were ever there. But the possibility is enough to bring a smile, and I return to the main cabin.

Once arrived, I discover that Haines's surroundings feature many attractive camping possibilities. I decide to investigate Chilkat State Park, an out-of-the-way haven overlooking the Chilkat Inlet. A soft mist blankets the bay. After setting up camp, I hike along the rock-strewn shore, peering out through the fog, listening to the raucous gulls. I sit down, enveloped in the haze, and hear a mournful foghorn echoing through the evening. Eventually, the chill of night drives me to my tent. I lie down and soon fall asleep, the rhythmic rocking of the ferry passage still in my bones.

Crawling out of my tent the following morning, I find two bald eagles—one adult and one immature—standing sentry over my campsite. Bald eagles thrive in this area, catching salmon in the nearby bays and along the Chilkat River. In fact, the Chilkat American Bald Eagle Preserve is host to the largest gathering of this large-bodied raptor in the entire world.

With a tip of my cap, I bid farewell to my two centurions and head out for the day. Driving the Haines Highway along the Chilkat River is a pleasure for any lover of nature. During the fall especially, birdlife is plentiful and active. While eagles fish the river, seagulls stand by patiently, anxious to pick over any leavings that might be available after the great birds eat their fill. An abundance of mallards in full plumage, red-breasted mergansers, coots, crows and shorebirds line the river.

As I drive further along, I discover a salmon weir that has been constructed to count the sockeyes, so important to the economy of this region. The weir obviously serves as a favorite fishing location for the area's brown bears.

As I drive by, I do a double-take, spotting a large grizzly sow on the weir teaching her two cubs to fish. I make a sudden U-turn and return to a spot where I can exit the car to better photograph the lesson with my telephoto lens. As it turns out, I am not the only observer. A crow is patiently perched directly behind the sow, watchful for an opportunity to grab any leftovers.

This intriguing scenario continues for the next hour or so—the bear leaping with a mighty splash and employing her powerful claw to spear her catch, then holding the flopping fish against a nearby rock and devouring it. Over and over, fish after fish, the bear repeats this routine until, satiated, she gathers her waiting cubs. Fishing lesson over, mother and cubs amble deftly along the struts of the weir and back into the surrounding foliage. I return to my vehicle.

Continuing along the Chilkat, I stop frequently to view the birdlife, reluctant to leave this sanctuary, so full of the drama of everyday life. However, upon reaching the Pleasant Camp Border Crossing into British Columbia, the road veers away from the river and, wistfully, I commence the drive north.

I have not proceeded far before I come across a small gravel road winding off to the east. True to my nature, I cannot help but check it out. Content that my viewing of the mother grizzly and her cubs will be the highlight of my day, I am nonetheless about to discover another mother with her two offspring—equally captivating—and a lot more up close and personal.

Pet a Moose?

If somebody told me this story, I might consign it to the

"tall tales" division of my gullibility. When discussing moose, the topic always seems to center around how these large animals can be aggressive and dangerous. Most experts would caution, "Keep your distance." And I don't disagree. However, my personal experience with moose is more of the "gentle giant" description.

Like so many animals I encounter in the wild, moose are, at the most, curious about my presence—at the least, disinterested.

For example, there was the time a dam and her near-grown calf came trotting across the Koyukuk River to check me out as I camped on the opposite bank. They approached to within about twenty yards and simply stood there, trying to ascertain just whom I might be. Once they determined I was no threat, they wandered away. In other instances, the moose I've come across could have cared less, entirely ignoring my activities.

Today, I proceed down the small gravel road with no particular expectation. The road snakes its way around a small pond, eventually reaching a meadow bordering a copse of trees. In the meadow stands a moose, grazing quietly with her two yearling calves. After some time, seemingly oblivious to my presence, they wander into the nearby trees. The road circles around this same copse, so I follow it, hoping to capture additional photos of this contented family.

Hearing the threesome slowly clumping through the trees, I stop and exit my vehicle—careful to shut the door softly—and peek cautiously into the surrounding bush. Suddenly, before I can react, the dam emerges just a few yards to my right. Now she moves beside me, no more than ten feet away. She is so close I have to resist the irrational temptation to sidle over to pet her. Instead, I slowly raise my camera—careful not to make any sudden movement—and take a picture of my new neighbor. She stands there silently—munching a leaf, not even glancing my way. After a few more snapshots, she ambles back into the forest to rejoin her offspring.

I walk the circular gravel road to the front of the copse where I expect the moose family to emerge. Soon the three of them approach, about to exit the tree coverage. Upon taking in my presence, they stop, unsure of whether to proceed. Finally—after snapping a quick photo—I withdraw, and they continue to exit the forest and graze their way forward. Thus we part.

I return to the main highway and resume my journey north toward my reunion with the Yukon Territory, greatly satisfied to have taken the road less traveled.

Back Roads

Since my first days of driving, I have never outgrown the temptation to investigate seldom-traveled roads. Who knows where you'll end up? Thus it is—not long after my episode with the moose family—I come across yet another gravel road to investigate. Aside from myself, it appears to have no recent takers.

The early September day has turned bright. It is crisp and sparkling—a Monet canvas of mackerel clouds dabbling a cerulean sky. Golden aspen—its smooth bark tinged chartreuse by the surrounding green of the conifers—colonnade the road as it curves into the distance. Bright red fireweed bursts at the foot of this autumn palette. The perfect backdrop for this entire scene, a majestic, snow-clad peak rises in the distance at the southern end of Kluane National Park. The park itself is but a portion of a larger spectacular wilderness area that neighbors Glacier Bay to the west.

I proceed no more than a mile before I happen upon one of those pristine lakes that populate our great northern wild spaces. Dazzling sunlight dances across the glittering surface.

Accepting nature's invitation to escape the confines of my automobile, I stop. Shutting off the engine, I open the door, and, upon stepping out, close it gently. Stretching, I breathe in the invigorating air, pulling it deep into my lungs before exhaling it with a sigh of satisfaction. Every cell in my body feels restored. I look down at the sparkling lake.

It's only about a quarter-mile down there. Wanna hike it? Kind of steep. Don't be such a wimp. Easy to turn an ankle. Wouldn't be havin' this debate thirty years ago. That was thirty years ago. You don't have to hike it. Don't have to do anything. Stop doing. Just sit. Let this be what it is.

I search for a chair-sized boulder and lower myself down on it. I sit. Drifting in the silence. Doing nothing. Saying nothing.

Janet would like to see this. Janet's doing what Janet's doing. You came here to be alone. So be alone. Stop being a critic. Breathe.

The chatter ping-pongs through my mind. Occasionally slowing. Very occasionally stopping.

Suddenly I'm back in the middle of another monologue. This time, I can't even remember when it started or what started it. It's not important. I tell myself, "Clear the slate. Reboot. Breathe." I turn my gaze outward and once again embrace the stillness.

And so goes an hour or so of this beautiful day. Eventually, the chatter ebbs away. I sit, enjoying the quiet, both external and internal. Finally, relaxed in body and mind, I rise from my rock, glad I stayed put.

Gazing again at my surroundings, I take one last mental picture, then depart—reminded that these languid moments are one of the great gifts of the wilderness. It is elusive territory—and sometimes hard to remain there—but one worth revisiting.

On the Road Again

Retracing the gravel back to the Haines Highway, I resume my drive up the southern and eastern boundary of Kluane National Park. As I proceed northward, Kluane now forms the eastern border to its sister park on the western side of the range, Alaska's Wrangell-St. Elias. Together with the Glacier Bay wilderness, these parks form part of an enormous UNESCO World Heritage site known for its magnificent glacier landscapes and wildlife. Kluane is home to a number of spectacular, snow-clad peaks, including Mt. Logan, the second-highest summit in North America.

The afternoon passes, and a sign informs me that I have arrived at Kathleen Lake. To the west, down yet another gravel road, I reach a remote and inviting campsite that is walking distance from the lake. A welcome respite, Kathleen Lake presents an opportunity to hike, take photos, and rest—a welcome change from my daylong journey. I set up camp and—as it turns out—end up staying here for a couple of days.

During my time here, I occasionally wander down to stroll and explore the lakeshore. On one particular sparkling afternoon, the wind whips up froths of whitecaps. Watching the lively breakers, I recall the cold, bracing spray that leaped over the bow of my canoe and into my face as I battled even more demanding waters just a couple of years ago in Wood-Tikchik. For now, I'm content to stand here, but I know that someday soon I'll feel the need to resume the challenge.

I look across to the far shore, where the turquoise lake is edged gold and green with aspen and white spruce. Lurking behind the cumulus clouds that drift on today's remarkably blue sky are the peaks of the Kluane. I stroll around the lake to the far side of the bay, squatting at times to inspect the shoreline—examining a piece of driftwood or a peculiarly shaped stone.

I try skipping some of the flatter stones and find my skill is a woeful reflection of that which I possessed in my boyhood. Nonetheless, this aimlessness is a pleasure after my long days on the road. As I look up, the breeze caresses my beard and a crow perched on a barren tree branch scolds me raucously, while even higher above a red-tailed hawk effortlessly glides the thermals.

Eventually, rounding a point on the opposite shore, a wide expanse of wilderness stretches out before me. I feel my aloneness. "There are grizzlies out here," I suddenly think, but let this bit of apprehension quickly wash over me. I look down, see no telltale tracks, and remind myself that no matter where I travel in the northern wild, I'm always accompanied by unseen eyes—real and imagined. I also remind myself that those eyes are as wary of me as I feel now.

I chuckle at this familiar internal dialogue. I've learned over these many years of traveling alone in the wild, it is easy for doubt to become obsession. Watchfulness is prudent, but fear is crippling. I will the chilling thoughts away, but nonetheless prudently start back for the campsite. Darkness and the chill of evening will soon set in.

After a couple of restorative days at Lake Katherine, I break camp, repack my car, and resume my drive. I proceed no more than a couple of miles down the road when I pass a delightfully rustic, small compound consisting of three cabins and a store nestled in a circle of spruce. Giving way to impulse, I pull over to the side of the road and reconsider. Realizing how reluctant I feel to leave this blissful corner of the Yukon, I swing my car around and pull into the little parking lot.

Stepping inside the sparsely furnished office, I meet a chatty and welcoming proprietor.

"Did you happen to see the grizzly down the road?" she asks, before I can say anything.

"No, where exactly was it?"

"Just about a hundred yards back. Folks have seen it off and on for a couple of days now." She explains. "I just wondered. I've lived here all my life, and I still love seeing them."

"I'll be sure and keep an eye out," I say. "Have you got a cabin available?"

"No other guests right now. You've got the pick of the

litter. Stay as long as you like."

I immediately book a simple, one-room cabin with a view of Kluane's peaks just out my front window. After inspecting my new abode—a comfortable chair to read in, outlets to charge my batteries, a table to review the day's photos, and a bed with a firm mattress—I decide on the spot to employ this as a base of operations for the next few days. Each morning, I roam further afield and return in the evening, ready to flop onto my single bed, gaze out my window, and contemplate the day's adventures.

Shadows and Light

The Yukon is a study of changing light and shadow. Bright autumn mornings awaken a fresh array of color, sparkling in the dew of early dawn. By contrast, the afternoons glow in silvery sub-arctic shadows. Driving back to my cabin one late afternoon, a monumental outcropping rises before me. Its shimmering cliffs reflect metallic in the late afternoon sun, dwarfing a landscape of yellow umber aspen, spread out like a field of sunflowers—a painting awaiting the hand of a Van Gogh.

Towards the end of my long day's drive, I stop by a wayside to wade an inviting stream, my camera strapped around my neck. Exiting the ice-cold water, I sit down on a rock to fix a late lunch, laying my camera beside me.

No sooner have I put the camera down than a bald eagle glides into my peripheral vision and heads my way. Her immense wings outstretched to cushion her landing, she prepares to alight in the crown of a spruce on the other side of the stream. Hurriedly, I grab my camera and snap a photo just as the enormous bird is touching down. Each of us settles in to watch the other. Having satisfied her curiosity, she abruptly turns her head—first downstream and then upstream, alert for any fish swimming just below the surface. I've plenty of time to photograph this imposing bird.

Finally, tiring of our photo session, with a powerful leap and a repeated flapping of her wings, the enormous raptor lifts off her perch and fishes her way downstream—eyes down, head sweeping back and forth—alighting on another spruce about a hundred yards away. After one last gaze downstream, I lower my camera and we each continue on our respective journeys.

Bald eagle sightings have always been special for me. Each time they appear I feel inspired—at once rejuvenated and serene—as if someone truly has my back. Smiling, I gather my gear and—with a spring in my step that belies my age—hop into my car.

I return to my cabin retreat in the early evening, tired—yet rejuvenated—by my experiences on this sixteen-hour excursion. In only a couple of days I will be on the road again, this time to travel back into Alaska and retrace my journey west along the Tanana River and then north to Fairbanks.

For now, I take advantage of the fact that I have electricity available, settle myself at my little desk, and plug in my computer. This is one of those rare occasions that I have an opportunity to review my photos. My last such opportunity was in Skagway, and I'm in for a treat. The bear and her cubs, the moose and her calves, Lake Kathleen, the ranges of the Kluane, and most recently the bald eagle, all reappear for my pleasure.

I work into the night processing and cataloguing these images, lost in the journey of the past few days. Finally my eyes grow heavy. Turning off my computer and stowing it in my gear, I flop onto the bed. Next thing I realize, the morning sun is streaming through my cabin window.

*   *   *

Enjoyable as it has been to settle down for a few days, I am ready to be back on the road. My luck has held. It is yet another sun-spangled morning. Thanking my host for her hospitality, I set out north for Haines Junction—the diversely populated town of about 600 that sits dwarfed at the foot of the magnificent Yukon Mountain Range. Located in Southern Tutchone territory, this historic village is now the administrative home of the Champagne and Aishihik First Nations.

The colors of Kluane National Park are exuberant on this spectacular autumn day. The high tundra wears a cap of white powder under cumulus clouds in a cyan sky, fronted by the blue ribbon of the Alsek River. Coming to the top of a rise, the splendor of this endless view confronts me. Row after row of snow-clad peaks march into the distance, displaying one of the largest non-polar ice fields in the world.

Almost stunned to a stop, I exit my vehicle and set up my tripod. It's the perfect time to try out my newly purchased panorama attachment. I spend the next hour experimenting with how best to capture the beauty spread out before me. Finally, I repack my gear and prepare to drive the breathtaking descent that will take me to Haines Junction.

Once I reach Haines Junction, I have a choice: to continue west to the Al-Can border or to explore what further gems of the Yukon Territory lay to the east. Realizing I may never again have this opportunity, it is no contest. Turning east at the junction with the Alaska Highway, I once again head in the direction of Whitehorse. About a half-hour later, I come across a signpost for Otter Falls.

Intrigued, I head north to investigate. The winding gravel road crosses an old prospector's bridge that spans the Aishihik River, namesake of the First Nation people who have made this land their home for centuries. The rugged, rutted road follows the Aishihik north, stretching on and on. I doggedly continue.

Finally, I pause on this bone-jarring journey to stretch my legs and scan my surroundings. Upon exiting, I immediately recognize a piercing cry and scan the shimmering sky. High above, I spot what appears to be a red-shouldered hawk, circling its way slowly in my direction, eyes locked below for possible prey.

Transfixed, I stand there as the great bird slowly advances, describing one circle and then another—gliding effortlessly. Escaping my stupor, I rush to the car, fish my camera out of my gear and, attaching my longest lens, point it upward. Obligingly, the hawk continues my way. Click! Click! Click! Finally, he circles away and, grateful for both the interaction and the adrenalin—which enlivens the plodding pace of my drive—I return to my car and continue toward Otter Falls, alert to whatever might next occur.

The Aishihik Herd

I don't have long to wait. The first time I ever lay eyes on a wood buffalo is about thirty minutes later. Unexpectedly, I come across a herd grazing peacefully in a large, grassy expanse at the foot of an aspen-clad hill. Inspecting a nearby plaque, I learn that this herd—and many like it—has recently been reintroduced in various locations throughout northern Canada and Alaska.

I feel transported in time—suddenly confronted by a pastoral scene that had essentially passed from the North American landscape a century ago. Now here they are in the present—in the wild, protected in these Aishihik lands—greatly diminished in number, but not in grandeur. A somewhat larger cousin of the American bison, a male buffalo, with its great horns and an enormous shaggy head and body astride spindly legs, mounts a willing female. Several yearling calves graze alongside their mothers. I linger for some time, taking photos as if to verify to myself that I am actually witnessing this bygone scene.

The herd is clearly aware of my presence, frequently lifting their heads and staring in my direction. Eventually—as if on cue—they turn as one and run off, determined to protect themselves from any possible predator. Watching their departure, I can almost hear the echoing hoofbeats of their ancestors as they thundered over this same landscape and down into the Dakotas and my native Iowa. I feel sad to see them disappear, as if the entire experience had been a chimera.

Otter Falls

My reverie is soon dislodged, as the rumble of the imaginary hoofbeats becomes the very real roar of the nearby Aishihik River cascading down the steepening slope. Otter Falls comes into view. Bounding its way for over a mile, it's more than a falls—it's an avalanche of water cavorting down the mountain. It is hard to imagine that this is the same river that has flowed so peacefully on my upward drive to the falls.

Exiting my car, I walk to the edge of the river, stepping carefully from boulder to boulder lest I slip into the cascade and dunk my camera. Settling down on a particularly accommodating boulder that offers stability and a mid-river view of the falls, I carefully select the lens I want and start taking photos. After a time, satisfying myself that I have captured the cascade as best I can, I lie back on the large rock, close my eyes, and allow myself to be enveloped by the cacophony of sound and spray. I nearly fall asleep.

Finally, an hour or so later, I return to my car. Retracing my journey along the Aishihik back to the Alaska Highway, I turn west. In the far distance, the sun is lowering over the Yukon Range, inviting me back to the splendors of Kluane. Soon I arrive once again in Haines Junction, at the foot of the towering peaks.

As evening approaches, I leave Haines Junction and proceed along the southern shores of Kluane Lake—the largest lake in the Yukon and home of the Kluane First Nation. In the deepening dusk, the lake is painted with a surreal impression of the sky above. I travel mile after mile along this immense body of water, the colors becoming more and more brooding. Behind me, a waning moon rises in the eastern sky above the now darkened foothills, casting an eerie indigo shadow over a rocky riverbed.

Nearly an hour later, as the moon ascends the opposite horizon, the western sky is now painted with ever-deepening colors. Royal purple clouds embrace the west horizon under a rich mauve sky. Still proceeding along Lake Kluane toward Destruction Bay, it feels as if a spell has been cast across a landscape in thrall of the sky—the mountains silhouetted, and the calm peaceful lake bathed in the color of a Yukon midnight.

It is past one in the morning when I finally spot a campground alongside the bay at Burwash Landing. I stop for the night, and fall into my tent—awash in visions of raptors, buffalo, cascading falls and deep purple.

A Shared Heritage

Morning dawns with a bright sun highlighting the glacier-clad peaks. Back on the road, I haven't proceeded half an hour when I notice a unique collection of roadside sculpture that bids me stop and investigate. I am drawn to a tablet, taller than myself, and carefully read its inscription. It tells the story of Douglas Richard Twiss II from Whitehorse, a "southern Tutchone man," whose native name is "Mbayata"—meaning "Sheep Daddy."

The memorial goes on to tell of Mbayata's pride in his family, how he danced with the Dakwakada Dancers (carrying on the traditions of the Southern Tutchone and Tlingit) and how he was taught the traditional ways by the Beaver Creek and Burwash Landing elders. Finally, the stone expresses its thanks to the Kluane First Nation for providing their traditional land for this memorial.

Surrounding the tablet are sixteen beautifully carved wooden and stone tributes to the Native land, wildlife and culture that nurtured Mbayata. As it turns out, Douglas's father, Doug Twiss, a celebrated Native artist in the Yukon Territory, created these works of art.

Standing here, I think back to my teenage self, when as an Explorer Scout in Des Moines, Iowa, I participated in a ceremonial group called the Mitigwa Dancers. Celebrating Native American culture, we made our own costumes—modeled on traditional Native feathered headdresses, beaded wampum belts, bone breastplates and leather breech clouts, and we learned to drum, chant and dance—emulating Native dances such as the Hopi Rain Dance.

Some twenty years later the Mitigwa Dancers became the object of protests by a group of Mesquakie Indians from Tama, Iowa who succeeded in replacing Mitigwa dance performances with their own at the Iowa State Fair. Was I participating in a romanticized stereotyping of Native peoples back then? The Mesquakie protesters seemed to think so.

My mind wanders to even earlier memories of Native American culture in the Midwestern heartland. I think of the street names of my Lincoln, Nebraska neighborhood—Otoe, Pawnee, Arapahoe and Cheyenne; the counties in Iowa paying homage to Chief Black Hawk, Chief Appanoose, and the Cherokee; and towns named Ottumwa, Osceola, Sioux City, Altoona, and Chillicothe. And, of course, the very name Iowa derives from Native America.

Suddenly, I'm a kid on one of my many trips to Minnesota (another Native name) to visit my relatives in Bemidji (yet another) and Blackduck. I'm seven years old and we're driving through Tama. Tama, my parents tell me, is an "Indian town" and looking out the car window through my child's eyes I see dusty streets, buildings in disrepair, and other children sullenly staring back at me as I pass through what feels like forbidden territory.

I feel confused. The "Indians" I have known have been those depicted in comic books and the movies: some brave and heroic like the Lone Ranger's sidekick, "Tonto"; others savage and threatening, as in the cowboy and Indian battles of Hollywood's Old West. These are neither. I am learning about stereotypes.

At about that same age, I remember wandering through a gift shop in Minnesota's Itasca State Park, where, fascinated, I look wide-eyed at the Native crafts—moccasins, tiny totems, toy canoes made of real birch-bark, dolls dressed in fringed deerskin, and books celebrating the "Land of the Chippewa." Next to them are displays of postcards, grotesque caricatures of a grinning "Injun Joe" (a character from Mark Twain) saying, "Wish'um you were here," and "Hav'um a wonderful time." Again, something didn't add up. It was all too simple— and too mean-spirited.

I jump ahead to when I am fifteen, standing with one of my uncles in the Red Lake Trading Post, on the edge of Minnesota's Red Lake Indian Reservation. In walk three Native Americans with a five-horsepower Johnson outboard. As we stand there, they trade it for a six-pack of Pabst Blue Ribbon. They leave the store, and someone mutters, "likely stole it," and for one of the first times I feel my whiteness and am ashamed to be a part of this sordid scene. Years later, this isolated reservation would explode with anger and frustration, garnering national headlines—as if the results of a century of broken promises, conquest, neglect, and a missionary zeal for acculturation should be a surprise to a wider public that had long ago averted its eyes.

Through the coming years, as I traveled through the North American continent, I came to more fully understand and appreciate those who have inhabited these lands for centuries. Just last year, canoeing through four villages along arctic Alaska's Kobuk River, I was welcomed by the Inupiat—Native Alaskans who generously invited me into their fish camps, their homes and their lives to share food and exchange stories.

Standing here today, I realize that for me, this is a

memorial not only to Mbayata, but to all those past and present who watch over these lands—honoring the environment and its inhabitants in a world too often in pursuit of short-term gain—a world disconnected from its heritage. It is this heritage that brings me to this spot today. I've come to this land with childhood memories of Sergeant Preston and the gold rush, only to be reminded that the real gold resides in the beauty of these hills and in the resilience of their inhabitants—a gold that cannot be mined, and that will be here for all who would find it long after I have departed.

I return to my car and proceed toward the Alaska border.

*   *   *

The drive from Burwash Landing along the Al-Can highway to its junction at Tetlin with Alaska's Top of the World Highway is less than five hours. However, if you are stopping to drink in the breathtaking scenery, it takes as long as it takes. The backdrop of Canada's Kluane National Park merges into that of Alaska's Wrangell-St. Elias once you cross the border, though borders and names mean little to the endless landscape.

But for me, crossing the border means saying goodbye to the Yukon and to some childhood fantasies as well. Goodbye to Sergeant Preston. Goodbye to his wonder dog Yukon King. The theme music from this radio classic once again courses through my memory and brings tears to my eyes.

Clearly the Yukon I beheld in Dawson City continues to harken back to those now mythic days. But what that radio series had best captured for me was the sweep of this vast country called the Yukon Territory, and its indescribable wild beauty.

I had started this journey not quite sure how it would feel to abandon my canoe. Indeed, I miss paddling the lakes and rivers of the north, and feel the pull to return to those waters.

However, the car has offered me a different kind of freedom, and I have used it to full advantage. My wanderings have allowed me to explore the intimate corners of this country and realize that there is a far richer heritage in this landscape and its inhabitants than my childhood imagination could possibly conjure. Far from regretting it, I thank myself for breaking the mold and venturing forward to explore the Yukon in this new format.

Crossing into Alaska, I am once again following along the Tanana, where I first attempted river-canoeing some three years previous. The mountains that watched over me on that expedition now loom in the distance, their purples and lavenders perfectly reflected in hushed waters. Reluctant to conclude my adventure, I stop to spend one last night in these wild surroundings before completing my circular journey back to Fairbanks.

It's strange how driving on the same highway can be such a different experience simply by traveling the opposite direction. Now, two weeks since I started this grand tour, the fall colors have deepened and the chill of seasonal change whispers through the landscape. Wildlife are active, foraging the meadows along the highway. Roadside plants beg you to stop and admire them before they succumb to winter.

Tundra and trumpeter swans grace almost every lake and pond with their regal presence, silently gliding—frequently in pairs—occasionally dipping their heads to sift through the nutrients beneath the water's surface. This is their migratory path, and I know that in a few months, upon returning home, I will see them again at Blackwater, my local wildlife refuge on the East Coast some three thousand miles distant.

Each time I observe these elegant creatures, I can't help but pull over to the side of the road and walk to the edge of the water, where I sit tantalized—finally getting up to drive on, only to be seduced by the next idyllic happen-stance. In one instance, I come across a single trumpeter, floating silently among the lily pads in a small, coffee-colored lagoon, surrounded by a dense spruce forest.

As I sit silently by the edge of this isolated pool, the great bird leisurely glides, circumnavigating the pond, occasionally rising up to stretch her wings. Then she dips her head far below the surface, searching the pads for sustenance. Instinctively, I raise my camera. Finally satiated, or perhaps just restless to be on her way, she coasts to the far end of the pond, rises up, and, creating an incredible racket, races across the water—beating her enormous wings furiously in order to lift her body into flight. Startled by this sudden flurry, my heart takes flight with her, straining to help her aloft. Nonetheless, I manage to capture the moment with my camera. Soon she disappears, winging through the forest. "See you at Blackwater," I call after her.

I am relieved that she is able to make a successful exit over the nearby surrounding spruces. As she lifts above the evergreens and flies off, I think back to the time when I paddled the headwaters of the Chisana years ago. Following along a rivulet, I suddenly noticed a break in the foliage on my left, revealing a small lake.

At the far end of the lake were a bevy of very large trumpeters. I no more than realized their presence than—perhaps startled by my intrusion—they rose up as one. I scrambled for my camera, but to no avail. By the time I had it in hand, they had thrashed their powerful wings and, shattering the wilderness quiet, formed a perfect wedge. Rising in the evening sky—they reminded me for all the world of a 747 on takeoff.

Now, watching my solitary swan soaring in the distance, the serendipity of this photograph is not lost on me. "Turn, turn, turn." I think. "All things come to those who wait."

One Last Look

In only a matter of hours, I am on a plane back to

Anchorage, there to be welcomed by John and his family and offered a comfortable bed for the night. It's hard to believe that only this morning I was saying goodbye to the Yukon.

Now, the following morning, John and I head out to the Lake Hood seaplane base to resume our yearly tour of his favorite Alaskan venues. We hop aboard his Cessna and head south over the Turnagain Arm of the Cook Inlet toward the glaciated mountains of the Kenai. Once again we glide high over the tundra, dipping down and sweeping so near the glaciers that it seems like they are gigantic toboggan runs. Though our weather is overcast, it provides yet another dramatic perspective on the ever-changing light and shadow that plays over the Alaskan landscape.

John and I discuss what I might plan for next year. With his usual jocular enthusiasm, he sings the praises of the Tongass National Forest—the Pacific's northernmost rainforest—that today is again under threat from those who would harvest its lush resources. John describes the remote fly-in wilderness cabins, maintained by the state, that are available for rental. Before long we agree to spend a week in one of his favorite cabins near the Tongass, after which he will fly me to my own cabin to reside alone in the rainforest for an additional week.

Thus is the seed planted for yet another kind of wilderness adventure. This time, instead of canoeing or driving over hundreds of miles, I will stay in place to experience the solitude and mysteries of the rainforest—an opportunity to meditate on both exterior and interior landscapes.

For the present, this journey through these mountains and valleys is my farewell excursion for 2008. Appropriately, as the sun dips behind the mountains, a radiant burst of gold paints the late afternoon sky. We turn towards home.

Chapter 13

2009 – MEDITATIONS – THE TONGASS

What can you see in a drop of rainwater? Get really close. Observe how its spherical shape magnifies the veins of the leaf to which it clings. Now notice how these intricate veins are like rivers flowing through a lush landscape. These rivers appear to flow to a sea, until you discover that the sea is actually a reflection of the sky above—and bits of this sky silhouette the elegant Sitka spruce that tower overhead and converge in the vertex of this raindrop.

Now, refocus and notice how the raindrop, perfectly sculpted in a half-moon of reflected light, glimmers and pulses, clinging tenaciously to the leafy surface. If you're really quiet as you lie on the rain forest floor underneath this clinging drop, you can feel your own pulse, as if in vicarious response.

And so it goes: my week alone in the Tongass. I've come to this largest and most northern rain forest in North America to experiment with yet another way of being alone in the wilderness. Located in Alaska's southern panhandle, I have arrived here by way of Juneau, the remote capital of this multifaceted state. From Juneau I hopped a commuter plane to spend some time with John and his wife at one of the many beautifully rustic and isolated Alaska State Park Service cabins that dot the inland waters south of Glacier Bay National Park. Following our time together, during which I had the opportunity to advise John on how to make best use of his new Nikon SLR, he then flew me in his Cessna to this secluded location.

Time has slowed. I have slowed. Nature is nurturing me. I am like this drop of water, taking in and reflecting all that surrounds me. I am forced to stop, and observe, and contemplate, and rest. Nights I spend finishing my reading of Barry Lopez's marvel, *Arctic Dreams*. Days I wander the forest, lazily discovering new wonders with almost every footstep.

The trekking isn't easy. One has to tread carefully. I slow down, cautiously planning the placement of each foot. The forest floor isn't really a floor. It's a spongy muskeg of lichen, bearberry, caribou and sphagnum moss, fern, rotted branches, and fallen trees. I keep to the winding trails frequented by moose, bear and other forest denizens—not only to avoid sinking up to my thighs, but also to preserve this gloriously primal environment.

The beavers have been busy here. Near the shore of Distin Lake, on which my wilderness cabin is situated, tree after tree confirms their gnawing presence. Bark has been stripped, leaving the trunks raw and exposed—awaiting the beaver's return to finish their harvest. Given the freshness of this evidence, the beaver must live nearby. I remind myself to keep an eye out for a dam or a lodge when I explore my lake in the flat-bottomed rowboat that the park service has provided.

I continue my trek, breathing in the aroma of the incredibly verdant understory. Enormous shelf mushrooms proliferate—bright orange and edged in yellow. They cling to the base of a tree, or perhaps a stump cut long ago, now the home of lush green sphagnum moss.

One afternoon, when the constant drizzle of the rain forest has paused and the sun and the clouds vie for supremacy, I walk down to the lakeshore. Gazing out over the barely rippled watery expanse, I decide it's time to investigate Distin Lake's further reaches. Tugging with all my strength, I manage to haul the bulky metal rowboat from high on the shore. Screeching as its flat bottom scrapes over the rocky beach, the craft finally settles heavily into the water. I'm used to effortlessly paddling a sleek, lightweight Kevlar. But like everything in my Tongass environment, the clunky boat forces me to slow down—its cracked, thin oars creaking in their rusty locks.

Settling into this more measured pace, I proceed unhurriedly, stopping to inspect the lily pads that populate the shallow shoreline waters. Holding the oars aloft, the boat drifts. I become fascinated with the drip, drip, drip of droplets from the tip of the blade, producing concentric circles as they plop into the water—eventually dissipating—to be followed by the next drop, and then the next.

The boat aimlessly floats into a colony of pads. Leaning over the side to inspect a blossom, the ripe lemon-yellow fall colors of the petals surround and accentuate its deep brown circular seedpod. Cradling these blooms, each heart-shaped green pad seems to levitate gracefully against the background of the tea-black water, tethered only by their slender stems.

Finally, careful not to disturb the delicate pads, I carefully row backwards out of the encircling plants and, once extricated, head toward the north end of the lake. After some time, absorbed in the rhythmic creaking of the oars, my musings are interrupted by a loud thwack echoing across the water. Instantly, I realize my beaver is nearby and swing around in my seat searching for him. Again his tail smacks the water, warning his intruder.

Respecting his message, I stay where I am, marveling at the power of his tail, as he thwacks the water over and over, raising an impressive fountain of spray. I'm transported to the afternoon my daughter Laurie and I spent canoeing the backwaters of Maine, playing hooky from the Parents' Day activities her college was sponsoring. During that excursion, a beaver almost soaked us, whacking his tail repeatedly while swimming alongside our canoe. Both of us preferred the pleasure of sharing this experience to listening to a lecture on school policy or attending a cocktail reception.

Each of my three children—Laurie, Geoff and Kelley—from the time they were toddlers—have grown to love the outdoors. Now they spend camping vacations with their own families and friends. I am reminded of how they recounted with pride the first time they went camping without their mom and dad. They traveled to Acadia National Park, set up their own tents, gathered firewood, cooked themselves a fine meal, and shared stories around the campfire. I've often wondered if those stories elaborated on those they had heard as children, when I would spin tales describing the perilous adventures of "Running Deer and Soaring Hawk"—trying to be as accurate as possible in passing on my own limited knowledge of Native American lore.

Finally—apparently satisfied that he has warded off any potential threat—the beaver goes his way. I go mine. For some time, I explore this end of the lake in a vain attempt to find his lodge. Unsuccessful, I'm ready to return to my cabin in the woods, and start rowing back. After hauling the boat well up onto the shore, I inspect one of the many driftwood logs scattered along the shoreline.

A circular eye, harboring a small colony of lichen that serves as an iris, stares out from the driftwood's knotty brow. The patterns in the sun-bleached wood seem to reflect the constantly repeated graceful swirls found in so many of the neighboring forest plants.

Sure enough, on my walk the next morning, I find this circular, swirling pattern repeated in the skunk cabbage and other broad-leaved plants that carpet the rainforest floor. Overhead, streams of sunlight etch the sphagnum moss that adorn the branches of spruce and western hemlock in spidery backlit radiance. I'm reminded of the old-growth swamps of Georgia and South Carolina.

I spend the remainder of my day wandering deep into these lush surroundings, craning my neck to scan the treetops. At waist level, lush, intricately symmetrical ferns surround me, joined by plants of every description, some with six-foot razor-thin sword-shaped leaves reaching out to find the sun. Wide-leaved umbrella plants serve to protect the vegetation nearest the forest floor. Kneeling to inspect the tiny plants that populate the miniature-carpeted world beneath me, I struggle back to my feet and stretch languidly. The sun has shifted. Can it be that I have already spent most of an entire day wandering through this plant paradise?

Feeling the need to get my blood pumping, I remember the woodshed that stands near the cabin. Ready for some real exercise, I walk back to the generous stash of precisely sawed logs—some measuring six feet or more around the girth—stacked neatly by park rangers in an open-faced shed that stands about ten feet tall. An axe, maul and wedge are thoughtfully provided.

Laying aside my camera and other gear, I climb a homemade ladder to the top of the shed and dislodge one of the enormous logs. It falls thudding to the ground, and—grabbing the axe, maul and wedge—I set to work cutting the oversized log into wedges that will fit into my fireplace. I repeat the process with several logs. After such an unhurried day in the consistent fifty-degree temperatures of the rainforest, my body is chilled throughout. It's good to work up a sweat.

I'm no stranger to this kind of work. During my college years, I spent my summer days on the CB&Q Railroad swinging a twelve-pound spike maul—windmilling that hammer from one side of the rail while my partner did the same from the other side—in order to drive a five-inch spike into the creosote-soaked tie. Over and over this cooperative process was repeated until, arm-weary, each of us would stop, sweat-soaked and exhausted, and catch our breath before continuing on to the next tie.

It was dangerous work. You could not afford to miss your target, lest your maul bounce off the steel rail into your leg or that of your partner. Necessity demanded skill, and—difficult as it was—this work rewarded you with a deal of satisfaction. To this day, that skill and accuracy—as well as the pleasure of hard work well done—has remained a part of my muscle memory.

Thus, taking advantage of the relatively dry afternoon (as dry as it gets in a constantly dripping rainforest), I chop a supply that I figure will last me of number of chilly nights to come. I gather up the cut wood and kindling and make several trips to my cabin to fill the log-bin.

Tired—but pleased with my accomplishment—I clean and replace the tools and then turn to prepare and cook my evening meal. Having purchased a week's supply of food in Juneau, I choose spaghetti and marinara sauce for my entrée with a simple lettuce and tomato salad. Dessert consists of a protein bar. It's quite a luxury to eat fresh food instead of freeze-dried—part of the trade-off between camping and cozying up in this cabin.

After dinner and cleanup, I stroll down to the lakeshore to bid the evening sky goodnight. The ever-present mist has abated as I gaze over the water and a few stars peek through. I stand in the quiet, breathing in the crisp cold air. Finally the chill drives me back inside.

Back in the cabin, I cozy up to my fire twice warmed—once by chopping the wood and once by burning it—open my book, and read myself sleepy by lantern light.

A good day in the Tongass.

Misty Morning

A fine sleep and breakfast behind me, I step out onto the

cabin porch to greet the new day. A light fog hangs over the lake, turning it monochrome. I stroll down to the bank. The placid water is pearl gray, the now-muted lily pads lining the shallows. A hundred yards off to my right, the silhouetted forest ascends from the shore, marching upward and inland— mimicked by its reflection. In the far distance, beyond the misty north shore, silvered mountains huddle in silence. Only the rustic, orange oars, resting in the gunmetal boat, lend color to this mist-laden tableau.

The lake beckons, and I decide to spend the day exploring in the boat. Retrieving some supplies from the cabin, I quietly step into the old flat-bottom, rocking it gently. The oars creak in their locks as if in parody of my own joints, slowly awakening after a night's sleep. Almost careful not to disturb the mirror of surrounding water, I back away from shore and swing the boat southward. Lazily, I row through the haze, occasionally stopping to listen to my surroundings.

Déjà vu. I've been here before. In another boat. Where? When? Then it comes to me.

I'm on the French River, deep in the Ontario wilderness. Years ago. Like now, I'm sitting in a boat, surrounded by quiet. But at that time I'm hunched over, intent on crafting something. What? Now it comes to me. I'm trying to make a cotter pin! The cotter pin on my outboard had broken. I recall the surprise and shock of being miles and miles from anyone, when suddenly my boat stopped moving, even though the Evinrude's engine was running. I had wondered why. I revved the engine, but the boat wouldn't advance. I revved it more. It whined in response. Still no movement.

Leaning down over the back of the boat, I could see the water wasn't churning. Slowly, I tipped the motor forward so I could see the propeller and revved the engine. The propeller didn't move.

My imagination began to race. *This is not good. I'm at least thirty miles from my outfitter. How am I going to get back?*

It's snowing and getting colder. This could be bad. Wait a minute. Stop it. Don't panic. Take a breath. Figure this out.

Cutting the engine and hanging over the back of the boat as far as I dared, I took hold of the propeller and spun it. It spun freely. Though I knew little about the actual mechanics of outboard motors, I knew this couldn't be good. Bracing myself on the motor housing for balance and leaning even farther over, I inspected the prop mechanism and eventually discovered there was a little pin that fastened the propeller to the crankshaft. It looked sort of like a cotter pin, but broken in half. No wonder the propeller wasn't spinning, I thought.

Climbing back into the boat, I considered my dilemma. I didn't have a cotter pin, or anything like it. How ironic—the intrepid outdoorsman stuck in the middle of nowhere for lack of a cotter pin no larger than a safety pin. There was only one answer—I would have to make one. I opened my tackle box and searched. Nothing. But I did have a pair of needle-nosed pliers and an assortment of hooks. I took one of the larger hooks out and—using the pliers to leverage the hook against the boat seat—I straightened it out. Then I bent it in half to mimic the shape of a cotter pin.

Finally, crawling out over the motor to install my new fashioning, I replaced the broken pin, careful not to drop my pliers into the river. Having done this, I restarted the outboard to see if the propeller would spin. Success! I eased the motor into gear and slowly tried it out. The boat began to move. I revved the engine a bit more. The boat responded. Finally, I really gave it some gas, and the boat leaped to life.

"Who-o-o-e-e-e-e!" I shouted. Elated, I decided that my new pin worked just as well as the old one, and, evening approaching, I headed back to my campsite.

I recall now that my French River excursion was in the month of October. There was snow on the ground, and I had realized as I got back to my campsite that I was really cold. And it was getting dark. Gulping down a Power Bar, I got into my tent, threw off my clothes, and zipped myself into my sleeping bag.

Night descended and I lay there freezing. I decided to put on some clothes. Still freezing, I huddled in my bag, unable to sleep. I got up and put on all the clothes I had, including my parka. Back in the sleeping bag, if anything, I felt colder.

What to do? I was wearing everything I had, and still felt cold to the bone.

My answer? In desperation I got out of my tent, threw off all my clothes, and jumped naked into the ice-cold river. I swam vigorously back and forth along the shore. For some reason, it felt invigorating as I swam lap after lap.

After about ten minutes, I got out of the water and, unbelievably, felt great. Still naked, I gathered some dry wood from my stash and built a roaring fire. I sat down and gazed into the blaze, amazed at how warm I felt. I looked up and my amazement only increased. Pulsating in the sky was an incredible display of shimmering lights, seeming to rise up from all horizons to a focal point high in the heavens. Reds, greens and whites vibrated upward, over and over, in luminous, dancing sheets of gossamer.

It was my old friend, the northern lights. The fact that I hadn't seen them for many years made this occasion even more special. I sat there by the fire—naked but warm—for about an hour, the light show constantly changing, but always climbing from the horizon to a central meeting point overhead. Eventually, the heavenly display ushered me into sleepiness. I crawled back into my tent, burrowed into my sleeping bag, and contentedly nodded off.

Two days later, I motored back to my outfitter. He greeted me at the dock. Proudly, I told him the story of my broken cotter pin and the replacement I had fashioned.

"I guess you didn't see the spare we always tape on the back of the motor," he said after patiently hearing me out. He pointed to a piece of masking tape I had never thought to look under.

"Oh," I said, more than a little chagrined, "I guess I didn't."

Remembering that experience, I still feel embarrassed to this day. At the same time, I'm still proud of my own homemade cotter pin.

As for jumping into the river, whenever I've described this crazy experience, nobody has had an explanation for what was going on—until I told John. "Oh," he said, not missing a beat, "You had hypothermia. People with hypothermia do all kinds of nutty things!"

"Could be," I mused, "Could be."

Up to this moment on Distin Lake, that was the last time I can remember being in a boat. Soon after, I had taken up the canoe, and I've been canoeing ever since. Now, here I am, back in a boat once again—minus the outboard—headed south through the lifting fog. As I approach the south end of the lake, I spot an impressive beaver lodge beyond the lily pads near the western shore. No sign of my beaver. For all I know, he's back near my cabin continuing his harvest. I give him and his family a silent salute and head homeward.

Alone

More than once I have been asked what it's like to be alone with one's thoughts over an extended period of time.

"I'd go nuts," some friends have said.

"I would be so bored," others speculate.

"I'd need to hear another human voice," still others comment.

Whenever I hear these questions and comments, I can't help but think of Jon Kabat Zinn's caveat, "Wherever you go, there you are." In other words, changing my circumstances doesn't necessarily change who I am. However, admittedly, changing my circumstances can bring out aspects of myself that might otherwise be dormant. Thus, I find it always refreshing and sometimes challenging to be away from the demands, if not the cacophony, of modern life.

Being alone in the wilderness presents an opportunity to re-center—to get in touch with a me that might otherwise have little opportunity for expression. Sometimes that means confronting a somewhat daunting situation. More often, it means finding the opportunity to slow down and to listen more carefully to my surroundings and myself. Simply said, my solo wilderness trips give me a chance to restore my place in the natural world, if not the cosmos.

Not that I care to romanticize this experience. I'm not talking about religious conversion. I'm not talking about reclaiming my life. And I'm not advocating that everyone should go to the wilderness and "find" herself or himself. More, I'm simply saying that the wilderness gives me an opportunity to rediscover what has always been a part of my total self, and perhaps to better understand the environment of which I am one small part.

I'm not a hermit. I don't wish I could escape to the wilds forever. I'm not the consummate outdoorsman. Rather, this time apart is a way of nurturing myself in such a way that I can return to my everyday environment feeling more balanced and whole.

In sum, my response to "What is it like to be alone?" is that it's an opportunity to discover what happens—internally and externally—when I remove myself from the distractions and cacophony of modern life. It's not so much a quest or an exploration as it is a listening, a waiting, and an openness to what comes next.

Farewell to Tongass

Perhaps like no other expedition, my trip to the Tongass has provided an extended opportunity to be quiet in nature— to listen and to appreciate, to rest and to restore. It's been a week now, and once again—as I have over the years—I am scanning the skies for the single-engine aircraft that will pick me up and begin my journey back to Takoma Park, Maryland, back to my working life, and back to Janet and my family.

Surrounded by my backpacks and other gear, I sit quietly on Distin's shore until I hear the familiar drone in the distance. One thing has become clear in my time here in Alaska's southern reaches—I've yet to explore the far north. I've decided that next year I will be back in my canoe, ready and anxious to paddle the arctic environs of the Koyukuk River. But for now, I am happy to have had the experience of staying put for one whole week—a far cry from breaking camp and traveling each and every day.

One last visitor is here to bid me farewell. Quietly, she spins her web as the roar of the plane echoes over the water. Wishing her luck, I get up to continue my journey.

Chapter 14

2010 – THE RECKONING – THE KOYUKUK

I've chosen the North Fork of the Koyukuk because of its allure as one of arctic Alaska's designated "Wild Rivers." Having read of the sweeping vistas of the "Gates of the Arctic," where the Koyukuk flows between Boreal Mountain and Frigid Crags in the storied Brooks Range—which stretches some seven hundred miles across northern Alaska and the Yukon Territory—how could I resist?

Once again I am starting this adventure in Bettles, just as I did three years ago when I canoed the Kobuk. At that time I didn't feel sufficiently accomplished as a paddler to attempt the Koyukuk, but now I feel confident and ready. My outfitter will fly me north to the Gates, from which I will canoe some one hundred miles back to Bettles, where I can hop a return plane to Fairbanks and on to Anchorage.

It's good to be back in Bettles. When last here—in 2007—I flew south to Walker Lake after two days waiting out unflyable weather. This year, the weather is again iffy, but it looks like—with a bit of luck—we should be able to take off on time.

On my previous visit, I was intrigued by the Cub bush planes that were parked on the grassy field outside our lodge, featuring fat tundra tires that make it possible to land at speeds as slow as thirty miles per hour. Now, for this expedition, I'll board one of these planes and land on the Koyukuk's rock-strewn shores.

I have a few hours before we're scheduled for takeoff, so I decide to check in with the Gates of the Arctic park rangers. Coincidentally, when I walk into the ranger station I discover two of them are also preparing to go up near the Gates, getting into their gear and inspecting their inflatable canoe.

"That's a beauty," I comment, eyeing their streamlined black craft with more than a little envy. "Really looks sleek."

"Yeah, it's a Grabner," they tell me. "Handles just like a canoe. It's the latest thing."

They ask me about my route and I tell them I'm putting in at the Gates.

"We'll see you up there!" they say.

Ambling back to my outfitter's cabin, I check in, anxious to be on my way.

"How's the weather looking up at the drop now?" I ask.

"Not bad," he replies. "Might as well give it a go."

And with that we walk out to the Cub, stow my gear behind the seats and taxi down the gravel runway. Soon we are aloft, and once again I feel the excitement abuzz throughout my body as my anticipation rises. In a couple of hours I'll be setting down at my final destination. I'm more than a bit curious about how it's going to feel landing on a riverbank.

Soon we are gliding north up an endless valley, the mountains embracing our tiny craft from either side. The nearly magical beauty of our surroundings enfolds us.

It's difficult to describe, with any justice, early autumn in the arctic. In September, the mountain tundra is ablaze with ochers, reds, oranges, rusts, siennas and purples. On an overcast day like today, the sun playing tag with the clouds, there is an ever-changing lightscape over the land—a dancing, shimmering kaleidoscope of color.

As we ride the bumpy air currents, occasionally a pond or

small lake appears below, throwing back the dazzling arctic sun and mirroring the azure sky and marshmallow clouds. Edged by a boreal forest of spruce, birch, aspen and poplar, these bodies of water look like vibrant Matisse cutouts in the vast expanse of the green taiga.

The Koyukuk twists and turns like an unspooling ribbon. As with all rivers when seen from this height, the mind is tricked into seeing an unpretentious, benign stream, when—quite possibly—a torrent rages where one perceives only ripples. The river's expanse may stretch fifty yards across a space that the eye apprehends as a slender stream. I am reminded of the headwaters of the Kobuk as seen from Kyle's Cessna when we scouted the rapids that gave me—a neophyte observer—only a hint of the actual tumult below.

However, as I lean forward to peer through the whirling propeller at the immense mountain guardians that loom in the far distance forming the Gates of the Arctic, the Koyukuk truly looks like a wild river. It sculpts an untamed swath through the broad, verdant valley—its sandy shores surrounded by lush willows, shrub thickets and scrub spruce.

As we finally begin our long and gradual descent, I see that what first appeared to be a sandy beach is actually a rock-strewn shoreline. No matter. The rocky runway feels baby smooth under the tundra tires, and we land without incident.

No sooner have we touched down than a bank of dark, low-hanging clouds moves in to assert itself. Rain begins to fall, first in a drizzle, then in wind-blown chill-inducing sheets. Ducking our heads against the elements, we offload my gear. My pilot wishes me a good journey and climbs back aboard the Cub—anxious to leave before the weather gets truly nasty.

Getting underway without delay seems like the best alternative for me as well. I should inflate my canoe, load up and be on my way rather than pitch my first campsite in the rain. Unlike some previous trips, I have little time to react to my sudden isolation. Pelted by icy raindrops, rather than wishing that conditions were different, I try to organize my thoughts.

I hardly notice as the Cub roars away.

Scrambling into my newly purchased PVC-coated seaman's gear, I thank myself for deciding to buy this coat. After years of experimentation, I'd decided the only truly water- and storm-proof outfit is the raingear favored by mariners. Even Gore-Tex has its limits. Rather than damp and clammy, I'm reasonably dry, even if my new mackintosh is a bit bulky. This new slicker, layered over my new all-weather lightweight jacket, is already earning its keep.

Fighting off the shivers, I hurriedly arrange my gear in my now-inflated canoe, and—checking one last time to make sure I have left nothing behind in my rush—shove off. Quickly orienting myself to this new river, I test the current and move into open water. Despite my two-year layoff from paddling, my old skills come racing back into form. This lifts my spirits.

"Wooo-ee-ee!" I whoop through the rain and the wind. "I'm here, I'm solo, and I'm back in the saddle! Weather be damned!" As if to acknowledge my uplifted spirits, the rainclouds begin to move away, and soon the late afternoon arctic sun has returned, spreading joy as it spreads its light. My exhilaration lasts for about a mile.

Suddenly, after all the rush to beat the weather and be underway, the long day catches up with me and the broad riverbank beckons. Again, as on the first day of so many of my previous trips, I have to remind myself that I'm not in the city anymore. I no longer have a schedule. I'm not on deadline. Seeing no reason not to, I decide to pull in for the evening and set up camp. I've been awake for nearly twenty hours, and I'm beginning to crash. That's the thing about the arctic in September—it's light for eighteen or twenty hours. Sometimes you forget to stop.

I stop.

I put up my tent, and immediately crawl in to stretch out

and enjoy. Opening both flaps, the chilly late afternoon breeze quickly dries the tent. Removing my rain gear, my clothes underneath are nice and dry as well, and I settle in to survey my surroundings through the frame of my tent door. A golden-leaved scrub willow crouches just outside my door. Far upriver, the sun highlights the late-day colors of a distant cliff, fronted by a spruce forest marching up the west bank of the Koyukuk.

Unable to resist the now beautiful and beckoning day, I exit the tent, stand tall and stretch—reaching down to touch my toes and up to grab the sky—a poor imitation of the Sun Salutation I was taught in my yoga days. It's a good time for an evening stroll up the beach. I grab a Power Bar and start off.

I haven't wandered fifty feet before I stop and peer down at a set of very impressive moose tracks, so large that I can almost fit my size twelve boot in one. The tracks ramble off towards the foothills to the east. I figure the moose must have come down to the river for a drink and a bath, and then continued on its way. I kneel down, checking to see if there are any other tracks—especially on the lookout for grizzlies—but find no trace. After an hour or so I return to my campsite, eat a light meal and turn in for the night. My first night back in the arctic wilderness is a welcome return.

The next morning dawns once again under partly cloudy skies—but fortunately, no rain. Not that I mind the rain, but it's much more convenient when you can keep your gear dry. Sometimes, when the wet weather goes on for days, you begin to feel like a clammy prune and wonder if your shoes and socks will ever be dry again.

In the arctic, you never know for sure when the weather might turn. One can easily wake up in a blizzard. So, given the opportunity, I cook a leisurely breakfast of eggs and hotcakes, with hot chocolate. Satiated, I resist the temptation to flop back down into my sleeping bag. Instead, I pack up my gear and prepare to proceed downriver.

I'm making pretty good time today. The Koyukuk is swift, but not overly challenging, and I take advantage of this opportunity to hone my somewhat rusty skills. Given that it's been two years since I've been solo canoeing, I'm pleased to find myself in sync with the river. Soon I'm crossing from bank to bank, leaning into the flow as the river bends—enjoying the swift current as it repeatedly sweeps along the shoreline, arcs back to midstream, and races toward the opposite shore.

Broad sandy and rocky shores prove plentiful along the entire Koyukuk, and locating a campsite is not a problem. Given my rapid progress, I decide I'll knock off early today and take a hike into the eastern foothills. Setting up camp, I fill a daypack with food and lenses and take off across the scrub-filled flats. Low-lying crystal clear pools of water abound—the same pools that looked like Matisse cutouts from high above—displaying the tracks of small animals and birds.

Hiking further back into the brush, I start to ascend carefully. It's getting steeper and now I'm panting. "Need to get in better shape," I scold myself. As I climb further into the hills, I come upon the tundra, with its delicate lichen and ground cover. Given the lowering light, I stop to sit and eat.

I look for a barren spot in the tundra, and finding one I lie back and gaze up at the sky, which the clouds have almost abandoned. No avian life wings overhead, and I suddenly realize what a dearth of sound there has been. No birds calling. No wolves howling. Only quiet. In the stillness a breeze begins to stir and I notice an afternoon chill setting in. Eventually, I rouse myself and, getting to one knee and leaning on my hiking stick for support, I manage to stand up and prepare for the trek back to camp.

I've come further than I realize. It takes nearly an hour to make my way back. Upon reaching camp, I walk over to the river, where I skip a few stones and examine others—gray ones the size of my fist that seem to have a thin white line running through them. No geologist, I can't surmise what would create such a pattern. After taking a couple of photos of these unique rocks, I return to my tent to prepare for the evening.

The River Wild

The next day dawns under a gray, rainy blanket. I layer on my full regalia—mackintosh, life vest, all-weather jacket, hiking shorts, Gor-Tex pants and hiking boots, and exit the tent. For some reason, my mood does not match the gloomy weather. Rather, I feel ready to take on a day of paddling, no matter the weather. After consuming a Power Bar and some trail mix washed down with water, I pack up and head for the river.

Out on the wind-swept Koyukuk, the temperature must be in the lower forties, but I'm comfortable in my gear. As I paddle, I notice the current picking up a bit of speed as the river bends and the water races by the shore. Soon—as I did yesterday—I get into the spirit, swinging back and forth from bank to bank, leaning into the curves and enjoying what feels like a sleigh ride. As I approach the east bank, riding the swift current, a sweeper appears some twenty yards ahead.

Despite the stories I've heard of sweepers catching and holding even the most experienced paddlers under icy waters while their empty craft is borne downstream, I'm not worried. There is only a single branch immediately ahead. I realize the proper thing to do is to steer around this low-hanging branch, avoiding it altogether. However, I misgauge the speed of the current and suddenly it's too late to paddle away from the oncoming obstacle.

In that instant, rather than duck under the branch (the next proper thing to do), I decide to catch hold of it and use it as a springboard to shove my canoe away from the onrushing rocky shore. This maneuver is easy to describe in hindsight.

However, it is not so simple to perform in real-time. As I approach the branch, I grab it with my left hand. To my surprise, instead of bending a bit and allowing me to swing around it, it holds fast. Suddenly, surrealistically, I'm airborne. My canoe continues downriver, while my body is propelled— as if time were frozen—toward the icy water.

"No," I think, as I plunge headfirst into the river, "This can't be!"

The momentum of my plunge propels me to the very bottom of the river. Strangely, everything feels as if it's happening in slow motion. Concerned that my heavy hiking boots will weigh me down, I twist my body and kick vigorously to reverse my plunge and return to the river's surface— helpfully buoyed by my life jacket. As I break through the surface I see my canoe moving downstream. It's already out of reach and quickly gaining distance.

Behind it trails the lashing rope, a ten-foot length that I had tied to the aft bow to let it follow behind the canoe—a precaution I had taken so that in the very unlikely event I were to be thrown overboard, I would have something to grab unto. Clearly, I dare not lose the canoe out here in the middle of nowhere. Even though I carry some emergency gear on my person—compass, dry matches, protein bars, high-tech foil blanket—my satellite phone, food and other essentials are headed downriver.

The trailing lashing rope is my one chance. Scissor-kicking in its direction, I grab for the rope and, luckily, catch hold of it on my first attempt. I then haul myself hand over hand alongside the canoe and throw my leg over the inflated side, attempting to roll in. No luck. I do so again—and then repeatedly—with the same result. Water-logged in all my heavy gear, I am tiring quickly. I have been told that survival in these frigid arctic waters is only a matter of minutes. Trying not to panic, I nonetheless begin to consider my plight and whether I will survive it.

Then something very peculiar happens—I tell myself not to worry, that I don't know how, but I will live to tell this story. All I need to do is take a breath and think. If I can't get into the canoe, then what is my alternative? I can't hang on indefinitely in these waters.

Meanwhile, my canoe and I are being swept by the current towards the middle of the river. At first I despair at being carried farther and farther from shore. Then it occurs to me that since I'm adrift in the main current, I will next be conducted nearer to the opposite shore. But as we approached that riverbank, the current again swings away and carries me and my canoe back to the middle of the river and, once again, toward the opposite shore. For a moment, I have a vision of being transported back and forth down river indefinitely, never quite gaining the safety of the shore. Again, I tell myself not to despair, but to think!

An idea finally comes. I realize that while I still have the strength and energy, I should work my way from the side of the canoe to the back. If I can obtain that position, by kicking my legs and using the canoe as a giant paddleboard, I can act as both propeller and rudder, and in doing so, I can try to steer the canoe out of the current to the opposite shore.

By now, it feels as if several minutes have passed, and I'm amazed that I'm not frozen. I begin the process of working my way hand over hand to the back of the canoe. Once there, I grab onto each side of the aft bow and begin kicking, trying to escape the current and guide the craft to shore. However, I am tiring, and finally, when the shore is only about ten yards away, I decide to see how deep the water is at this point.

Fortunately, my legs find a purchase on the bottom of the river, and I push off as hard as I can in the direction of the shore. Repeating this process several times, I am finally able to grab some vegetation along the riverbank and hug my body against the rocky shore, all the while clinging to the rope of the canoe. I rest here both exhausted and ecstatic, hanging onto the steeply sloping edge of the riverbank. However, even here the current is pulling me and the canoe back into the river. Using nearby rocks as leverage to ease myself further onto the shore, I carefully raise up into a crouch and duck-walk the canoe to a nearby eddy, which is bordered by a friendlier slope. There I scooch into a notch in some larger rocks, sit back, and gather my wits. After accomplishing this—soaked but alive—I think through my dilemma.

"I'm not out of the woods yet," I tell myself. I need to get to the opposite side of the river where there is level ground and an opportunity to rest and make a plan. Now I discover that I've lost my paddle when I was thrown into the river. However, following standard practice, I carry a spare for just such an event.

Hunched over, low to the ground, I gingerly step back into my canoe—with the same trepidation one must have when driving a car after an accident. I hunt for my spare paddle, and, relieved to see that it is still where I secured it, paddle to the opposite shore. Breathing a deep sigh of relief, I beach the canoe and drag it far onto the gravel bar—not about to let it get away! Finally, shedding my mackintosh and life vest, I open the zipper on my lightweight tech jacket. Out pours a rush of river water. Astonished, I loosen the waist on my rain pants and another torrent ensues. Working my way through my clothing, turning out pockets and loosening straps, I finally divest myself of the river.

Concerned about hypothermia, I check my pulse. Low seventies. Ok there. Though my teeth are chattering in this chilly weather, my thinking seems clear and other bodily functions normal. No numbness. Not even shivering. Of course, I realize the irony is that when you are in the midst of hypothermia, one symptom is that you don't realize it.

What surprises me most is that though my clothing is sodden, I'm not actually cold. Clammy? Yes. Soaked? Yes. But freezing? No. "This new tech gear really does work," I tell myself. "Kept me warm even after a dunk in an arctic river. Quite amazing!" During this entire time, the rain continues. Not a hard, driving rain, but one that promises to persist indefinitely under these steel blue-gray clouds.

It seems as if a whole day has passed already, but it is, in fact, only late morning. Should I stop and camp here? It doesn't make much sense because I will have to pitch my tent in the rain and risk getting my sleeping bag and other gear wet, with little likelihood of drying my clothes even if I build a roaring fire. Additionally, I'm on an expansive, wind-swept gravel bar with no dry wood in sight. I decide that, counterintuitive as it might seem—having just dragged myself out of the river—it will be best to re-launch my canoe and continue my journey.

I proceed to do just that.

However, no sooner do I get underway than a couple of bends downriver I confront a considerable stretch of rapids. I gauge them to be no more than Class II or III, but after my recent experience in the river, I proceed with extreme caution. Putting aside my fears, I manage to negotiate the hundred yards or so that I must travel to reach an eddy along the east shore that is bounded by a series of smooth rocks where I can rest and regain my confidence.

Finally, pushing off from the eddy and venturing back into the main current, fortune smiles on me. Not only do I survive my ordeal, but by late afternoon the skies clear and out comes what is—for me—the most beautiful sun one could hope for, casting a welcome rainbow in its rays. It feels like it has warmed to the high forties and I quickly take advantage of this break in the weather and head for shore to make camp.

After I pitch my tent, I strip off all of my clothes and scatter them about on the rocks to dry, the sun aided by a gentle breeze. And dry they do. I lie down with the pebbles as my bed, grateful to be alive. As evening approaches, I dress in my now warm, dry gear and sit down in front of a toasty fire. Here the

Koyukuk is peaceful—no hint of the racing river I had come through earlier today.

Two moose—a dam and her grown calf—come across from the opposite side of the river to check me out. Splashing their way across an expanse of shallow water, they pause about twenty yards away and stand quietly, perusing this strange presence in their midst. Finally, deciding I pose no threat, they return to their side of the Koyukuk. I return to my tent. Suddenly exhausted, I sleep like a baby through the night.

The next morning, hungry almost beyond reason, I devour a breakfast of hotcakes, coffee, and freeze-dried scrambled eggs. Feeling only comfortably full, I gather my now thoroughly dry gear and load up the canoe. Bowing east, west, north and south—thankful as any guest might be for the comfort this wilderness space has offered—I once again embark down the Koyukuk.

After no more than a couple of hours on the water, I come across the two park rangers that I had met in Bettles, camped along the west riverbank.

After pulling ashore and hopping out of my canoe, I ask, "You didn't happen to run across a canoe paddle?" trying to sound casual.

They glance at each other nervously. "Nope," one replies. "What happened?"

"I ran into a sweeper and took a dunk in the river yesterday morning during that rain." I say, sounding as if these things happen all the time.

"Geez, are you ok?"

"Yeah, I'm fine. But I lost my paddle. I've got a spare, though."

Looking somewhat reassured that all is ok, they promise to keep an eye out for the paddle. Digging my SLR out of its bag, I ask them, "How about a photo?" Obligingly, they pose proudly by their sleek new canoe, and, shaking hands all around, I shove off down the river. "See you back in Bettles," one of them calls as I continue downstream.

Proceeding downriver, that afternoon I spot a grizzly ambling up the west shore—head down, preoccupied. We pass within a few yards of one another, but he pays my paddling no mind. We might as well be two strangers passing on a street. I'm amused how an event that would have stirred such excitement in me at one time now seems so normal—so every day. There's something pleasant about this change. Moose come and go. Grizzlies come and go. It's the passage of life in the wild, and I am just another creature making his way.

The day yawns lazily before me, quite a contrast to the events of yesterday. The Koyukuk may be a wild river, but here it flows quietly and peacefully. Each bend offers a new visual experience. Around the next one, steep cliffs tower over me. I crane my neck as they rise dramatically along the western shore. Hearty spruces anchor themselves in its rocky crags, while overhead, wispy clouds sweep a brilliant sky.

I recline back in my canoe, resting my paddle across my chest, letting the gentle current escort me downriver. I am glad to adopt the Koyukuk's lazy pace, letting it rock me in its bosom. As the afternoon melds into evening, I find another friendly gravel bar and stop early to enjoy the approaching night. After setting up my campsite and gazing out at the smoothly flowing water as it murmurs downstream, I'm reminded of an old camp song of my youth, and I sing a few bars of "Peace, I ask of thee O river. Peace. Peace. Peace."

My thoughts drift back to one particular four-day autumn weekend many years ago when, impulsively, I drove round-trip from Washington, D.C. to a deserted campground on the Atlantic Coast of Florida. There I sat for two nights, contemplating the river, the saw grass, the pine trees and the sunset. I meant for it to be a songwriting weekend, and I jotted down a tune called "My Time":

If my time were this river,
Wandering to the sea,
Just like this old river,
I'd take it slow and free.

Goodbye to the Koyukuk

My last two days are delightfully uneventful. The brittle colors of the arctic autumn are beginning to announce the onset of colder weather. On a distant bluff high above the east bank of the river I can make out a small fishing shack, a sure indication that I am nearing Bettles and the end of my paddling. About a mile downriver, I pull into shore, unload my gear, and deflate my canoe. I've got about a mile to hike from here to my outfitter's cabin.

By the time I walk through his door, I'm sure I look somewhat bedraggled. He greets me with a hearty handshake and asks, "How'd it go?"

"Fine. Good to see you!" I grin, pumping his hand. Suddenly I realize how tired I actually am.

"I lost a paddle," I blurt out, embarrassed. "Of course, I'll pay for it."

"Forget it," he replies, as if this is a common occurrence, and that's the last mention of the missing paddle. I'm almost too tired to be relieved.

"Let's go get your gear," he suggests, and with that, we hop into his pickup and backtrack to where I've left my canoe and packs. By the time we return and schlep all my gear into the cabin where I will spend the night, I fall into my bunk—the pace and grind of my trek still coursing through my body and my psyche.

That night, in my feverish dreams, I break camp, I battle the currents, I set up camp, and I cook my dinner over and over again—seemingly unable to escape the cycle.

All too soon, bright sunlight streams through my window as—body aching from my night's labors—I startle awake in what must be the early dawn. Rolling over, I bury myself in my sleeping bag and try to catch a bit more precious sleep. But the rhythms of morning just outside my cabin door refuse to be ignored, and finally I sit up on the side of my bunk, rub my eyes, and try to shake the cobwebs loose.

Suddenly there's the sound of hurried footsteps approaching and a loud, insistent knock at my door. Still in the groggy throes of sleep, I throw open the door, and startled by the blinding sun, realize it is high in the sky.

"Yes?" is all I manage to ask my outfitter, who—in my blurry vision—appears to be in an awful hurry.

"Turns out they've got a seat available on an earlier flight back to Fairbanks. Grab your stuff. They're waiting on you!" he says, nearly out of breath.

"What? What time is it?" I ask.

"Almost noon," he replies. "No time. Get your stuff."

And with that—in record time—I pull on my clothes, throw my gear together, check under the bunk to make sure I'm leaving nothing behind, and race out to the tarmac where a ten-seater Otter sits impatiently revving its engines. The pilot throws my stuff into the cargo hold and I hop on board the plane, where a few Native locals and a couple of fishermen wait stoically for my arrival. I flop down in the one empty seat, the door slams shut, and we're off for Fairbanks, as Bettles fades quickly into the distance below.

Getting Real

Touching down in Fairbanks, I gather my gear and head for the rental car counter. Since I'm only a couple of hours north of Denali, I'm tempted to take in the mountain up close and personal once last time.

I drop my gear at the Alpine Lodge, FedEx John's satellite phone back to him with my thanks, hop in my car and head south. However, exhaustion soon overtakes ambition. I'm running on nervous energy. "Stop," I tell myself, "Take a breath and head back to the Alpine. Denali will still be there tomorrow."

After a plate of delicious stuffed shrimp at Pike's on the sunset deck, I saunter back to the lodge, where I spend a couple of hours in my room reviewing photos of the Koyukuk. Finally, too tired to continue, I crawl into the comfort of a king bed. What a luxury after a week on the water.

Next morning, as I travel the Parks Highway towards Denali, I come to the Nenana River Bridge. It is but one of Alaska's many impressive engineering feats. I exit my vehicle and walk out onto the high expanse. Looking far below, I see what appears to be Class III or IV rapids roaring through the chasm. Ever drawn by such water, I walk back and then scramble down under the bridge, hiking the steep slope for a better view. Every river I see is a temptation to paddle. But despite the lure of the rushing water, I content myself to look. Faced with the steep climb back up to my car, I smile at how my ambition does not seem to keep pace with my advancing age. I remind myself of what I used to tell my kids, "It's alright to want!"

Turning one last time to gaze at the Nenana, I think about this. What is it about this trip that seems to signify an ending—not a dramatic, "music-swelling-as-the curtain-falls," ending—but a simple, "enough is enough"?

My journey was inspired by childhood fantasies, which over these years have dissolved into a much richer reality of real places and real animals and real people inhabiting a fragile, endangered, and extraordinary environment. In the process, I have discovered realities about myself that are far more valuable than any ego-driven perceptions that I had constructed.

I am human. I have limitations. There is risk. And, yes, nature can be unforgiving. But, given reasonable precautions, the wilderness can help you discover inner resources that will delight and inform you. You may find that when you cease to strive, you move forward; that when you calm your fears, you find connection; and that when you decide to trust your particularly human faculties, they respond in ways that can—quite literally—save your life.

I remember myself, so many years ago, standing in our bedroom and saying to Janet, "I've *got* to go to the wilderness. Alone. It's something I've been harboring in the back of my mind all my life, and if I don't do it now—while I'm still able—I'll never do it."

And now the wilderness is part of me. I'll carry it with me always.

It's time to go home.

- End -

Epilogue

Only after finishing the last chapter of this book did I realize that a song I had written some twenty years before I headed north for the Boundary Waters foreshadowed this writing. I was so taken with how the song described my life quest that I decided to share it here.

A Matter of Time

My heart is an ancient prospector,
Traveling these foothills of mine,
Through the heat and the cold,
Looking for gold,
Panning the rivers of time.
Now fool's gold is often deceiving,
It glitters, it gleams and it shines,
But the gold that will last,
Is the time that you've passed,
Searching the depths of the mine.

It's an old miner's tale,
A baby's first wail,
It's a reed in the river of time,
It's the wind in the pines,
The dark in the mines,
And it's only a matter of time.

When your heart is a barnacled sailor,
Seeking lost treasures of old,

The waves climb so high,
They blot out the sky,
And shudder the ribs of the hold.
Lost treasures are often deceiving,
They can rot with the bones of the deep.
Keep a watch on the shore.
The breakers bring more,
Of the treasures you're likely to keep.

It's an old sailor's tale,
A ship in a gale.
It's a calm on the mirror of time.
It's the moon o'er the sea,
Reflecting in me,
That it's only a matter of time.

Someday I'll be reaching safe harbor,
My prospecting it will be through.
I'll put down my gold,
My treasures untold,
And tell this old world,
"Hey, I'm through."
I won't even try to remember,
No, I won't even try to forget.
My fortune, in time,
Will be down to a dime,
And I'll have spent it without a regret.

On an old timer's tale,
A baby's first wail,
On a reed in the river of time,
On the moon, and the sea,
They're all deep in me.
And we're only a matter of time.

From *A Matter of Time* © Music and Lyrics
by Dick Anderson, AnderSongs 2020

Acknowledgements

"Where to start?" must be the question facing every author when trying to acknowledge the debt they owe to all who have so generously contributed their time, expertise, resources and love to such a project as this. Let me start by thanking all of you, named and unnamed, who extended your kindness, knowledge, and assistance to me during these journeys. Had I not experienced it for myself, it would be hard to imagine exhibiting such generosity to a stranger.

I am indebted to my family, my friends and my colleagues for their patience and support during the two-plus years that have been devoted to this effort.

Specifically, my thanks to those who have read all or portions of this book and offered their suggestions. They have greatly improved my meager efforts. I would especially thank Mary Wylie, whose editing and encouragement have so improved this presentation and spared the reader of many passages that were clearly of interest only to me.

Janet, Laurie, Geoff, and Kelley, you all know what a truly important role your love, support and insightful suggestions have played in bringing this vision to fruition. Thank you again and again!

About Atmosphere Press

Atmosphere Press is an independent, full-service publisher for excellent books in all genres and for all audiences. Learn more about what we do at atmospherepress.com.

We encourage you to check out some of Atmosphere's latest releases, which are available at Amazon.com and via order from your local bookstore:

Emotional Liberation: Life Beyond Triggers and Trauma, nonfiction by GuruMeher Khalsa

The Bond: How a Mixed Bag of Foster Kids Became a Family for Life, a memoir by A.M. Grotticelli

License to Learn, nonfiction by Anna Switzer

Between Each Step: A Married Couple's Thru Hike on New Zealand's Te Araroa, a memoir by Patrice La Vigne

Ordinary Zenspiration: Find Your Chill, Find Your Fun, Find Yourself, by April Cacciatori

Waking Up Marriage: Finding Truth In Your Partnership, nonfiction by Bill O'Herron

Eat to Lead, nonfiction by Luci Gabel

A Converted Woman's Voice, nonfiction by Maria Covey Cole

An Ambiguous Grief, a memoir by Dominique Hunter

My Take On All Fifty States: An Unexpected Quest to See 'Em All, nonfiction by Jim Ford

About the Author

Dick Anderson resides with his wife Janet in Takoma Park, Maryland and River Ridge, West Virginia. A father and grandfather, Dick has traveled throughout the United States, Canada, Mexico, and Europe. His work has ranged from railroad Gandy dancer, U.S. Senate Foreign Relations Committee researcher, and inner-city high school teacher, to co-founder of Art for People, a graphics design firm assisting not-for-profit clients. He is currently Editorial and Creative Consultant for the National Magazine Award-winning *Psychotherapy Networker*, a position he has held for four decades. A songwriter, avid bird-watcher and photographer, Dick often frequents the Eastern Shore of Maryland and Virginia.

CPSIA information can be obtained
at www.ICGtesting.com
Printed in the USA
BVHW071709250521
608094BV00004B/703